Davis, R.M. & Maurice. <u>Caliph of Bagdad</u>

Contains new material about O. Henry's
southern years, about his literary methods,
about the originals and settings of his
stories and the money he receives for them,
and for the first time prints several of
his letters.

THE CALIPH OF BAGDAD

7

Photograph by Vanderweib

*"He no longer saw a rabble, but his brothers seeking
the ideal."*

BRICKDUST ROW

THE CALIPH OF BAGDAD

BEING ARABIAN NIGHTS FLASHES OF
THE LIFE, LETTERS, AND WORK OF
O. HENRY ✾ ✾ WILLIAM SYDNEY PORTER

ROBERT H. DAVIS *and* ARTHUR B. MAURICE

D. APPLETON AND COMPANY ✾ ✾
NEW YORK ✾ LONDON ✾ MCMXXXI

FOREWORD

TWENTY-ONE years have passed since O. Henry died in the Polyclinic Hospital in New York City. His last jesting words were in echo of a popular song of the hour. There are two versions of the exact phrasing. One was that it began, "Pull up the shades"; the other, "Turn up the lights." Then, as both agree, he continued: "I don't want to go home in the dark." In that little conflict of evidence we have one aspect of his life in epitome.

O. Henry had no conscientious Boswell; no faithful Forster. The importance of his work, his destined preëminence as a master of the American short story were hardly recognized in his lifetime. Most of the men who were in close contact with him in the years of his achievement, the men who were best fitted by training for the task of historians, were more concerned with the problem of extracting from him the promised and overdue tale than in jotting down notes for the benefit of posterity. Therefore O. Henryana to-day is largely a matter of memories, more or less shadowy, and often conflicting. That condition is reflected in the following pages.

When C. Alphonso Smith's *Biography* appeared in 1916 it provoked criticism that was neither kindly nor fair. Professor Smith wrote his book with the full approval of those by right most closely connected with O. Henry. But many readers who did not understand

v

that felt it was too soon to bare to the public the facts of O. Henry's shadowed years: those spent in the Federal Penitentiary at Columbus, Ohio, to which he was sent as a result of certain irregularities found in his accounts when he was employed in a Texas bank.

Now the full story may be told. The lapse of time justifies that. His daughter Margaret, his only near blood relative, has long been in her grave. Also, with the years, there has been the growing feeling that the crime for which O. Henry was sentenced was a crime of which he was relatively if not entirely innocent.

The authors of the present book have drawn from, and here wish to make acknowledgment to, many sources. For the record of the early years they have naturally gone to many of the authorities used by Professor Smith in the preparation of his *O. Henry Biography*. A book that has proved highly serviceable in throwing light on O. Henry's first wife, Athol Estes, is Frances Goggin Maltby's *The Dimity Sweetheart*, published by the Dietz Printing Company of Richmond, Virginia.

Thanks are also due to Doubleday, Doran and Company; to the Century Co.; to Dodd, Mead and Company, formerly the publishers of *The Bookman*, which during the editorship of one of the authors of this book, printed a vast amount of original O. Henry material; to the Dallas *News;* and to the editor of the *Saturday Evening Post.*

Also to Arthur W. Page, author of *Little Pictures of O. Henry;* to Al. Jennings, author of *Through the Shadows with O. Henry* and *Beating Back;* to Will Irwin; to Lindsay Denison; to Franklin P. Adams;

to William Griffith; to George Barr Baker; to Alexander Woollcott; to Roy Norton; to Gilman Hall; to Richard Duffy; to R. P. Conway; to Vivian Richardson; to Edmund Travis; and to many others.

R. H. D.
A. B. M.

CONTENTS

PART I

Aladdin

PART II

Sinbad

PART III

Haroun

PART IV
Scheherezade

ILLUSTRATIONS

xi

PART I
ALADDIN

I

A BOYHOOD IN RECONSTRUCTION DAYS

"Do you see those hills over there? Well, I was born and raised on the other side. You ole fool nigger, can't you tell people from other people when you see 'em?"   *A Municipal Report*

I WAS born and raised in No'th Ca'lina and at eighteen went to Texas and ran wild on the prairies. Wild yet, but not so wild. Can't get to loving New Yorkers. Live all alone in a big two rooms on quiet old Irving Place three doors from Wash. Irving's old home. Kind of lonesome (since the April moon commenced to shine). How I'd like to be down South, where I could happen over to Miss Ethel's or Miss Sallie's and sit on the front porch—not on a chair—on the edge of the porch, and lay my straw hat on the steps and lay my head back against the honeysuckle on the post—and just talk. And Miss Ethel would go in directly (they say presently up here) and bring out the guitar. She would complain that the E string was broken, but no one would believe her; and pretty soon all of us would be singing the "Swanee River" and "In the Evening by the Moonlight" and—oh, gol darn it, what's the use of wishing.

Such is the fairy tale of the life of William Sidney Porter, better known to the world as O. Henry, as told by himself in a confidential moment that, under analysis, proves to be far from confidential. Through the fairy tale there runs a vein of truth. It conveys the flavor of the hero's youth, not exactly as he lived it, but as he liked to think of it in looking back across the

3

years. Actually the boy Will Porter was not out of
his teens when he left his native Greensboro, and the
Miss Ethel and Miss Sallie of the dream were probably
wondering how they could get rid of "that Porter boy"
to devote themselves to some more mature and therefore
more desirable suitor. The thoughts of the Aladdin of
the Greensboro years were hardly yet turned towards
the Beautiful Princess.

Some years after O. Henry's death, the family Bible
of the Porter family came to light. It recorded that on
September 11, 1862, at Greensboro, North Carolina,
there was born to Dr. Algernon Sidney Porter and his
wife, *née* Mary Jane Virginia Swaim, a son who was
christened William Sidney Porter. Both the name and
the date have direct bearing on the story told in this
book. When O. Henry was in his brief hour of celebrity, it was his habit to represent himself as having
been born in 1867. The white lie was due, not to a
vanity of middle age, but to the wish to eliminate, even
from his own thoughts if that were possible, the memory of certain years of his life that were more happily
forgotten. Then, in later days, occasionally dropping
his first name, he formed the habit of spelling his
middle name "Sydney." That seems to have been
merely a harmless affectation.

Let us suggest briefly the environment of the first
formative years. To the Greensboro of that early
autumn of 1862, according to O. Henry's own words
"a somewhat somnolent Southern town," came echoes
of stirring events. President Lincoln—the name was
execrated in Greensboro as standing for a tyrannical
ogre—was drawing up the Emancipation Proclama-

tion, not as a pronouncement of any humanitarian principle, but as a war measure, a threat of property confiscation to be held over the heads of the states that persisted in remaining in secession from the Union. Grant was still in the West. McClellan had been reinstated in command of the Army of the Potomac. The Confederates were invading Maryland. Late in the month the Battle of Antietam was fought. In the great struggle between North and South the tide was beginning to turn, but neither side knew it.

In many of his stories O. Henry guyed gently the tradition of the baronial splendor of the old South— the legend of marble halls and troops of slaves. The boy William Sidney Porter was not born to that estate; nevertheless, his was a fine inheritance. His father, Dr. Algernon Sidney Porter, was a skilled and highly esteemed physician, with a strong inventive turn. That talent stood in the way of his material prosperity. His riper years were devoted more to his often impractical inventions than to his practice. William Sidney Porter's grandfather had come down to North Carolina from Connecticut in 1823 as an agent for a clock company.

The ink in Will Porter's blood came through his mother's side of the family. Mary Jane Virginia Swaim Porter's fondness for writing verses was an inheritance from her father, William Swaim, who had been the editor of the Greensboro *Patriot* from 1827 till his death in 1835. The Swaims came originally from Holland about the year 1700, and settled in North Carolina some years before the Revolutionary War.

The career of William Swaim reflects an aspect of

the South of the early half of the nineteenth century. An ardent Whig, a foe to Jacksonian principles, the Quaker in him made him an implacable opponent of Negro slavery as an institution. But he had little sympathy with the Abolitionists of the North. His idea was that the slaves should be gradually emancipated—the view held by many Southerners. As early as 1816, a society pledged to that solution of the problem had been formed at Center, a Quaker settlement ten miles from Greensboro. Through another line, Will Porter's ancestry traced back to that Quaker community. Center's most influential family was the Worth family, to which Will Porter's grandmother on his father's side belonged.

In the *Patriot* for May 30, 1832, William Swaim wrote the following characteristic editorial. What was known as the "nabob gentry" of Greensboro had evidently sought to use the paper to their own ends, which moved Swaim to the following defiance:

They soon learned from our tone that we would sooner beg for bread and be free than to compromise our principles for a seat upon a tawdry throne of corruption. Still bent upon the fell purpose of preventing, if possible, an unshackled press from growing into public favor, their last resort was to ransack hell, from the center to the circumferance, for slanderous fabrications; and these have been heaped upon us, without cause and without mercy, even until now. But thanks to a generous public, they have thus far sustained us "through evil as well as through good report," and we would rather bask for one hour in their approving smiles than to spend a whole eternity amidst the damning grins of a concatenation of office-hunters, despots, demagogues, tyrants, fools, and hypocrites.

So might Colonel Aquila Telfair of "The Rose of Dixie" have written; so might Major Pendleton Talbot of "The Duplicity of Hargraves" have thundered. Like Colonel Telfair when "The Rose of Dixie" languished as a result of dwindling circulation, Editor Swaim had his troubles with subscribers. For the admonition of delinquents the *Patriot* one day expressed itself in an article headed "Stop the Runaways!":

The following is a list of gentlemen who, after reading our paper for a time, have politely disappeared and left us the "bag to hold." We give the names of each, together with the amount due, and the place of his residence at the time he patronized us. Should this publication meet the eye of any delinquents and should they yet conclude to forward to us the amount due, we will publicly acknowledge the receipt and restore him who sends it to better credit than an act of the legislature could possibly give. Any person who will favor us with information of the residence of any or all of the absentees shall have the right to claim the homage of our sincere thanks.

Joseph Aydelotte, Esq., Guilford County, North Carolina. Twelve dollars.

John Lackey, Tarboro. Nine dollars.

James Hiatt, not recollected. Nine dollars.

William Atkinson, unknown. Nine dollars.

Jacob Millers, not recollected. Nine dollars.

Joseph Bryan, whipt anyhow and may be hung. Six dollars.

Is there not, suggested Professor C. Alphonso Smith in his *O. Henry Biography*, at least a hint of O. Henry in this "unexpected crack of the whip at the end"?

The Greensboro of Will Porter's boyhood was a little town of some twenty-five hundred inhabitants, a

typical democratic community of the old South before
the industrial invasion. It had contributed its con-
tingent of soldiers to the Confederacy, and in April,
1865, after hearing the news of the surrender at Appomattox, President Jefferson Davis repaired to
Greensboro to hold there his last conference with the
members of his cabinet. Later soldiers of both sides
gathered in Greensboro, thirty thousand men from
Sherman's army, and then thirty-seven thousand Confederates under General Johnston who were being
paroled. The women of the town were in a mood to
keep up the war, but the soldiers fraternized, and one
day there was a grand review of the Union troops.

Then, after the war, Reconstruction. In the story
of the misrule by revengeful extremist and carpetbag-
gers Greensboro has a particular significance. It was
there that Albion W. Tourgee found the material for
his *A Fool's Errand*, the most famous novel of its day.
Greensboro is easily recognized as the Verdenton of the
story. Judge Tourgee, "the fool," is Colonel Servisse;
and most of the other characters are Greensboro men
who were quickly identified. Tourgee came to Greensboro as a carpetbagger; in fact was the first carpetbagger to enter the town. Unlike most of the other carpet-
baggers he was just, honest, and intelligent. These
qualities won him a certain respect in the community,
but never liking. He was always an alien and an in-
truder whose presence was resented. He was in constant fear of an unfriendly visit from the Invisible
Empire, as the Klan of the early days was known. It
never materialized. To the boys of the town the
Tourgee home was a sort of demon's haunt. When,

in 1879, Judge Tourgee left Greensboro never to return, Will Porter, then a youth of seventeen, drew a cartoon to celebrate the departure.

When Will Porter was three years old, his mother died. Consumption was the cause of her early death at thirty. The malady was one of the shadows of O. Henry's life. Athol, his first wife, was later to die of it. His father, who had been the best-known and best-liked physician in Guilford County, had, in his passion for invention, lost much of his interest in his practice. Neglecting his patients, he seems also to have rather neglected his son, though in the neglect there was nothing of unkindness. In consequence, Will Porter's formative years were under the influence of his father's sister, Miss Evelina Porter, better known as Aunt Lina. She ran the Porter household as well as a private school that adjoined the Porter residence.

This book is made up of many stories; of the reminiscences of men and women who knew William Sidney Porter at various periods of his life. Tom Tate was Will Porter's desk mate at Miss Lina's school. Of their teacher and Will's aunt he has written:

Miss Porter was a maiden lady and conducted a private school on West Market Street, in Greensboro, adjoining the Porter residence. Will was educated there, and this was his whole school education (with the exception of a term or two at graded school). There was a great deal more learned in this little one-story, one-roomed school-house than the three R's. It was the custom of "Miss Lina," as every one called her, during the recess hour to read aloud to those of her scholars who cared to hear her, and there was always a little group around her chair listening.

She selected good books, and a great many of her
old scholars showed the impress of these little readings
in after life. On Friday night there was a gathering
of the scholars at her home, and those were good times,
too. They ate roasted chestnuts, popped corn or barbecued quail and rabbits before the big open wood fire
in her room. There was always a book to read or a
story to be told. Then there was a game of story-
telling; one of the gathering would start the story and
each one of the others was called on in turn to add his
quota until the end. "Miss Lina's" and Will's were
always interesting. In the summer time there were
picnics and fishing expeditions; and in the spring wild-
flower hunts, all conducted personally by "Miss Lina."

Of that boyhood in Reconstruction days, and the
reactions of youth to the presence in the community
of Judge Tourgee, Tom Tate has recorded:

Of course Will and I played Ku Klux. My mother
was a past master at making masks out of newspapers
which she folded and cut out with her scissors. I remember how the Negroes used to pretend to be ter-
ribly frightened and how pleased we were with our
efforts. The old Presbyterian High School used to
be the meeting place of the genuine article and was
always held in awe by us boys for a long time on that
account. You will remember that it stood vacant and
gloomy in the grove just opposite our home place for
many years.

As to Judge Tourgee, we looked upon him as some
sort of a pirate, mysterious and blackened by a thousand crimes, and we glanced at him covertly when he
happened around. He was a sort of ogre, but even
then we admired him for his courage and wondered at
it, coming as he did from the North. Very dark stories
were whispered of his doings out in far-off Warners-

ville, the Negro settlement out by the Methodist graveyard. He held meetings out there that we were almost
prepared to say were a species of voodooism.

You will remember that he had a beautiful country
place out on the Guilford College Road. There were a
greenhouse, flowers, shrubbery, and an immense rustic
arbor there and it was used for dances and had an
upper and lower floor. Miss Sallie Coleman was visiting in Greensboro and either expressed a desire for
magnolias or Will conceived that she would like to
have some, so we started about midnight on the six-
mile hike to West Green to spoil and loot. Strange to
say, the memory of the moonlight night is with me now
even after all these years. It was a perfect night. The
moon was full and showering down her mellow radiance
in great floods. I can see the long white line of road
stretching out, hear the whippoorwills and smell the
good night air laden with fragrance and I can see the
long row of magnolia trees out in the wheat field and
orchard with their great white flowers gleaming out
from the dark foliage. I can also feel the creepy sen-
sation that I felt when we mounted the fence and
started across the open field for the trees and the
relief that came when we crossed the fence with the
loot. We carried them back and laid them on Miss
Sallie's doorstep.

The boys in Miss Lina's school were divided into
two clubs, the Brickbats and the Union Jacks. The
members of the Union Jacks were Percy Gray, Will
Porter, Jim Doak, and Tom Tate. Tom Tate, the
only one of the four to live beyond middle life, wrote
of the Union Jacks:

This club had headquarters in an outbuilding on the
grounds of the old Edgeworth Female College, which
some years previously had been destroyed by fire. In

this house they kept their arms and accoutrements, consisting of wooden battle-axes, shields, and old cavalry sabres, and on Friday nights it was their custom to sally forth armed and equipped in search of adventure, like knights of old from their castle, carefully avoiding the dark nooks where the moonlight did not fall. Will was the leading spirit in these daring pursuits, and many was the hair-raising adventure these ten-year-old heroes encountered, and the shields and battle-axes were ofttimes thrown aside so as not to impede the free action of the nether limbs when safety lay only in flight. Ghosts were common occurrences in those days, or rather nights, and arms were useless to cope with the supernatural; it took good sturdy legs.

Meanwhile, in the Porter home, all was not prosperity. Dr. Porter had never been a practical man. In his younger days it was his mother who saw to it that his bills were sent out. That procedure was regarded as a violation of the conventions. It was not good form for a physician to send a statement of the amount due. The patient was supposed to settle once a year without a reminder. Professor Smith has recorded an anecdote illustrating the troubles of a country doctor of the old South. Dr. Porter had visited two maiden ladies and when a bill was sent to their father he sent back indignant word that the visits were only "social calls." "Social calls," wrote O. Henry's grandmother, "I want you to understand that my son Algernon don't make social calls on maiden ladies at two o'clock in the morning and they a-suffering with cramp colic."

After the death of his wife, Dr. Porter became more

visionary than ever. According to one of Will Porter's schoolmates, John H. Dillard of Murphy, North
Carolina, Dr. Porter fell a victim to the delusion that
he had solved the problem of perpetual motion and
spent nearly all his time working on his machines. In
the words of Professor Smith, a perpetual motion
water-wheel, a new-fangled churn, a washing machine,
a flying machine, a horseless carriage to be run by
steam, and a cotton-picking contrivance that was to
take the place of Negro labor became obsessions with
him. His mother, who was still the strength of the
household, consigned these inventions to the barn, and
it was at her orders that Will and young Dillard often
demolished them during the doctor's absences.

Naturally the home of this inventive Micawber was
not one of plenty. There were originally three Porter
boys, Will, and his brothers Shirley Worth Porter,
born August 6, 1860, and David Weir Porter, born
March 26, 1865. David Weir died in childhood.
Until 1882, when he left for Texas, Will lived with
his grandmother, his father, his Aunt Lina, and his
brother Shirley Worth. It was to help out the meager
family income that Will Porter at an early age went to
work in the evenings as a clerk in the drug store of his
uncle, Clarke Porter. Here Will gathered experience
that was to serve him in his darkest hour. Here
also he acquired much of the knowledge that was later
to be used in such stories as "The Love Philtre of
Ikey Schoenstein" and "Makes the Whole World Kin."
That was the second phase of his practical education
as a story-teller. The first phase was the reading of
his boyhood years.

His schooling ended when he was fifteen, and before he was out of his teens he had done most of the reading that was to influence his writing life. One of his cherished treasures was a dictionary, which he studied from cover to cover. It was the foundation of his later style.

I did more reading [he once recorded] between my thirteenth and nineteenth years than I have done in all the years since, and my taste at that time was much better than it is now, for I used to read nothing but the classics. Burton's *Anatomy of Melancholy* and Lane's translation of *The Arabian Nights* were my favorites.

But there were other books read that were far from being classics. In an English magazine Will Porter found two serial stories called *Jack Harkaway* and *Dick Lightheart*. These tales suggested the two school clubs, the Brickbats and the Union Jacks.

Also, like most healthy minded boys of his age, Will Porter fell under the spell of the dime novel, and his childhood was enriched with adventures with *The Red Rover, Three Fingered Jack, The Miller and His Men, The Terror of Jamaica,* and *The Wood Demon*.

We had [Tom Tate recorded] the biggest collection of dime novels I have ever seen outside of a cigar stand, and I don't think we could have been over seven or eight years old. Will soon imbibed the style and could tell as good a thriller as the author of *Red-Eyed Rube*. I can see the circle of wide-eyed little fellows lying around in the shade on the grass as he opened up with: "If you had been a close observer you might have descried a solitary horseman slowly wending his way," or "The sun was sinking behind the western hills."

But besides *The Arabian Nights*, which were to be reflected in his own life, and the *Anatomy of Melancholy*, there was much early reading of a sound nature. There were the inevitable novels of Scott, Dickens, Thackeray, Charles Reade, Bulwer-Lytton, Wilkie Collins, Auerbach, Victor Hugo, and Alexander Dumas. His favorite among Dickens's novels was *Bleak House*, and among Thackeray's *Vanity Fair*. Like many other men, his interest in the unfinished Dickens story, *The Mystery of Edwin Drood*, led him to attempt to complete the plot. One book of Charles Reade held him above all the others. He once said: "If you want philosophy well put up in fiction, read *The Cloister and the Hearth*. I never saw such a novel. There is material for dozens of short stories in that one book alone."

Professor Smith made a very careful study of O. Henry's early reading:

His love of Scott came *via* an interest which he soon outgrew in *Thaddeus of Warsaw* and *The Scottish Chiefs*. Three other novels made a deep impression on him at this time: Spielhagen's *Hammer and Anvil*, Warren's *Ten Thousand a Year*, and John Estes Cooke's *Surry of Eagle's Nest*. He thought Warren's character of Oily Gammon the best portrait of a villain ever drawn and always called one of Greensboro's lawyers by that name. Stonewall Jackson and Jeb Stuart, among the characters introduced by Cooke, were the Confederate heroes of whom he talked with most enthusiasm.

In "The Emancipation of Billy," O. Henry drew the picture of a drug store in a southern town. Probably in that fleeting description of the emporium of Mr. Appleby R. Fentress, his mind went back to the drug store of his uncle where so many of his boyhood nights

were spent. No Governor Pemberton graced it with
his patronage, but it was the social club of the little
town in the 1870's. In the back room there was usually
a game of chess or checkers going on. There was a
stove behind the prescription counter and round it
gathered many of the local celebrities, the judge, the
colonel, and the doctor among them. Ponderously the
war was refought from Sumter to Appomattox and,
in the winter of 1878-79, the counting out of Mr.
Tilden heatedly denounced. Meanwhile, behind the
counter, there was a quiet, reticent boy making his
drawings, and storing up impressions. The talk to
which he listened was not of the kind to inspire hero-
worship; and perhaps from those evenings dated his
life-long distaste for what he called the professional
Southerner.

Meanwhile his pencil was busy, delineating the scene,
drawing portraits and caricatures. From his earliest
years he had shown a decided talent as an artist. When
he was ten he drew a picture of a playmate that, though
crude in execution, was striking in its accuracy. In
the drug store on Elm Street, opposite the old Benbow
Hotel, he was forever making sketches. At times the
pictures served a practical end. Those were the days
of lax business methods and easy credit. In the owner's
absence a stranger would enter the drug store and run
up a bill. Later Will Porter would report the matter
to his uncle. "Who was it?" the question would be.
"I never saw him before, but he looks like this." Uncle
Clarke would survey the drawing on a piece of wrap-
ping paper and say: "Oh, that's Bill Jenkins out here
at Reedy Fork. He owes me $7.25."

THE O. HENRY DRUG STORE AT GREENSBORO, NORTH CAROLINA

There Will Porter worked for five years for his uncle, Clarke Porter, dispensing drugs, soda water and notions among the patrons. There he first distinguished himself as a caricaturist.

That pictorial talent was quickly recognized. From Greensboro the fame of his cartoons spread to neighboring towns. Some years before Will Porter left his birthplace, never to return to it, an opportunity came that might have changed his entire career. Colonel Robert Bingham, a relative by marriage and superintendent of the famous Bingham School, then at Mebane, North Carolina, urged him to come at once to Bingham's where an education free of charge would be given him. "My only direct connection with William Sidney as a boy," writes Colonel Bingham, "was to offer him his tuition and board in order to get use of his talent as a cartoonist for the amusement of our boys. He was an artist with chalk on a blackboard. But he could not accept my offer for lack of means to provide for his uniform and books." Though O. Henry was never heard to allude to this opportunity, it was probably one of many of life's chances that was in the back of his mind when he wrote "Roads of Destiny."

The night work in the drug store was playing havoc with Will Porter's health. He had a hacking cough and those who knew his physical inheritance feared for him. Always opposed to any form of violent exercise, he spent the leisure hours of his Sundays in pleasant indolence, reading a book or building daydreams. Far horizons were beckoning to him, and an immediate change in his method of life was necessary. The opportunity came in the spring of 1882, when he was rounding out his twentieth year.

II

HEARTS OF THE WEST

"Son, there are plenty of things in the chaparral, and on the prairies, and up the cañons that you don't understand. But I want to thank you for listening to a garrulous old man's story. We old Texans love to talk about our adventures and our old comrades."

Friends in San Rosario

IN 1882, when Will Porter, a pale-faced anæmic boy who weighed hardly a hundred pounds went to live on a sheep ranch in La Salle County, Texas, forty miles from Cotulla, and fourteen miles from the nearest post office at Fort Ewell, the West was still the West, wearing its sombrero not as an affectation, taking its whisky straight, rugged in its virtues and its code of honor, somewhat boyish in its enthusiasms and its extravagances, sound in its principles, but at times inclined to be lax and lawless in the application of these principles. Will Porter was destined to be a tragic victim of that laxity.

For fifteen years, off and on, Will Porter lived in Texas. It was there that he stored up some of his richest memories. No one of his stories was definitely placed in his native North Carolina, though the inference is that he had that state in mind when he wrote "The Emancipation of Billy" and "The Guardian of the Accolade." But he began his career by writing tales against the Texas background. Some forty of his stories are Texas stories. They comprise practically all of *Hearts of the West*, and run through *Options, Roads of Destiny, Sixes and Sevens, Whirligigs*, and

18

naturally the collection, *Rolling Stones*. They reflect every phase of his career—his activities on the sheep ranch, as a pharmacist, as a bookkeeper for a real estate firm, in the General Land Office, in the bank at Austin, and as a journalist with *The Rolling Stone* and the Houston *Post*.)

The manner of Will Porter's migration from Greensboro to Texas was as follows: The doctor to whom reference has been made as one of the habitués of Clarke Porter's drug store was Dr. James K. Hall. When Will Porter's father drifted away from steady practice to pursue his inventive will-o'-the-wisp, Dr. Hall succeeded him as Greensboro's leading physician. He had always taken a keen interest in the son of his fellow practitioner, despite the fact his great height, his stoop, and the pose of his head, made him the frequent target of the boy's cartoons.

Dr. Hall had three sons of his own who had settled in Texas and there made good. They were Lee, Dick, and Frank. Dick, as Richard M. Hall, had become a leading citizen. Well educated, he had lived the adventurous life of a Texas Ranger and served in various local offices. Later he was to attain to greater political distinction. From 1887 to 1891, he was State Land Commissioner. In 1891, he ran for governor of Texas against James Hogg and was defeated by a narrow margin. His wife came of a family of educators and lawyers who had been eminent in the state's history. Texas born, she had been educated in Virginia and Louisiana, and in the broadening of Will Porter's reading she carried on the work begun in his early life by his Aunt Lina.

In March, 1882, Dr. and Mrs. Hall were planning a visit to their sons in Texas. Dr. Hall, worried over Will Porter's health, invited him to accompany them. He felt that the mild, dry climate of La Salle County and the open ranch life would do the boy a world of good. "Will," said Dr. Hall, "I want you to go with us. You need the change, and ranch life will build you up." Three months later, when Dr. and Mrs. Hall left the Richard M. Hall house to return to North Carolina, Will Porter did not accompany them. He was staying on as "one of the family."

The Texan of those days was still a legendary figure. In fiction he was reflected in a novel, now relatively forgotten, but in the middle of the 1880's as much discussed and far more widely read than Albion W. Tourgee's *A Fool's Errand* had been a few years earlier. That was Archibald Clavering Gunter's *Mr. Potter of Texas*, a book from which Europeans and Americans of the eastern seaboard largely derived their impressions of the state.

Dick Hall was a personage. His brother Lee, better known as Red Hall, was more of a personage. As Professor Smith has said, it was Lee's personality and Lee's achievement that opened the doors of romance to Will Porter in Texas and contributed atmosphere and flavor to the nineteen stories that make up *Hearts of the West*. Ten years before Will went to La Salle County, Red Hall's fame spread throughout the state. He had led the Rangers in the last battle with the Comanches in northeast Texas. "He did more to rid Texas of desperadoes," wrote John G. Elgin, "than any officer that Texas ever had. He has made more

bad men lay down their guns and delivered more desperadoes and outlaws into custody than any other officer in Texas."

Major-General Jesse M. Lee called him "the bravest
of the brave." Edward King, in *The Great South,*
wrote of him as one who seemed to bear a charmed life.
"He moved about tranquilly every day in a community
where there were doubtless a hundred men who would
have delighted to shed his blood; was often called to
interfere in brawls at all hours of the day and night;
yet his life went on. He had been ambushed and shot
at and threatened times innumerable, yet he always exhibited a scorn for his enemies, which finally ended in
forcing them to admire him." In April, 1877, he was
made Lieutenant of the Texas Rangers and received
his commission as Captain later in the same year. At
the head of his company of thirty men—the largest in
Texas—he patrolled the vast territory from the mouth
of the Rio Grande to the head of the Nueces. But by
1882 he had retired from the service and was acting
as agent and general manager for the Dull Brothers.

Even this more peaceful occupation had its dangers.
The ranchmen of La Salle County had been in the
habit of turning out their cattle to graze over what
had been from time immemorial a boundless prairie.
They resented Captain Lee Hall's action in having his
ranch fenced—one could ride for forty miles without
coming to the end of the fence—and there ensued a
fence-cutting war, famous in Texas annals. To put a
stop to the fence-cutting, the Captain enlisted the
services of a force of cowboys and Mexicans. But his
wife, a beautiful and highly educated woman of a

family originally from Pennsylvania, lived in the continual fear that her husband would be killed. Of the life in 1882 and Will Porter's association with it she has written:

At the time Willie Porter was with us in Texas, Captain Hall had charge of the ranch in La Salle County belonging to the Dull Brothers, of Harrisburg, Pennsylvania. He had a contract with these gentlemen to buy the land, fence and stock it, and then operate the ranch as Superintendent. And it is this ranch and his life thereon that O. Henry has immortalized in many of his Texas stories. Captain Hall had to rid La Salle County of a notorious band of fence-cutting cattle thieves, and his famous result is chronicled in the Bexar County Courts of 1882. He finally succeeded in electing "Charlie" McKinney, a former member of his company of Rangers, as Sheriff of La Salle County, and this officer proved himself most efficient and capable, securing peace to that community until his untimely death.

When we first went to the ranch, we occupied a small frame house of one room, about 12 by 8 in size. This room was sitting-room, bedroom, dining-room, etc., in fact, the whole house. They then built a log house, about 12 by 35 feet, for Captain Hall and myself, and Mr. and Mrs. Dick Hall took possession of the log house, and it was here that Will Porter first stayed with them.

We lived a most unsettled, exciting existence. Captain Hall was in constant danger. His life was threatened in many ways, and the mail was heavy with warnings, generally in the shape of crude sketches, portraying effigies with ropes around their necks, and bearing the unfailing inscription "Your Necktie." We usually traveled at night, nearly always with cocked guns. It was at this period of our life, during the struggle be-

tween the legitimate owners and the cattle thieves, that
O. Henry saw something of the real desperado.

Willie Porter himself had a most charming but shy
personality at this time. I remember him very distinctly and pleasantly. At the time he was on the
ranch with us he was really living with Mr. and Mrs.
Dick Hall, though he was a frequent visitor at our
house. The intercourse between O. Henry and Captain
Hall was more of a social than a business nature,
though he acted as cowboy for a period under Captain
Hall about the year 1882.

In the Dick Hall household there was at the time
another permanent visitor. That was B. F. Hughes,
Mrs. Hall's brother. With the Dick Halls and their
infant daughter, this made a family of five. There were
no hired men and usually no servants. Will Porter had
no regular work, nor was he hired by Dick Hall. He
lived with the family just as Mr. Hughes was living.
The sheep ranch itself required little work. But Will
was naturally brought into contacts with the cowboys
who thronged the neighborhood. From them he
learned to ride and rope, and like Curly of "The
Higher Abdication," received the puncher's accolade
that made him "pardner" and stirrup brother, foot to
foot.

"In six months' time he had developed into a regular
broncho-buster," writes Mr. Hughes,[1] "and was as
valuable as any man in Lee Hall's service. Porter was
then initiated into the cowboy fraternity by an initia-
tion similar to that of Curly in 'The Higher Abdication.'" Whatever linguistic attainments he afterwards

[1] Hyder E. Rollins, "O. Henry's Texas Days," *The Bookman*,
1914.

possessed he acquired at this period. On the ranch he
took up the study of French and German. At least a
smattering of these languages is reflected in many of
the stories. But more serious and much more important was his pursuit of Spanish. That language was
used by all the cowboys as well as the Mexicans. In
three months Will Porter was conceded to be the best
speaker of Spanish on the ranch. Naturally, Mr.
Rollins says, he spoke a "greaser" dialect, but he
bought a grammar, mastered it, and learned to write
and speak correct Spanish as well. It was to serve
him in Central America and in the writing of
Hearts of the West, of *Cabbages and Kings*, and in his
occasional tales of Spanish-Latin-American life in New
York.

With the cowboys Will Porter learned to ride and
manage his horse, shoot from the saddle, dip and shear
sheep, lasso cattle, and break the will of a stubborn
broncho. With them he also first experimented with
the culinary art, which he was later to practice in
strange surroundings. But there were long hours of
seclusion. When his stirrup brothers would be in
Laredo, where the trouble began that moved the
Laredo Kid of "A Double-Dyed Deceiver" to migrate
to South America, playing conquian, or monte, or
poker, or taking in the bailes, Porter would remain at
the ranch, and, stretched on a cot under a shady tree,
would read from morning to night.

But in the evenings he would emerge from his solitude and with a rickety guitar in his hands, he would
thrum a tune, and sing cowboy songs; or else with a
pencil and a piece of cardboard draw caricatures of

his friends, or make pictures illustrating the day's happenings. Once in a great while he would invent a story for the entertainment of those in the Dick Hall home. But according to Mrs. Hall, no one suspected his talent for story-telling. It was obscured by his cleverness with his pencil. Yet it was while he was living on the Hall ranch that he wrote, and at once destroyed, his first stories of western life.

It was there, too, that he drew the now famous series of illustrations for a book that was never printed. The author of the book was "Uncle Joe" Dixon, who had been a prospector in the bonanza mining days in Colorado. The book was to have been called *Carbonate Days*, and to have been a narrative of personal experiences in novel form. Uncle Joe has left the story of the origin of the Will Porter drawings. Here is his story:

Years before I went to Colorado, John Maddox—now one of the most influential men of Texas—and myself had been intimate friends in Texas, which state was my home. In 1877, he and I learned of the gold excitement in the Black Hills of Dakota and had started for that region and were stranded in Chicago, where we were fleeced like lambs by the Chicago Board of Trade, when we tried a little flier in the wheat market. Maddox returned to Texas, where he made a fortune in the land business, but I stopped in Kansas City, got into newspaper work and made that my home. It was from there I went to Leadville in 1879 and spent several years in the Rockies prospecting for gold and silver.

One day Maddox wrote to me, after I had been in the Rockies some time, and said: "Joe, your carbonates lie at the bottom of an inkwell. Come back and put

down the pick for the pen and you'll make a fortune.
A man who can see what you can see in the common
things of life, and write of them as you can write of
them, can create a gold mine of his own. Come back
to Austin and write a book. I will stake you for six
months or longer, and you write of your life in the
Rockies, as you can write of it, and your fortune is
made."

I hesitated, but John kept writing to me so in 1883
I went.

In the Maddox house in the suburbs of Austin, Uncle
Joe settled down to work early and late on *Carbonate
Days*. Maddox promised that when the book was
finished he would have it illustrated and published in
the very best style, and that the two of them would
take the boat from Galveston to New York to see that
the masterpiece was properly launched.

One day he [Maddox] came in and said: "Joe,
there is a young fellow here who came from North
Carolina with Dick Hall named Will Porter, who can
draw like blazes. I believe he would be the very one
to make the illustrations for your book. Dick Hall
owns a sheep ranch out not very far from here, and
Porter is working for him. Now you go right out
there and take the book along and tell him just about
what you want, and let him have a crack at it."

It looked like a pretty good idea to me, for it seemed
to me that a man who had seen something of the same
life might be better able to draw the pictures.

I found Porter to be a young, silent fellow, with deep,
brooding, blue eyes, cynical for his years, and with a
facile pen, later to be turned to word-painting instead
of picture-drawing.

I would discuss the story with Will in the daytime,
and at night he would draw the pictures. There were

forty of them in all. And while crude, they were all good and true to the life they depicted.

The ranch was a vast chaparral plain, and for three weeks Porter worked on the illustrations, and he and I roamed about the place and talked together. We slept together in a rude little shack. I became interested in the boy's personality. He was a taciturn fellow, with a peculiar little hiss when amused, instead of the boyish laugh one might have expected, and he could give the queerest caustic turn to speech, getting off epigrams like little sharp bullets, every once in a while, and always unexpectedly.

Uncle Joe Dixon's story is much longer. It tells how he recognized Will Porter's latent ability as a writer and urged him to try his hand at writing for the magazines, a suggestion which the boy did not follow. Candidly, like many other original discoverers of O. Henry, Uncle Joe in that rôle is not to be taken too seriously. Uncle Joe goes on to describe the adventures of the manuscript of *Carbonate Days*. Uncle Joe, with what the reader of his quoted reminiscences is likely to consider a sound sense of literary values, reached the conclusion that the book was not turning out to be the masterpiece on which his friend Maddox was counting. In a moment of doubt he tore the manuscript into fragments and consigned them to the waters of the Colorado River. Then he wrote a note to Maddox telling him what he had done.

Maddox organized a searching party that put off in a boat and found what remained of *Carbonate Days* lodged against a sand bar. With the salvaged paper in his possession Maddox then took a train to New York where he employed an expert in the hope that the manuscript could be patched together. But the damage had been too great. To placate him, Uncle Joe wrote a burlesque called "An Arrested Movement in Southern Literature," in which he told of his brief career as a novelist and of the irretrievable damage done southern literature by the destruction of his novel. Whatever Uncle Joe may have lacked in literary quality, he seems to have possessed a sense of humor. Will Porter also illustrated the "Arrested Movement," but the illustrations have been destroyed.

From the Texas ranch Will Porter wrote often to his friends in Greensboro but only a few of his letters have been preserved. These were the letters to Mrs. Hall, the wife of Dr. Hall and the mother of Dick and Captain Lee Hall, and to Dr. W. P. Beall, a physician associated in practice with Dr. Hall. Dr. Beall was a member of the Vesper Reading Club of Lenoir, North Carolina, and it was his suggestion that Will Porter be elected to honorary membership. Acknowledging the honor the young ranchman wrote a letter to "The Ladies and Gentlemen of the Vesper Club." The letter follows in part:

Some time ago I had the pleasure of receiving a letter from the secretary of your association which, on observing the strange postmark of Lenoir, I opened with fear and trembling, although I knew I didn't owe anybody anything in that city. I began to peruse the document and found, first, that I had been elected an honorary member of that old and world-renowned body amidst thunders of applause that resounded far among the hills of Caldwell County, while the deafening cheers of the members were plainly heard above the din of the loafers in the grocery store. When I had recovered somewhat from the shock which such an unexpected honor must necessarily produce on a person of delicate sensibilities and modest ambition, I ventured to proceed and soon gathered that I was requested to employ my gigantic intellect in writing a letter to the club. I again picked myself up, brushed the dust off, and was disappointed not to find a notice of my nomination for governor of North Carolina.

The origin of the idea that I could write a letter of any interest to any one is entirely unknown to me. The associations with which I have previously corresponded have been generally in the dry goods line and my letters for the most part of a conciliatory, pay-you-next-week tendency, which could hardly have procured me the high honors that your club has conferred on me. But I will try and give you a truthful and correct account in a brief and condensed manner of some of the wonderful things to be seen and heard in this country. The information usually desired in such a case is in regard to people, climate, manners, customs, and general peculiarities.

The people of the State of Texas consist principally of men, women, and children, with a sprinkling of cowboys. The weather is very good, thermometer rarely rising above 2,500 degrees in the shade and hardly ever below 212. There is a very pleasant little phase in the weather which is called a "norther" by the natives, which endears the country very much to the stranger who experiences it. You are riding along on a boiling day in September, dressed as airily as etiquette will allow, watching the fish trying to climb out of the pools of boiling water along the way and wondering how long it would take to walk home with a pocket compass and 75 cents in Mexican money, when a wind as cold as the icy hand of death swoops down on you from the north and the "norther" is upon you.

Where do you go? If you are far from home it

depends entirely upon what kind of a life you have led previous to this time as to where you go. Some people go straight to heaven while others experience a change of temperature by the transition. "Northers" are very useful in killing off the surplus population in some degree, while the remainder die naturally and peacefully in their boots.

The letter concludes:

But I must bring this hurried letter to a close. I have already written far into the night. The moon is low and the wind is still. The lovely stars, the "forget-me-nots of the angels," which have blossomed all night in the infinite meadows of heaven, unheeded and unseen by us poor sleepy mortals for whom they spread their shining petals and silvery beams in vain, are twinkling above in all their beauty and mystery. The lonely cry of the coyote is heard mingling with the noise of a piece of strong Texas bacon trying to get out of the pantry. It is at a time like this when all is quiet, when even nature seems to sleep, that old memories come back from their graves and haunt us with the scenes they bring before us. Faces dead long ago stare at us from the night and voices that once could make the heart leap with joy and the eye light up with pleasure seem to sound in our ears. With such feelings we sit wrapped in thought, living over again our youth until awakening comes and we are again in the present with its cares and bitterness. It is now I sit wondering and striving to recall the past. Longingly I turn my mind back, groping about in a time that is gone, never more to return, endeavoring to think and convene my doubting spirit whether or not I fed the pup at supper. But listen! I hear the members of the V. R. C. rushing to the door. They have torn away the man stationed there to keep them inside during the transactions of the evening, and I will soon close with the request that the secretary in notifying me not to send any more letters may break the terrifying news as gently as possible, applying the balm of fair and delusive sentences which may prepare me at first by leading up gradually to the fearful and hope-destroying announcement.

In that letter to the Vesper Reading Club we have a picture of the mind of Aladdin in the formative years, of the Will Porter of the "smart-Alec" days. The awkward English, the obvious imitation, the extravagance of expression, the feeble attempts at wit, were to follow him throughout all his prentice years. It was only by the blackening of much paper that O. Henry won through to his style and his individuality.

A letter to Mrs. Hall:

La Salle County, Texas

DEAR MRS. HALL:

Your welcome letter, which I received a good while ago, was much appreciated, and I thought I would answer it in the hopes of getting another from you. I am very short of news, so if you find anything in this letter rather incredible, get Dr. Beall to discount it for you to the proper size. He always questions my veracity since I came out here. Why didn't he do it when I was at home? Dick has got his new house done, and it looks very comfortable and magnificent. It has a tobacco-barn-like grandeur about it that always strikes a stranger with awe, and during a strong north wind the safest place about it is outside at the northern end.

A colored lady is now slinging hash in the kitchen and has such an air of command and condescension about her that the pots and kettles all get out of her way with a rush. I think she is a countess or a dukess in disguise. Catulla has grown wonderfully since you left; thirty or forty new houses have gone up and

thirty or forty barrels of whiskey gone down. The bar-
keeper is going to Europe on a tour next summer and
is thinking of buying Mexico for his little boy to play
with. They are getting along finely with the pasture;
there are sixty or seventy men at work on a fence and
have been having good weather for working. Ed
Brockman is there in charge of the commissary tent,
and issues provisions to the contractors. I saw him last
week, and he seemed very well.

Lee came up and asked me to go down to the camps
and take Brockman's place for a week or so while he
went to San Antonio. Well, I went down some six or
seven miles from the ranch. On arriving I counted at
the commissary tent nine niggers, sixteen Mexicans,
seven hounds, twenty-one six-shooters, four desperadoes,
three shot-guns, and a barrel of molasses. Inside there
were a good many sacks of corn, flour, meal, sugar,
beans, coffee, and potatoes, a big box of bacon, some
boots, shoes, clothes, saddles, rifles, tobacco, and some
more hounds. The work was to issue the stores to
the contractors as they sent for them, and was light
and easy to do. Out at the rear of the tent they had
started a graveyard of men who had either kicked one
of the hounds or prophesied a norther. When night
came, the gentleman whose good fortune it was to be
dispensing the stores gathered up his saddle-blankets,
four old corn sacks, an oil coat and a sheep skin, made
all the room he could in the tent by shifting and arranging the bacon, meal, etc., gave a sad look at the
dogs that immediately filled the vacuum, and went and
slept outdoors. The few days I was there I was
treated more as a guest than one doomed to labor. Had
an offer to gamble from the nigger cook, and was allowed as an especial favor to drive up the nice, pretty
horses and give them some corn. And the kind of
accomadating old tramps and cowboys that consti-
tute the outfit would drop in and board, and sleep

and smoke, and cuss and gamble, and lie and brag, and do everything in their power to make the time pass pleasantly and profitably—to themselves. I enjoyed the thing very much, and one evening when I saw Brockman roll up to the camp, I was very sorry, and went off very early next morning in order to escape the heart-breaking sorrow of parting and leave-taking with the layout.

Now, if you think this fine letter worth a reply, write me a long letter and tell me what I would like to know, and I will rise up and call you a friend in need, and send you a fine cameria obscuria view of this ranch and itemized account of its operations and manifold charms. Tell Dr. Beall not to send me any cake, it would make some postmaster on the road ill if he should eat too much, and I am a friend to all humanity. I am writing by a very poor light, which must excuse bad spelling and uninteresting remarks.

I remain,

Very respectfully yours,

W. S. Porter

Here is another letter to Mrs. Hall, dated Kyntoekneeyough Ranch, November 31, 1883:

Dear Mrs. Hall:

As I have not heard from you since the shout you gave when you set out from the station on your way home I guess you have not received some seven or eight letters from me, and hence your silence. The mails are so unreliable that they may all have been lost. If you don't get this you had better send to Washington and get them to look over the dead letter office for the others. I have nothing to tell you of any interest, except that we all nearly froze to death last night, thermometer away below 32 degrees in the shade all night.

You ought by all means to come back to Texas this winter; you would love it more and more; that same little breeze that you looked for so anxiously last winter is with us now, as cold as Callum Bros. suppose their soda water to be.

My sheep are doing finely; they never were in better condition. They give me very little trouble, for I have never been able to see one of them yet. I will now proceed to give you all the news about the ranch. Dick has got his new house well under way, the pet lamb is doing finely, and I take the cake for cooking mutton steak and fine gravy. The chickens are doing mighty well, the garden produces magnificent prickly pears and grass; onions are worth two for five cents, and Mr. Haynes has shot a Mexican.

Please send by express to this ranch seventy-five cooks and two hundred washerwomen, blind or wooden legged ones preferred. The climate has a tendency to make them walk off every two or three days, which must be overcome. Ed Brockman has quit the store and I think is going to work for Lee among the cows. Wears a red sash and swears so fluently that he has been mistaken for a member of the Texas Legislature.

If you see Dr. Beall bow to him for me, politely but distantly; he refuses to waste a line upon me. I suppose he is too much engaged in courting to write any letters. Give Dr. Hall my profoundest regards. I think about him invariably whenever he is occupying my thoughts.

Influenced by the contents of the *Bugle* there is an impression general at this ranch that you are president, secretary, and committee, etc., of the various associations of fruit fairs, sewing societies, church fairs, Presbytery, general assembly, conference, medical conventions, and baby shows that make up the glory and renown of North Carolina in general, and while I heartily congratulate the aforesaid institutions on their having such a zealous and efficient officer, I tremble lest their requirements leave you not time to favor me with a letter in reply to this, and assure you that if you would so honor me I would highly appreciate the effort. I would rather have a good long letter from you than many *Bugles*. In your letter be certain to refer as much as possible to the advantages of civilized life over the barbarous; you might mention the theatres you see there, the nice things you eat, warm fires, niggers to cook and bring in wood; a special reference to nice beefsteak would be advisable. You know our being reminded of these luxuries makes us contented and happy. When we hear of you people at home eating turkeys and mince pies and getting drunk Christmas and having a fine time generally we become more and more reconciled to this country and would not leave it for anything.

I must close now as I must go and dress for the opera.

Yours very truly,
W. S. Porter

'A week later Will Porter was writing to Dr. Beall:

Dear Doctor:

I send you a play—the regular high art full orchestra, gilt-edged drama. I send it to you because of old acquaintance and as a revival of old associations. Was I not ever ready in times gone by to generously furnish a spatula and other assistance when you did buy the succulent watermelon? And was it not by my connivance and help that you did oft from the gentle Oscar Mayo skates entice? But I digress. I think that I have so concealed the identity of the characters introduced that no one will be able to place them, as they all appear under fictitious names, although I admit that many of the incidents and scenes were suggested by actual experiences of the author in your city.

You will, of course, introduce the play upon the stage
if proper arrangements can be made. I have not yet
had the opportunity of ascertaining whether Edwin
Booth, John McCullough, or Henry Irving can be secured. However, I will leave all such matters to your
judgment and taste. Some few suggestions I will make
with regard to the mounting of the piece which may
be of value to you. Discrimination will be necessary
in selecting a fit person to represent the character of
Bill Slax, the tramp. The part is that of a youth of
great beauty and noble manners, temporarily under a
cloud, and is generally rather difficult to fill properly.
The other minor characters, such as damfools, citizens,
police, customers, countrymen, etc., can be very easily
supplied, especially the first.

Let it be announced in the *Patriot* for several days
that in front of Benbow Hall, at a certain hour, a
man will walk a tight rope seventy feet from the ground
who has never made the attempt before; that the exhibition will be FREE, and that the odds are 20 to 1
that the man will be killed. A large crowd will gather.
Then let the Guilford Grays charge one side, the Reids-
ville Light Infantry the other, with fixed bayonets,
and a man with a hat commence taking up a collection
in the rear. By this means they can be readily driven
into a hall and the door locked.

I have studied a long time about devising a plan
for obtaining pay from the audience and have finally
struck upon the only feasible one, I think.

After the performance let some one come out on the
stage and announce that James Forbis will speak two
hours. The result, easily explainable by philosophical
and psychological reasons, will be as follows: The minds
of the audience, elated and inspired by the hope of
immediate departure when confronted by such a terror-
inspiring and dismal prospect, will collapse with the
fearful reaction which will take place, and for a space

of time they will remain in a kind of comatose, farewell-vain-world condition. Now, as this is the time when the interest of the evening is at its highest pitch, let the melodious strains of the orchestra steal forth as a committee, appointed by the managers, of lawyers, druggists, doctors, and revenue officers, go round and relieve the audience of the price of admission for each one. Where the person has no money let it be made up from another, but on no account let the whole sum taken be more than the just amount at usual rates.

As I said before, the characters in the play are purely imaginary, and therefore not to be confounded with real persons. But lest any one, feeling some of the idiosyncrasies and characteristics apply too forcibly to his own high moral and irreproachable self, should allow his warlike and combative spirits to arise, you might as you go, kind of casually like, produce the impression that I rarely miss my aim with a Colt's forty-five, but if that does not have the effect of quieting the splenetic individual, and he still thirsts for Bill Slax's gore, just inform him that if he comes out here he can't get any whiskey within two days' journey of my present abode, and water will have to be his only beverage while on the warpath. This, I am sure, will avert the bloody and direful conflict.

Accept my lasting regards and professions of respect.

Ever yours,
BILL SLAX

Perhaps even more than the letter to the Vesper Reading Club, this letter to Dr. Beall, in straining after effects that the writer believes to be comical, reflects the callowness of youth. Obvious is the delight of the boy in his riotous use of the words, culled from study of his constant companion, Webster's Dictionary; words that he had swallowed, but had not yet digested.

But Will Porter was to write few more letters from the ranch. Dick Hall had bought another ranch near Florence, Williamson County, and thither he moved his family and his sheep. Will did not go with him. His ranch days were over. The open life had done much for him: restored a health that had been seriously threatened, built up his body, and toughened his muscles. But he was twenty-one, and the isolation of the life had begun to pall. He wanted the excitements of the city. He went to Austin.

III

A YOUNG MAN IN AUSTIN

If you should chance to visit the General Land Office, slip into the draughtsmen's room and ask to be shown the map of Salado County. *Georgia's Ruling*

THE Aladdin of the Wonderful Lamp was a lazy, idle boy, much given to dreaming. Will Porter at the Aladdin period of his life had many lazy, idle hours, in which he builded dreams. There were many of them in the life on the ranch which had lasted for two years. It was in the spring of 1882 that he had migrated from Greensboro; it was in the spring of 1884 that he moved to Austin. He was then in his twenty-third year. The last letter that he is known to have written from the ranch was one to Mrs. Hall in Greensboro bearing the date of March 13. It reflects his restlessness:

MY DEAR MRS. HALL:

As you must be somewhat surprised that I haven't been answering your letters for a long time, I thought I would write and let you know that I never got any of them and for that reason have not replied. When the *Bugle, Patriot,* and your letters stopped, I am way behind in Greensboro news, and am consumed with a burning desire to know if Julius A. Gray has returned from Fayetteville, if Caldcleugh has received a fresh assortment of canary bird cages, or if Fishblate's clothing is still two hundred per cent below first cost of manufacturing, and I know that you will take

pity on the benighted of the far southwest and relieve
the anxiety.   Do you remember the little hymn you
introduced into this country?

> Far out upon the prairie,
> How many children dwell,
> Who never read the Bible
> Nor hear the Sabbath bell!
>
> Instead of praying Sundays,
> You hear their fire-arms bang,
> They chase cows same as Mondays
> And whoop the wild mustang.
>
> And seldom do they get, for
> To take to church a gal,
> It's mighty hard you bet, for
> Them in the chaparral.

But I will not quote any more as of course you know
all the balance, and will proceed to tell you what the
news is in this section. Spring has opened and the earth
is clothed in verdure new. The cowboy has doffed his
winter apparel and now appeareth in his summer cos-
tume of a blue flannel shirt and spurs. An occasional
norther still swoops down upon him, but he buckles on
an extra six shirts and defies the cold. The prairies
are covered with the most lovely and gorgeous flowers
of every description—columbine, jaspers, junipers,
hollyhocks, asteroids, sweet-marjoram, night-blooming
cereus, anthony-overs, percolators, hyoscyamuses, ber-
gamots, crystallized antlers, fuchsias, and horoscopes.
The lovely and deliciously scented meningitis twines its
clustering tendrils around the tall mesquites, and the
sweet little purple thanatopsis is found in profusion
on every side. Tall and perfumed volutas wave in the
breeze while the modest but highly-flavored mega-
therium nestles in the high grass. You remember how
often you used to have the train stopped to gather ver-

benas when you were coming out here? Well, if you should come now, the engineer would have to travel the whole distance in Texas with engine reversed and all brakes down tight, you would see so many rare and beautiful specimens.

I believe everybody that you take an interest in or know is well and all right. Everything is quiet except the wind, and that will stop as soon as hot weather begins. I am with Spanish like Dr. Hall's patients, still "progressing," and can now tell a Mexican in the highest and most grammatical Castilian to tie a horse without his thinking I mean for him to turn him loose. I would like to put my knowledge of the language into profitable use, but am undecided whether consulship to Mexico or herd sheep. Doctor Beall suggests in his letter to me the other day that I come back to North Carolina and buy a shovel and go to work on the Cape Fear and Yadkin Valley Railroad, but if you will examine a map of your State you will see a small but plainly discernible line surrounding the State and constituting its border. Over that border I will cross when I have found some United States bonds, a knife with six blades, an oroide watch and chain, a taste for strong tobacco, and a wild western manner intensely suggestive of cash.

I figured up that I made two thousand five hundred dollars last spring by not having any money to buy sheep with; for I would have lost every sheep in the cold and sleet of last March and a lamb for each one besides. So you see a fellow is sometimes up and sometimes down, however large a capital he handles, owing to the fluctuations of fortune and the weather.

This is how I console myself by philosophy, which is without a flaw when analyzed; but you know philosophy, although it may furnish consolation, starts back appalled when requested to come to the front with such little necessities as shoes and circus tickets and clothes and receipted board bills, etc.; and so some other science must be invoked to do the job. That other science has but four letters and is pronounced Work. Expect my next letter from the busy marts of commerce and trade.

I hope you will write to me soon, when you have time. Give Doctor Hall my highest regards, and the rest of the family. I remain

Very truly yours,
W. S. PORTER

A few weeks later he was in what he called the busy marts of commerce and trade, although the Austin of that day, though the State capital, was merely a little town of some ten thousand inhabitants. Will's first home was with Mr. Joe Harrell at 1008 Lavaca Street. He went there at Dick Hall's suggestion and found a genuine old-time Texan welcome. The Harrells were Greensboro people. They had known Will's father and mother. Mr. Harrell accepted the young man at once as a member of the family, a fourth son to be added to the three boys of his own, and for a time would not listen to Porter's suggestion that he contribute to the household expenses by paying board. The Harrell boys, all near Will's age, were equally friendly and hospitable. They were impressed by the Webster's Dictionary that the newcomer always carried with him. When Will was not poring over the dictionary, they would search it for hard words and triumphantly propound them, only to be dumfounded by the ease with which he would spell and define them.

Will Porter lived with the Harrells for the three years from 1884 to 1887. One of his first moves after reaching Austin was to present himself at the offices of

Morley Brothers, a big wholesale drug firm. The experience acquired in Clarke Porter's drug store in Greensboro was his only practical asset, but to back it up he had testimonials that had been forwarded to him by Dr. Hall and Clarke Porter. He was employed as a clerk and entered upon his new duties late in May, 1884. But after the freedom of the ranch the work proved confining and irksome, and he stood it only a few months.

Then began another Aladdin-like period of comparative idleness. For months he spent his time prowling about the Lavaca Street house, reading and drawing and playing the guitar. Mr. Harrell had a cigar store on Congress Avenue, and Will occasionally helped there, behind the counter, or in keeping the books. There was no business arrangement. Will worked when he chose to do so and received no salary. In time he grew weary of this lazy, haphazard existence. In the autumn of 1885, he went to work for the real estate firm of Maddox Brothers and Anderson. With this firm he remained for two years, at a salary of one hundred dollars a month. His work was apparently thoroughly satisfactory. He resigned of his own free will, and the firm reluctantly accepted the resignation. All the partners liked him. Mr. Anderson, after the resignation, persuaded him to move into the Anderson home on West Sixth Street, a house in which Austin society enjoyed a continual round of entertainments. Porter lived there for more than a year. The senior partner, John Maddox, wanted to send him to New York to study drawing. But Porter, perhaps doubting his own ability, refused to go. Had he done so the whole course of his life might have been changed. Again, as in the case of the hero of "Roads of Destiny," the end might have been the same.

This was the period of Will Porter's life when he was most normal in the keen enjoyment of the society of young people of both sexes. He was the beau he depicted in Ben Granger of "A Moment of Victory," who clerked by day for Brady and Murchison of St. Augustine and divided his evenings between the German Club, the athletic association, and the military company. The salary of one hundred dollars a month paid him by Maddox Brothers and Anderson meant comparative affluence to a bachelor without responsibilities in the Austin of the 1880's.

In Austin, as in most American small towns, the various churches were the centers of social activity. Will was a regular attendant at the Presbyterian Church and sang in the choir. He joined what was called the Hill City Quartet, composed of C. E. Hillyer, R. H. Edmondson, H. H. Long, and himself. The quartet sang frequently in the Baptist Church, and the Episcopal Church of St. David's. It formed the center of the social circle in which Will Porter revolved. An unnamed chronicler has left this picture:

Will Porter, shortly after coming to Texas became a member of the Hill City Quartette . . . Porter was the smallest man in the crowd, and, of course, basso profundo. He was about five feet six inches tall, weighed about one hundred and thirty pounds, had coal black hair, gray eyes, and a long, carefully twisted moustache; looked as though he might be a combination between the French and the Spanish, and I think he

Hill City Quartette

R. H. Edmondson Jr.   H. H. Long

W. S. Porter.   C. E. Hillyer

Austin Tex   1886.

once told me that the blood of the Huguenot flowed in
his veins.) He was one of the most accomplished gentlemen I ever knew. His voice was soft and musical, with
just enough rattle in it to rid it of all touch of effemi-
nacy. He had a keen sense of humor, and there were
two distinct methods of address which were characteristic with him—his business address and his friendly
address. As a business man his face was calm, almost
expressionless; his demeanor was steady, even calculated. He always worked for a high class of em-
ployers, was never wanting for a position, and was
prompt, accurate, talented and very efficient; but the
minute he was out of business—that was all gone. He
always approached a friend with a merry twinkle in his
eyes and an expression which said: "Come on, boys, we
are going to have a lot of fun," and we usually did.

The story of "The Green Door" in its spirit and
in its fact was just such a thing as might happen with
him any night. It is but justice, in order to give balance to this unique character, to say that he made no
religious professions; he never talked infidelity nor
skepticism; he had such reverence for other people's
views that he never entered into religious discussions;
and, personally, he seemed rather indifferent to the
subject, though in no wise opposed to it. . . .

He got interested in society and lost all taste for the
drug business. Being a fine penman, a good account-
ant, well educated, and with good address, it was an
easy matter for him to make a living without working
every day and Sunday, too, and most of the evenings
besides. The fact of the matter is, while W. S. P.
would not have admitted it for the world, I think he
really wanted a little more time for love making. So
during the time of our association, he went to work at
eight in the morning and quit at four. He always had
sufficient money for what he needed; if he had any
more, no one knew. He was very fond of going fishing

but he let you do the fishing after he went. He loved
to go hunting, but he let you kill the birds, and somehow I always thought that on these trips he got
something out of the occasion that he enjoyed all by
himself; they were not occasions which invited the introduction of sentiment, and I believe his enjoyment of
them was purely sentimental. He loved the mountains
and the plains; he loved to hear the birds sing and the
brooks babble, but he did not talk to the boys about it.

He was accomplished in all the arts of a society
man; had a good bass voice and sang well; was a good
dancer and skater; played an interesting game of
cards, and was preëminently an entertainer. There
were no wall flowers to Porter, and the girl who went
with him never lacked for attention.

If W. S. P. at this time had any ambitions as a
writer, he never mentioned it to me. I do not recall that
he was fond of reading. One day I quoted some lines
to him from a poem by John Alexander Smith. He
made inquiry about the author, borrowed the book and
committed to memory a great many passages from it,
but I do not recall ever having known him to read any
other book. I asked him one day why he never read
fiction. His reply was: "That it was all tame compared
to the romance of his own life"—which was really true.

On January 12, 1887, Will Porter began his four
years of service as a state employee in the General Land
Office at Austin. Six months before, at the July Democratic primary election, his old friend Dick Hall
had been nominated Land Commissioner. The nomination was equivalent to election. In August, Porter
wrote Mr. Hall asking for a position, and was told that
if he could prepare himself for work in the drafting
department within three months, a place would be
found for him. Equipped with natural talent the

young man applied himself to the task and when Mr.
Hall assumed office Will Porter was ready and entered
the Land Office as assistant compiling draftsman at
the same salary of one hundred dollars a month that he
had received from Maddox Brothers and Anderson.

In the routine life he found a measure of romance.
The office itself was an antiquated building dating
from 1857. It suggested stories. In the burlesque
"Bexar Script No. 2692," published in *The Rolling
Stone* in May, 1894, Porter described the office in a
passage that was curiously reflected many years later
in his picture of the Old Munich of "The Halberdier
of the Little Rheinschloss":

As you pass up the avenue, on a steep hill before you
you see a mediæval castle. You think of the Rhine; the
"castled crag of Drachenfels," the Lorelei; and the
vine-clad slopes of Germany. And German it is in
every line of its architecture and design. The plan
was drawn by an old draughtsman from the "Vater-
land," whose heart still loved the scenes of his native
land, and it is said he reproduced the design of a certain castle near his birthplace, with remarkable fidelity.

"Bexar Script No. 2692," "Georgia's Ruling,"
"Witches' Loaves," and "Buried Treasure" were some
of the fruits of Will Porter's observations when a
draftsman in the Land Office. The business of the
office brought daily crowds of land sharks, disreputable
lawyers, poverty-stricken leasers. The prodigal waste
of land and the negligence of early officials had thrown
everything into confusion. Lacking adequate records
the new Land Commissioner had to rely on his own
judgment of character.

There is no better commentary [said Mr. Rollins] on the business side of the office than "Georgia's Ruling," a story published by Porter in 1900. The story is based upon fact and is so frankly biographical of Mr. Hall that, after his pseudonym had been revealed, O. Henry forbade its publication in book form, and only after his death did it appear in *Whirligigs*. Porter himself once indulged in a little speculation. Having located some "stray land" in Willbarger County, he bought it for fifty dollars and in a few months sold it for nine hundred dollars.

Other stories, too, grew out of his work in the Land Office. The draftsmen, for instance, were in the habit of erasing the pencil marks from their drawings with stale bread. One day a clerk inadvertently used a piece of buttered bread, ruining his drawing. Hence the story "Witches' Loaves." [1] Here, too, a group of the younger men formed a party to search for treasure that had supposedly been buried in Pease Park, a mile from the city. They found nothing, but Porter's part in the search later resulted in the story "Buried Treasure."

But in the Land Office years, from 1887 to 1891, the idea of writing had not yet entered Will Porter's head. In that stage of his Aladdin period his rôle was that of the *rawi* of the East. He lived in an atmosphere of adventure that was largely the product of his own imagination, and was an inveterate story-teller. Many of these tales were told in the first person with himself

[1] See *Sixes and Sevens*. The story of a romantic old maid who keeps a bakery, and a customer, a middle-aged German, whose habit is to buy two or three times a week two loaves of stale bread. With pity for his supposed poverty, and the matrimonial bee buzzing in her bonnet, Miss Martha Meacham generously butters the bread, with the result of ruining three months' work on a plan for a new city hall that was to be submitted in a prize competition. Inferentially, O. Henry changed the scene of the story from Texas to New York.

as the hero or at least the chief protagonist. Listeners were often puzzled to know if the adventures related were real or invented. To the inquiry direct, his stock reply was: "Never question the validity of a joke."

But he was incorrigibly the caricaturist, just as he had been in his clerking days in Clarke Porter's drug store. Every unusual looking person who entered the drafting room was sure to be a target for his pencil. Even the maps that he drew with landscapes or portraits had a humorous twist. They are still preserved in the Austin Land Office, for their value as records and for their associations. Mr. Rollins has told of one of Kent County, drawn July, 1889:

Though dimmed with age, the sketch at the top of the map presents some amusing features. In the immediate foreground, at the two sides of the picture, are two telephone poles (an anachronism), on whose sagging wires a jay bird is resting. Between the wires and to the left a sombreroed cowboy rides complacently along, watching his hound, who has driven a rattlesnake from under a clump of prickly pears, chase a jack-rabbit. Behind him, and in the center of the picture, meanders a clear stream, on the surface of which floats an enormous fish. Nearby two longhorn steers are grazing. In the background to the right is seen a prosperous looking ranch house overtopped by a windmill; while at the left appears the bunk house. In the extreme background rise hills, thickly covered at the foot with small cedar trees.

A characteristic adventure of the early Austin days involves Will Porter's connection with the military company that he joined soon after reaching the city. Mr. Page, in telling it, attributes it to the same unnamed contributor who furnished the description of the Hill City Quartette.[2]

In the great railroad strike at Fort Worth, Texas, the Governor called out the State Militia, and the company to which we belonged was sent, but as we were permitted a choice in the matter, Porter and I chose not to go. In a little while a girl he was in love with went to Waco on a visit. Porter moped around disconsolate for a few days, and suddenly said to me: "I believe I'll take a visit at the Government's expense." With him to think was to act. A telegram was sent to Fort Worth: "Capt. Blank, Fort Worth, Texas. Squad of volunteers under my command tender you their services if needed. Reply." "Come next train," Captain Blank commanded. Upon reaching the depot no orders for transportation of squad had been received. Porter actually held up the train until he could telegraph and get transportation for his little squad, because the girl had been notified that he would be in Waco on a certain train. She afterwards said that when the train pulled into Waco he was sitting on the engine pilot with a gun across his lap and a distant glance of her was all he got, but he had had his adventure and was fully repaid.

Another tale of adventure of amateur soldiering comes from the same source:

One night at the Lampasas Military Encampment of Texas Volunteer Guards, the Quartette, with others, had leave of absence to attend the big ball at the Park Hotel, with orders to report at 12:00 sharp. Somehow, with girls and gaiety and music and balmy Southern breezes and cooing voices, time flies, and before any of us had thought to look at a watch it was five minutes

[2] Arthur W. Page, "Little Pictures of O. Henry," *The Bookman,* 1913.

past twelve and we were in trouble. We had all gathered near the doorway looking toward Camp when we saw the Corporal of the Guard approaching the building to arrest us. Of course, what follows could never have happened in a camp of tried veterans, but Porter knew the human animal as few people do.

He got a friend with an unlimited leave of absence to meet the Corporal's squad at another door and suggest to them that they should not carry their guns in among the ladies. So the squad stacked their guns on the outside and went in the other door to arrest us. Up to this point Porter had worked the thing without taking us into his confidence. As soon as the guns were stacked he beckoned to us to follow and we did not stop for explanation. We knew where Porter led there would be adventure, if not success.

He took command; we unstacked the arms of the Corporal's squad; all our boys who did not carry guns were marched as under arrest. Now none of us knew the countersign, and our success in getting by the sentry was a matter of pure grit. As we approached the sentry we were crossing a narrow plank bridge in single file, at the end of which the sentry threw up his gun and Porter marched us right up straight to that gun until the front man was marking time with the point of the gun right against his stomach.

Porter just said to the sentry: "Squad under arrest. Stand aside." The whole thing was done with such courage, decision, and audacity that the sentry never noticed that we had never given the countersign, but stepped aside and let us pass. A few yards from the camp, we stacked our guns, and sneaked into our tents. When the real corporal came back to camp and told his story the sentry refused to accept it and had the whole squad placed in the guard-house for the night.

When the boys began to whisper the joke in their tents, the disturbance became so great that the Cor-

poral's Guard came down to ascertain the cause, but
in looking into the tent found only tired soldier boys
snoring as though they had been drugged. There was
quite a time at the court-martial next morning, at
which the corporal and his body were given extra duty
for their inglorious behavior on the previous night, but
no one ever knew our connection with the story.

IV

ATHOL

Holy is the wife; revered the mother; galliptious is the summer girl—but the bride is the certified check among the wedding presents that the gods send in when man is married to mortality.

Sisters of the Golden Circle

ONE afternoon in late November, 1905, in his apartment at 55 Irving Place, New York, O. Henry wrote, at a single sitting of three hours, "The Gift of the Magi," that touching Christmas tale of the young wife who sacrifices her glorious hair to buy for her husband a fob chain worthy of his treasured watch, only to learn that he has sold the watch in order to purchase a pair of side combs for her hair. The story of how "The Gift of the Magi" came to be written will be told in detail later in this book. But despite other molding circumstances, it is certain that in the writing O. Henry's heart and memory went back some twenty years to Athol Estes, the young wife of his early manhood.

The physical portrait of Della of "The Gift of the Magi" was drawn from O. Henry's memory of Athol, then in her grave for more than eight years. It was a word picture. Della's hair, "rippling and shining like a cascade of brown waters," had been Athol's hair. The sketch was rounded out with other personal reminiscent touches. "She had a habit of saying little silent prayers about the simplest everyday things," wrote O. Henry of Della. In the trying days of the

53

life of Athol Estes Porter, no sacrifice was too great, no weariness of the spirit too demanding, that Athol was not always ready for her husband with a smile and a word of cheer. The habit of "little silent prayers" was always with her. There was one sad Christmas season that she sold a lace handkerchief that she had made for twenty-five dollars. She was almost penniless herself, but like Della, she devoted the money to a Christmas box for Will, an exile far away in Honduras. She packed the box running a temperature of one hundred and five.

There is some little conflict of opinion about the exact age of Athol Estes. Both Professor Smith and Mr. Rollins speak of her as a "seventeen-year-old girl" in July, 1887, at the time of her runaway marriage to Will Porter. Also they set the day of the elopement as July 5th. Frances Goggin Maltby recently told the story of Athol's pathetic life in *The Dimity Sweetheart*, a charming little book upon which the present authors have drawn freely in this chapter. She wrote: "In all the accounts of the marriage of Athol Estes and Will Porter I have read, the date is given as Tuesday, July 5th. This is a mistake. It was Friday, July 1st. The files of the Austin *Statesman* in the State Library at Austin verify this."

In the matter of the girl's age Mrs. Maltby begins by saying that when William Sidney Porter was six years old, there was born some four hundred miles west of Greensboro, in the town of Clarksville, Tennessee, a little girl who was to play a vital part in the drama of his life. In July, 1887, Will Porter was just two months short of rounding out his twenty-fifth year.

Six years his junior, Athol would have been nineteen instead of seventeen. Again Mrs. Maltby definitely names April, 1868, as the month and year of Athol's birth.

The tragedy of Athol's life was foreshadowed in a tempestuous childhood. Clarksville, Tennessee, far more than Greensboro, North Carolina, had suffered from the grip of Reconstruction. "The dark period that followed the termination of the war between the States was intensified in this section of the South," writes Mrs. Maltby. Clarksville numbered so many Negroes among its population that it was sometimes called "Little Haiti." When Athol was a babe in arms, there was one night of terrible fear. Mrs. Estes was still convalescing from the child's birth, and Mr. Estes was seriously ill from tuberculosis. After nightfall word came through a faithful Negro servant of a plot for a general uprising among the Negroes of Clarksville.

The family home was a farm outside the town, defenseless against attack. Half mad with terror, herself ill and with a helpless husband and an infant, Mrs. Estes took counsel with the faithful colored girl who had brought the news of the impending outbreak. A Negro boy who lived on the place was sent to the authorities with a note of warning and a plea for assistance. Long hours of suspense followed. Would the boy prove true to his trust, or would he carry the note to the plotters? The boy delivered the note and the uprising was prevented by the arrest of the ringleaders. But in the morning the Estes family left the farm never to return. They went into Clarksville until they could make arrangements for removal to Nash-ville.

When Athol was six months old her father died, leaving her the heritage of his own malady. When she was six years old her mother remarried. The second husband was a widower of Nashville, a Mr. G. P. Roach. By a former marriage he had two daughters several years older than Athol. When he met Mrs. Estes, Mr. Roach was in comfortable circumstances. But before the marriage he met with business misfor-tunes and offered to break the engagement, a sugges-tion to which the young widow would not listen. Eventually the two decided to go West, and in 1879, Mr. Roach moved his family to Texas, buying a farm at Hornsby's Bend, a rural community near Austin. Athol, according to Mrs. Maltby, was then eleven years old.

The years passed. In 1881, Athol was enrolled in a public school of Austin, where she won the Peabody medal for the best record in English composition; and in time she moved through the various grades of the high school. Mrs. Maltby, who was Athol's desk mate during senior year at the high school, pictures her as having been "a belle from babyhood to maturity by sheer right of charm." As a schoolgirl her desk "fairly bristled with heart offerings"—glass marbles with vivid interiors, candy hearts with impassioned verses, flowers and fruit of varying colors and conditions.

In time Will Porter, with his waxed mustache, his uniform as a member of the Austin Grays, the military company that he had joined, his dictionary, his guitar, and his bass voice, came to join the ranks of Athol's

suitors. Like Cyrano de Bergerac, and like his own
Judson Tate of "Next to Reading Matter," he seems
to have relied much on his voice in those years in his
wooing. The Hill City Quartette was in full swing
with its sentimental songs designed to stir feminine
hearts. In addition to singing with Messrs. Long,
Hillyer, and Edmondson, Will Porter organized the
"Jolly Entertainers," principally for the purpose of
serenading the fair sex.

The Jolly Entertainers were not everywhere welcome. Their serenades were not always appreciated
by the fathers of families whose liking for music did
not extend to this orchestra composed of two fiddles,
a guitar (the one that Porter had brought from the
Dick Hall ranch), a triangle, and a melodeon. The
melodeon was carted about in an old surrey, while the
"orchestral artists," as Porter called them, found
transportation on the horse's back, in the surrey, or
wherever the whim of the moment seemed to suggest.
Among the young ladies serenaded by the Jolly Entertainers were the Roach girls, Nettie and Effie. Will
Porter's approach to Athol seems to have been by way
of her older half sisters. Among the irate fathers was
Mr. Roach.

Will Porter and Athol Estes probably first met
about 1885, when she was still a high school girl, and
he was working sporadically helping out Mr. Harrell
in the cigar store, before taking a regular position
with Maddox Brothers and Anderson. The suggestion
is that he first saw her at the "german" given by the
Austin Grays the night following the laying of the
corner stone of the new state capitol. Athol had been

chosen by her class in the high school to place in the corner stone the souvenirs contributed by the class. In accordance with her custom she wore a dress of dimity. When Porter saw her he forgot all about her stepsisters and had eyes only for his "dimity sweetheart." Many years later O. Henry was asked why he always dressed his heroines in dimity or crêpe de Chine. He replied: "That is all I know about women's clothes. Athol always wore dimity. We couldn't afford anything better. And my second wife wore crêpe de Chine."

In 1885, when Will Porter first enrolled himself among the swains dancing attendance upon Athol Estes, the girl was no more than seventeen, and Porter himself was in no position to consider such a step as matrimony. The two were thrown naturally much in each other's society. Their circles were the same. They sang together in the choir of the Southern Presbyterian Church. They had many tastes in common. Just as Porter was an unusual young man, Athol was an unusual girl. They talked poetry, and Will filled Athol's school books with cartoons. Athol herself had a knack for drawing, though her pictures ran to little boys with patched trousers, and little girls with sunbonnets and aprons.

But with the beginning of the year 1887 conditions were changed. Will was in the Land Office, drawing a salary of one hundred dollars a month. He could reasonably count upon that to last for the four years of his chief's tenure of office, if not for longer. In the United States of the 1880's a reasonably assured income of one hundred dollars a month went far in main-

ATHOL59

taining a household that was willing to practice a sensible economy. Also, perhaps, Will was spurred on by the activities of some of his rivals.

There was one such rival whose story had all the ingredients of an O. Henry tale. Incidentally, there is the suggestion of him in the Pinkney Dawson who figures in the tales, "Shoes" and "Ships" of *Cabbages and Kings*. His name was Lee Zimplemann. He was the admirer who caused Will Porter the most anxiety. His good looks were those of Fergus MacMahan of "Next to Reading Matter." Lee gave Athol a lock bracelet of which he carried the key. He also, in defiance of the ancient superstition, gave her an opal ring. When Athol was married it is said that she still wore the lock bracelet on her arm, her former sweetheart having refused to surrender the releasing key. Lee Zimplemann is reputed to have sought balm for his aching heart in melancholy song, entertaining a local concert with such selections as "When Other Hearts and Other Lips" and "A Heart Bowed Down." Of Athol and her heart affairs Mrs. Maltby has drawn a pretty picture:

Athol's romances were of deep interest to me. I had no romance of my own, so I fairly fed upon the heart interests she furnished. I was some two years younger than Athol, tall, lank, curlless, and freckled. I solaced myself with the thought that even if I had been the charmer that Athol was I should not have been allowed to do the things that Athol did. My mother was of the old school and held the belief that books and boys could not combine, that "beaux" in your head excluded study, so I dug away at our algebra problems while Athol carroled in the moonlight with Lee or Will. I used to trade her those problems for bits of English composition composed by her admirer, Will Porter.

I have often thought that we were, no doubt, the first copyists of O. Henry, but not the last by any means. I recall some delightful bits that came into my possession in this way. One of these fragments, written with characteristic absurdity, I have preserved. Our English assignment had been a description of an entertainment given for the benefit of a local church. I can now fully appreciate O. Henry's enjoyment in passing this on to us to be used as a schoolgirl composition: "The tableaux were all on a large scale, intricate, elaborate, and very elegant. Colored lights were burned, and the young ladies in their groupings and graceful draperies were very beautiful."

Of the cartoons with which Will Porter used to decorate Athol's schoolbooks, Mrs. Maltby tells at length of two—one, the caricature teasing Athol about the bashful and unmarried young high school principal—and the other throwing a light on the occasional unpopularity of the Jolly Entertainers. The occasion of the latter cartoon was an "orchestral serenade" given at the Roach home. Mr. Roach was the most indulgent and good-natured of men, but the "heart appeals" generated by the Jolly Entertainers failed to affect him in the intended way.

The Roach home was represented as a storm center. Chairs and tables were overturned. Mr. Roach, clad in night apparel, was breaking away from Mrs. Roach, pistol in one hand and candle in the other, while Mrs. Roach clung to him and plead with him to "spare the artists." The two Roach girls and Athol were shown hanging out of a window in rapt unconsciousness of their irate father. A second view depicted the hasty

retreat of the "Jolly Entertainers," as a pistol was
fired from an upper window. Two of the "artists"
were astride the steed and two on top of the surrey,
casting a guitar and triangle at the speeding horse.
Inside the surrey the violin and guitar "artists" continued to perform. The instruments were giving out
prolonged brays, as "cool as Nero." Beneath this
sketch was written: "The Only Time the 'Jolly Entertainers' Ever Declined an Invitation to Stop."

A uniform played its part in the romance. Will
Porter was now Lieutenant Porter of the Austin Grays.
The waxed mustache and the martial attire wrecked
Lee Zimplemann's last chances. The uniform gave
Porter added courage. He realized its influence. A
little play called "Waiter Drill" was presented for the
benefit of the Southern Presbyterian Church. Will
Porter had the principal part, that of the Captain,
and Miss Athol Estes was cast in the rôle of First
Sergeant. Three other young women completed the
company. During the rehearsals held in Turner Hall,
a converted German beer garden, Will pressed his suit.
He wrung from Athol the promise to remove the lock
bracelet from her arm and the opal ring from her
finger. But there remained the matter of persuading
Athol's family to listen to reason. The waxed mustache and the uniform were not effective with either
Mr. or Mrs. Roach, and the latter was frank in expressing her preference for Lee Zimplemann as a son-
in-law. Evading direct opposition, she argued that
Athol was still a child who did not know her own mind.
She urged delay and planned to send her daughter
away to Nashville with the idea that absence would help
her plans. Finally she gave a stronger reason for her

objections to the match. Bluntly she told Will that
Athol's father had died of tuberculosis as had his
mother, and on these grounds flatly refused her consent.

Facing the uncompromising edict, there was but one
course to pursue. On the afternoon of Friday, July
1st, or Tuesday, July 5th, Athol Estes slipped out of
her home, on the pretense of an errand, joined Will
Porter; and the two, accompanied by the inevitable
sympathetic and abetting friends, in this case Mr.
and Mrs. Anderson, drove to the home of Dr. Smoot
of the Southern Presbyterian Church, and there were
married. In the conflict of opinion as to the exact date
of the wedding, Mrs. Maltby has all the better of the
argument, quoting an account of the ceremony from the
Austin *Statesman* of July 2, 1887, in itself conclusive
evidence. Further, she insists that the elopement was
not premeditated, emphasizing the point that in a day
when the little superstitions of life were held to be of
high importance, no southern girl, brought up as Athol
had been, would have tempted Providence by deliberately choosing a Friday for her wedding day.

The convenient Andersons broke the news of the
marriage to Mrs. Roach. Her anxiety over Athol's
absence relieved, she accepted the situation in a wise
and kindly spirit. She had never been personally
hostile to Will Porter; her opposition to the match
had been based entirely upon his physical heritage
and her sound belief that her daughter's life would
prove happier and easier as the wife of Lee Zimplemann. The conventional forgiveness and blessing were
quick and sincere. She and her husband were to prove
Will Porter's best friends when the dark hour came.

Courtesy of Mrs. L. G. Maltby

THE DIMITY SWEETHEART

Athol Estes Porter, O. Henry's first wife, and the mother of Margaret

After the wedding Will and his bride went to the home of the Andersons, there remaining as guests during the summer and autumn of 1887. Then they set up housekeeping for themselves in a small house on Eleventh Street, close by the Land Office. It was a very small house, and most of the furniture was bought on the installment plan. Their social diversions remained much the same as they had been before marriage; they still both sang in the choir of the Southern Presbyterian Church; and shared in the usual church activities. But with a home to establish as well as maintain, Will's salary of one hundred dollars a month from the Land Office was spent almost as soon as it was received. He sought a means to augment his income. He thought he would try his hand at writing. It was in his first months of married life that O. Henry's career as a writing man began.

Apparently the first offerings sent out, only a few weeks after his marriage, were of odds and ends, for under date of September 4, 1887, there is a letter from the Detroit *Free Press* reading:

My DEAR SIR:
Please send your string for month of August. And it would please me to receive further contributions at once. Send a budget every week.
Sincerely,
A. MOSELEY

From the same source a letter in November, 1887:

My DEAR MR. PORTER:
Your string for November just in. Am sorry it is not longer. Check will be sent in a few days.
Can you not send more matter—a good big instal-

ment every week? I returned everything that I felt I could not use, in order that we might resume operations with a clear board. Hereafter all unavailable matter shall be sent back within two or three days. After you get a better idea of the things we do not want, the quantity to be returned will be very small.

But the real thrill came with the news that two sketches had been sold to *Truth*, a New York publication. Probably other contributions were offered with them, but the word that "The Final Triumph" and "A Slight Inaccuracy" had been accepted and that a check for six dollars would be sent in payment, caused hearts to beat high in the little home on Eleventh Street. Athol danced in her delight and hugged her husband. Six dollars seemed a fabulous sum. She was sure that they were on the way to fortune. Manlike, Will attempted to carry his success with a light air. "It will keep the chafing dish bubbling and buy steak and onions," was his comment.

There was one deep sorrow in that early married life. Their first-born, a boy, who was to have been named after his father, died. Mrs. Maltby records that the little house with the new bedroom suite bought on the installment plan, and the pomegranates bloomin the yard, was a sad place for a time. But Athol and Will were young, and the day came when they were singing again, and taking joy in the twitter of the birds and the blooming of the flowers. However, the passing of their first-born had left its scar. Late afternoons they would borrow Charley and the phaëton from Mrs. Roach, drive out to the cemetery and put altheas and pomegranates on the little grave.

Then a second child was born, the girl who was christened Margaret. Athol's recovery was slow and for a time her life was considered in danger. It was thought best to give up the little home on Eleventh Street, in order that Athol might stay at her mother's house and have constant care and attention. For both Will and Athol the break away from the little cottage that had meant so much in their young married life was a hard one. But the move was for the best. After a few months in the Roach home Athol's health was vastly improved. A house across the street from the Roaches was rented, and into it Will and Athol moved, with their well-beloved furniture. Then there was a trip back to Greensboro, where the young couple and their baby spent a very happy autumn month; Will proudly exhibiting little Margaret to his admiring relatives.

With the beginning of the year 1891, there was a radical change in the family fortunes. The term of Dick Hall, Will Porter's chief as Land Commissioner, expired, and under the political system the new Commissioner would naturally distribute the various office posts among his own friends and henchmen. On January 21, 1891, Will resigned his position as assistant compiling draftsman, drawing the sixty-six dollars and sixty-six cents that was still due him. He looked about for a new position. He found one as paying and receiving teller in the First National Bank of Austin. There he remained nearly four years.

But for the time being this is Athol's story rather than Will's. One of those characteristic self-sacrifices

that link her with Della of "The Gift of the Magi" and
Delia of "A Service of Love," marked the summer of
1893. That was the year of the Chicago World's Fair,
which called to the people of Austin as it did to the
people of all the other cities in the land. The Roaches
were planning to go, and Will Porter, who then had
saved a little money, wished Athol to accompany them,
believing that the trip would be of benefit to her health.
But the care of Margaret was a problem, and so it was
finally decided that Mr. and Mrs. Roach were to go to
Chicago first, and then return to take charge of the
baby while Athol made the journey with a party of
friends later in the season.

However, Athol had a change of heart. When Mrs.
Roach returned home she looked across the street at
Athol's cottage. There were crisp new muslin curtains
blowing from Athol's windows and two new wicker
chairs on the porch. She went over to see what this
meant. Athol met her at the door, her face wreathed
in smiles. She led her mother into the house and
showed her the new matting she had just finished putting down. "Isn't that a beautiful Japanese pattern?"

"But, Athol," gasped Mrs. Roach, "where did you
get the money?"

"Will gave it to me and I used it in this way."

"But your trip? Where is the money for your
trip?" her mother persisted. "Did you spend the
money for your trip for these things?"

"Yes, I did; and I'm glad I did. I just couldn't go
on a jaunt and leave Will here to work all summer and
not have any fun. Now he'll have just as much fun

out of the money as I do. You see I bought *two* rockers. I'm playing fair." She had done it all without Will's knowledge.

The fact that in the summer of 1893 Will had a little money saved, combined with the fact that early in the spring of 1894, while still holding his position with the bank, he bought the plant of Brann's *Iconoclast*, and tried to run a paper of his own, *The Rolling Stone*, on the side, may have had a bearing upon subsequent events. From the beginning the work at the bank had been irksome and uncongenial. It was an astonishing bank, run with an astonishing laxity. According to Mr. Rollins its affairs were managed so loosely that Porter's predecessor was driven to retirement, his successor to attempted suicide. On one occasion Porter spent two days hunting a shortage of one hundred dollars. Finding no solution he took the problem to one of the officers. "Oh, yes," said the latter, "I took out a hundred the other day when I went to San Antonio and forgot to file a slip for it. Sorry I gave you such a hunt."

Apparently such an occurrence was not exceptional. Finally the situation got on his nerves. He would rush home for the noon meal, change his limp collar for a fresh one, and hurry back to the bank. "You have an hour. Why don't you rest and cool off?" Athol would suggest. "No," he would answer, "I must get back. The longer I stay away, the more trouble I have. Sometimes I think I had best not leave at noon. I spend hours hunting up money that has been carelessly checked out."

One day in October, 1894, a United States Govern-

ment Bank examiner made his appearance at the First
National. Perhaps when, years later, O. Henry wrote
"Friends in San Rosario," his mind went back to that
morning as he described the precise and coldly righteous J. F. C. Nettlewick, with his determined face and
aggressive, gold-rimmed nose glasses. The details of
that examination will be told later. In Will Porter's
accounts certain irregularities were found. The bank
officials, understanding the muddled situation, made up
the shortage and refused to prosecute. But the Federal
authorities, long irritated by the manner in which the
bank had been run, sought to make an example. Will
Porter was the victim of that zeal.

Legal retribution, whether merited or unmerited,
was, however, not immediate. For the alleged defal-
cations of the autumn of 1894, Will Porter was not to
stand trial until early in 1898. Of course, his connection with the bank ceased at once; he was obliged
to turn to other fields to earn his living; to leave Austin
for Houston and there to stay until the summons to
return to stand trial drove him in panicky flight to
Honduras. All of that will be told in due time.

But for the moment this is still Athol's story. With
the first rumors of her husband's financial entangle-
ments her heavier trials began. One day, the perturbed
Mr. Roach brought the information home that Will
Porter had been held responsible for the shortage in
the bank. There was the question of breaking the news
to Athol. Mrs. Roach had not the heart to do so, so
it was Mr. Roach who took the tidings across the street.
Later Mrs. Roach went over to try to comfort her
daughter.

She found Athol crumpled up on the bed, crying bitterly. Then the clock struck four. Instantly Athol was on her feet. "It's four o'clock," she said. "Will will be home any minute. I musn't act like this. He shan't find me crying." Nor did he. He found her dressed in a crisp new dimity, his favorite, smiling and fresh and dainty, no traces of tears, her head held a bit higher than usual. The fire of courage that she showed in that hour never ceased to flame.

When Will Porter fled, Athol's unfaltering stanchness and faith, and the manner in which she defended her absent husband from the rising clamor of censure, won general admiration for herself and a more charitable feeling for the fugitive. The home of her mother and stepfather was open to her, but she preferred to be independent, and took a correspondence course with the idea of fitting herself to make a living for herself and Margaret. She made dresses for the neighbors and fancy work which she sold to a friendly merchant. Perhaps her resolution to be independent was stiffened by the fact that Mr. Roach, as one of Will Porter's bondsmen, was likely to suffer financial loss on account of his flight.

Her courage served a practical end. When Will Porter returned, so keenly in sympathy were the police and other authorities of Austin with the little wife, condemned to death and fighting her battle, that they not only ignored his presence in the city, but also privately sent him word that if he kept out of sight during his wife's illness they would not molest him. All that late winter, spring, and early summer of 1897 he was left free to stay in the Roach home and drive with

Athol in the shadows of the evening. The winter days
were spent mostly in a hayloft playroom which Mr.
Roach had prepared for Margaret as an inducement
to Athol to come and live with them.

For a time her joy at her husband's return wrought
a decided change for the better in Athol's health. Or
at least her animated spirits gave that impression to
those about her. She was pathetically cheerful and
hopeful, says Mrs. Maltby. Her prayer had been:
"Please, God, let me live to see Will once more." Her
prayer now was: "Please, God, let me live to see his
name cleared." She had never doubted his innocence,
although she realized that his flight had been a terrible
mistake that turned the tide of opinion against him.
Let him fight the thing out and all the world would
share her belief.

But that turn for the better was merely temporary.
With the spring she grew weaker again. Soon she no
longer had the strength to walk and her husband carried her. Borrowing the Roach phaëton and old Charley, he would drive her out through the country fields.
In the first days of his return, following the official
hint to the letter, he had kept himself within doors
during the daylight hours. But as Athol faded, he
threw discretion to the winds, no longer waiting for
night for these drives into the country. Day by day,
as the spring became summer, Athol wasted away. The
end came on Sunday, July 25th. The day she died
was the only one she stayed in bed. So no more of
Athol.

V

BOHEMIA

We discovered and enjoyed the only true Bohemia. Every night and day we repaired to one of those palaces of marble and glass and tilework, where goes on a tremendous and sounding epic of life. Valhalla itself could not be more glorious and sonorous.

The Plutonian Fire

WHEN, in the autumn of 1894, with the discovery of a shortage in his accounts, Will Porter left the employ of the First National Bank of Austin, there remained, as a possible means of support, his side venture, *The Rolling Stone*, which was rolling unsteadily along. The 1890's were the last days of a curious and distinctively American school of journalism that flourished particularly in the West and Southwest. Some eminent names are associated with that school, which was at times witty, at times rather inane, and at all times of a vitriolic quality that invited physical reprisal.

Brann's *Iconoclast*, the press of which Will Porter had bought in the spring of 1894 at a cost of two hundred and fifty dollars as a foundation for *The Rolling Stone*, had had a typically tempestuous career. Brann sold his paper to Porter to go to San Antonio to assume the editorship of the San Antonio *Express*. Two numbers of the *Iconoclast* for March, 1894, are said to have appeared under Porter's editorship. With the press, Porter had also bought the name, to which, for the moment, Brann apparently attached no im-

71

portance. Later, however, he moved from San Antonio
to Waco to start a paper of his own, and asked Porter
to give up the name *Iconoclast*. Porter consented. In
February, 1895, Brann brought out the first issue of
his new *Iconoclast*. He had raised it to a circulation of
ninety thousand copies when he was killed in a street
brawl in April, 1898. Will Porter, hoping to make
The Rolling Stone an asset, found it a liability. Yet
its acquisition marked an important and decided step
in his life. With it he first found Bohemia, which is a
state of mind, an aspiration of youth, rather than a
particular environment. Bohemia flowers in strange
places. It does not need a great city or a colorful
setting such as the Café Momus of Henry Murger's
Scènes de la Vie de Bohême; or the climbing, winding
streets of old Montmartre where Leonard Merrick's
Tricotrin and his companions lived in picturesque
privation; or London's Bloomsbury or Chelsea; or the
Washington Square neighborhood of yesterday; or the
Greenwich Village of the present. Red Gap had a
Bohemia of its own; so, in the 1890's, did Austin and
Houston.

In later life, O. Henry was to know intimately the
Bohemia, real or pseudo, of New York. But the
Sinbad the Sailor years had robbed him of many of
his illusions. He no longer believed in Bohemia, any
more than he believed in a material Santa Claus, or in
all-powerful jinns, or in enchanted horses, or in wonderful lamps. Derision of Bohemia is to be found in
many of the stories. It was in "The Halberdier of the
Little Rheinschloss" that he wrote of a certain restaurant that once it had been "the resort of interesting

Bohemians, but now only writers and painters and musicians frequented it."

It was different in the days when he was still Will Porter and Aladdin. Then the bank was Philistia. The ink that was in his blood called him to Bohemia with its freer air and its absence of trammeling conventions. Being very human he had his Dr. Jekyll side and his Mr. Hyde side. As a newspaper man he could, as a matter of business and without impropriety, frequent haunts where the presence of the bank teller who sang in the choir of the Southern Presbyterian Church would have been the subject of inevitable criticism.

The Rolling Stone enjoyed or endured just a year of life, the first issue appearing on April 28, 1894, and the last issue on April 27, 1895. Will Porter drew all his cartoons, and wrote most of the copy, although syndicated articles by Bill Nye, and contributed articles by Texas writers occasionally appeared. In the enterprise, Porter had two partners, first Dr. Daniels, known to Porter as "Dixie," and later an Englishman named Henry Ryder-Taylor. Mr. Arthur Page gives us the report of how Dr. Daniels told the story of his own association with the paper and with Will Porter.

It was in the spring of 1894 that I floated into Austin, and I got a place in the State printing office. I had been working there for a short time when I heard that a man named Porter had bought out the old *Iconoclast* plant—known everywhere as Brann's *Iconoclast*—and was looking for a printer to go into the game with him. I went around to see him, and that was the first time I met O. Henry. Porter had been a clerk in the Texas Land Office, and a teller in the

First National Bank in Austin, and when W. C. Brann
went to Waco decided to buy out his plant and run a
weekly humorous paper.

I talked things over with him, the proposition looked
good, and we formed a partnership then and there.
We christened the paper the *Rolling Stone* after a few
discussions, and in smaller type across the full-page
head we printed "Out for the moss." Which is exactly
what we were out for. Our idea was to run this weekly
with a lot of current events treated in humorous fashion, and also to run short sketches, drawings, and
verse. I had been doing a lot of chalk plate work and
the specimens I showed seemed to make a hit with
Porter. Those chalk plates were the way practically
all of our cuts were printed.

Porter was the most versatile man I had ever met.
He was a fine singer, could write remarkably clever
stuff under all circumstances, and was a good hand at
sketching. And he was the best mimic I ever saw in
my life. He was one of the genuine democrats that
you hear about more often than you meet. Night after
night, after we would shut up shop, he would call to
me to come along and "go bumming." That was his
favorite expression for the night prowling in which
we indulged. We would wander through streets and
alleys, meeting with some of the worst specimens of
down-and-outers it has ever been my privilege to see
at close range. I've seen the most ragged specimen of
a bum hold up Porter, who would always do anything
he could for the man. His one great failing was his
inability to say "No" to a man.

He never cared for the so-called "higher classes," but
watched the people on the streets and in the shops and
cafés, getting his ideas from them night after night.
I think it was in this way he was able to picture the
average man with such marvelous fidelity.

Well, as I started to say, we moved into the old

Iconoclast plant, got out a few issues, and moved into
the Bruegerhoff building. The *Rolling Stone* met with
unusual success at the start, and we had in our files
letters from men like Bill Nye and John Kendrick
Bangs praising us for the quality of the sheet. We
were doing nicely, getting the paper out every Saturday—approximately—and blowing the receipts every
night. Then we began to strike snags. One of our
features was a series of cuts with humorous underlines
in verse. One of the cuts was the rear view of a fat
German professor leading an orchestra, beating the air
wildly with his baton. Underneath the cut Porter had
written the following verse:

With his baton the professor beats the bars,
'Tis also said he beats them when he treats.
But it made that German gentleman see stars
When the bouncer got the cue to bar the beats.

For some reason or other that issue alienated every
German in Austin from the *Rolling Stone*, and cost us
more than we were able to figure out in subscriptions
and advertisements.

Another mistake Porter made was when he let himself be dragged into a San Antonio political fight—the
O'Brien-Callaghan mayoralty campaign. He was
pulled into this largely through a broken-down English writer, whose name, as I remember, was Henry
Rider-Taylor. How Taylor had any influence over him
I never was able to make out, for he used constantly
to make fun of him. "Here comes that man Taylor,"
he'd say. "Got a diamond on him as big as a two bit
piece and shining like granulated sugar." But he went
into the political scrap just the same, and it cost him
more than it was worth.

We got out one feature of the paper that used to
meet with pretty general approval. It was a page
gotten up in imitation of a backwoods country paper,

and we christened it "The Plunkville Patriot." That idea has been carried out since in a dozen different forms, like "The Hogwallow Kentuckian," and "The Bingville Bugle," to give two of the prominent examples. Porter and I used to work on this part of the paper nights and Sundays. I would set the type for it, as there was a system to all of the typographical errors that we made, and I couldn't trust any one else to set it up as we wanted it.

Porter used to think up some right amusing features for this part of the paper. I remember that about then we had on hand a lot of cuts of Gilmore, of Gilmore's Band, which played at the dedication of the State Capitol at Austin. We would run these cuts of Gilmore for any one, from Li Hung Chang to Governor Hogg.

The Populist Party was coming in for all sorts of publicity at this time, and the famous "Sockless" Simpson, of Kansas, was running for Congress. Porter worked out a series of "Tictocq, the Great French Detective," in burlesque of Lecocq, and in one story, I remember, had a deep-laid conspiracy to locate a pair of socks in Simpson's luggage, thus discrediting him with his political followers.

There was reason for Dr. Daniels's early optimism. The first two issues of *The Rolling Stone*, editions of a thousand copies each, were quickly exhausted. Curiosity about a new venture may have stimulated the sale. Of the third issue an edition of six thousand was published and distributed free, with the idea of enlisting the advertising of Austin business men. Thereafter the edition of *The Rolling Stone* in its period of prosperity was about fifteen hundred copies. Then the paper began to flicker. In March, 1895, two issues were skipped, probably due to Porter's illness at the time.

The issue for March 30th carried a paragraph humorously apologizing for the temporary suspension of publication. After that there were three more issues before *The Rolling Stone* came to an end.

From time to time, the work took Porter to San Antonio. First it was for the purpose of drumming up circulation there; later, with the issue of January 26, 1895, there was the announcement that the paper was "published simultaneously in Austin and San Antonio, every Saturday." Porter referred to San Antonio as the City of Tamales, and in a letter of December 20, 1894, wrote of it as "fearfully and wonderfully made."

During some of his visits he lived in an adobe shack, a few blocks from the business district. The shack long survived. For a time it was used as a store. Then, finally, a year or two ago, it was razed to make way for a street widening. In its last days it had a sentimental significance, being known as the O. Henry hut, and there was once a plan to preserve the flagstones and rebuild the fireplace in one of the local schools. To memories of days in San Antonio, Porter turned for the material that went to the making of such tales as "Hygeia at the Solito," "A Fog in Santone," "The Missing Chord," "The Higher Abdication," "The Enchanted Kiss," and "Seats of the Haughty."

Porter's work on *The Rolling Stone* has been praised to the point of extravagance. Hyder E. Rollins, for example, has suggested that if Porter had continued to edit the paper and had the financial side been well managed, it would undoubtedly have become one of the leading humorous weeklies in the United States.

In support of this conjecture he added: "Its crowning glory is the short stories written by Porter, and one can detect in them the touches and mannerisms that made O. Henry great." The mannerisms, yes, but hardly the touches. In that early work there were originality and promise, but at best it was the work of a talented prentice hand; and Porter had to go far and learn much before he began to master the mechanics of his craft, above all the art of compression.

However, the work had been good enough to win him a new post, providing a means of livelihood and a temporary refuge when both were sorely needed. He was in dire straits after the collapse of *The Rolling Stone*, in the late spring and the summer of 1895, eking out a precarious income by free-lance work, contributing odds and ends, particularly to the Cleveland *Plain Dealer*. Then Colonel R. M. Johnston of the Houston *Post* offered him a position on that paper, and Porter accepted and moved to Houston in the autumn of 1895. At a salary of fifteen dollars a week, he was put to work doing miscellaneous reporting. Athol and Margaret did not go with him at once, Athol again being seriously ill. The treasured belongings of the little home had all been sold in July when Porter had planned to go to Washington to accept a call there, but had been held in Austin when his wife's health took the turn for the worse.

Will Porter was with the Houston *Post* for nine months, from October, 1895, to July, 1896. His work was appreciated from the beginning. Starting as a reporter, he was assigned to the uncongenial task of gathering and writing society items. Athol helped

A HOME IN "SANTONE"

*Rear of house in which O. Henry lived in San Antonio,
showing ruins of steps which formerly led down to the river*

him with most of these. Then he started a department
of his own. On October 14th, he began to edit a
column of witticisms—brief paragraphs of narrative,
jokes and poems—called "Tales of the Town" and
later "Some Postscripts and Pencillings." On November 5th, the name of the column was changed to "Some
Postscripts." His salary was raised first to twenty
dollars, and then to twenty-five dollars a week, that
sum being the top wage then known in Houston journalism, and Colonel Johnston told him that he should
go to New York where his talents would be in demand
by the big newspapers.

When O. Henry died in June, 1910, the *Post* recalled his services in an editorial which said that in his
brief term of service he "became the most popular
member of the staff," and went on:

As a cartoonist Porter would have made a mark
equal to that he attained as a writer had he developed
his genius; but he disliked the drudgery connected with
the drawing and found that his sketches were generally
spoiled by any one else who took them to finish. In
the early days he illustrated many of his stories. Those
were before the present development of the art of illustration, whether for magazine or newspaper, and he did
most of the work on chalk, in which the drawing was
made, a cast of lead being afterward made with more
or less general results of reproducing the drawing in
the shape of printing. The generality of the result was
at times disheartening to the artist and Porter never
followed his natural knack for embodying his brilliant
ideas in drawings.

In themselves Porter's *Post* "pencillings" were
hardly deserving of immortality. They dealt lightly

with topics of the hour, or emphasized the rivalry between the various Texas cities. Thus a paragraph appearing December 1, 1895, tells of Cerberus informing a new arrival from Earth, with a passport for heaven, that he is at the gate to the wrong place: "I know it," says the shade, "but it allows a stop-over here. You see, I'm from Galveston, and I've got to make the change gradually."

Then there were his verses in memory of Eugene Field. Field had passed away in his sleep during the night of November 3-4, 1895. Two days later Porter wrote in his column:

> No gift his genius might have had,
> Of titles high in church or State,
> Could charm him as the one he bore
> Of children's poet laureate.
>
> He smiling pressed aside the bays
> And laurel garlands that he won,
> And bowed his head for baby hands
> To place a daisy wreath upon.
>
> He found his kingdom in the ways
> Of little ones he loved so well;
> For them he tuned his lyre and sang
> Sweet simple songs of magic spell.
>
> Oh, greater feat to storm the gates
> Of children's pure and cleanly hearts,
> Than to subdue a warring world
> By stratagems and doubtful arts!
>
> So, when he laid him down to sleep
> And earthly honors seemed so poor;
> Methinks he clung to little hands
> The latest, for the love they bore.

A tribute paid by chanting choirs
And pealing organs rises high;
But soft and clear, somewhere he hears
Through all, a child's low lullaby.

Very pretty in sentiment, but very far from being good verse. The Will Porter of *The Rolling Stone* and the Houston *Post* was not yet a genius.

Meanwhile in the newspaper world, both in Austin and in Houston, Porter had been finding a new circle of friends, a new orbit of life. From environment, or inclination, or necessity, he had shed something of what the world calls "respectability." He was cultivating Bohemia and finding it stimulating and pleasant; and Bohemia in a Texas town of the old days usually meant an establishment where men gathered together to talk and to blow foam from the tops of capacious glasses. Many hard things have been said of the saloon of pre-Volstead times, and with a certain measure of justice; but there were occasions when it served as the local Mermaid's Tavern or the local Cheshire Cheese.

Vivian Richardson, in the Dallas *Morning News* of August 4, 1929, described the old Bismarck Café of Austin where William Sidney Porter had his favorite table and chair. The Bismarck, or what remains of it, still exists, or at least did in the summer of 1929. It is a delicatessen now, but though the beer served is only "near beer," there is still the same mahogany bar, the same battered brass cuspidors, and the same cases filled with ham and cheese, and the same proprietor, George Zerschausky, as in the days, thirty-five years ago, when Porter sat there and carved his place card

on the table. But the table is no longer there. In its
place there is a shiny new piece, presented by an Austin
collector, Eugene Digges, who took the "O. Henry"
table and chair away and placed them for safe-keeping
in an Austin bank vault.

In its palmy days the Bismarck was very German
and very resplendent. Zerschausky was then a young
man who had arrived in Austin from the Fatherland
in 1891. On the walls of the Bismarck were nine huge
pictures, including portraits of the Kaiser and the
Iron Chancellor; side by side were arranged busts of
Falstaff and John Barleycorn. There were also displayed the United States flag and the Texas State flag.
"By 1895," writes Vivian Richardson, "the Bismarck
had become a sort of little Bohemia, the preferred of
those with *savoir-faire*, frequented by statesmen and
celebrities and the few literati, a man's place where
strong cigar smoke filtered over pungent cheeses and
habitués using little white paddles carefully spattered
golden horseradish over thick rosy slices of ham, and
the beer foamed white and cheerily."

Will Porter was not a statesman and not yet a celebrity. But he seems to have been the center of his little
circle, the "life of the party." That did not save him
from the proprietorial wrath when he ventured to carve
a V-shaped wedge out of his favorite table. "I gave
him hell," said Zerschausky, according to Vivian Richardson's account.

He made a long face and told me he was just "marking his place." After that he always sat directly in
front of the notch and in the low chair; if some one else
was occupying the place when he came in he would

courteously suggest that that person move. At this table, too, he often sat alone, quietly scribbling on notes for the *Rolling Stone*, his paper. Sometimes he drew caricatures which were later inked and used in the *Rolling Stone*, and once he did some queer ones of Indians and people which afterwards were elaborated to illustrate Wilbarger's "Indian Depredations in Texas."

Will Porter's vandalism, which was to preserve for posterity memories of the Bismarck, was apparently no more appreciated by its proprietor than was King Alfred's burning of the cakes by the cottage housewife.

There was also the flavor of Bohemia in the nine months in Houston. When Athol joined him, the two with little Margaret boarded in a house on Caroline Street, near the post office. From there he sallied forth in search of his "copy" which he found in the town's byways, in the resorts where men stood with their feet resting on brass rails, in the Grand Central Depot, where the train arrivals often meant news items, and in the old Hutchins House, a favorite stopping place for the drummers of St. Louis with their unfailing fund of stories.

Writing in the Houston *Post-Dispatch* of October 26, 1930, Elbert Turner recalled those Houston days and some of the opinions of Porter's associates on the paper.

It was [writes Mr. Turner] the day of the open saloon, sawdust floors, and the gastronomical gamble, the free lunch. . . . It was a wild time in the old town. Bloomers and bicycles were agitating the press. Somebody was fighting somebody else in Europe, but nobody seemed to care much, for everybody seemed to

think it was just another Balkan operetta, with a bad
score. . . . It was the day when ladies, heavily swathed,
and securely trussed in great bales of bunting, wiggled
inoffensive looking Indian clubs. . . . This was the
hot-bed that was Houston when O. Henry came to town.

Will Porter was then thirty-three years of age. His
contemporaries, according to Mr. Turner, recall him
particularly on account of his striking blue eyes, his
impassive face, his low, even voice, and his unusual
reticence. Then, as in after life, few men ever penetrated his armor of reserve; got to know him well.
Though he possessed a quiet, deliberate certainty of
action, he was as shy and timid as a stranger. Extremely sensitive, always effacing himself, usually silent
to the point of taciturnity, he obviously shrank from
persons who sought him out. Yet there were times
when, feeling entirely at ease among his fellow workers,
he talked freely. Then, "his conversation bubbled
with witticisms. He made no effort at being funny.
Jokes just oozed out of him, and he never laughed at
his own sayings. Sometimes there was just a small
smile."

A. E. Clarkson, present secretary-treasurer of the
Houston *Post-Dispatch*, is quoted as telling that he
used to hand Porter his pay envelope every week and
recalls that the columnist was always promptly on hand
to receive it—a statement that is likely to be accepted
without hesitation by the editors who were to know
O. Henry in the New York days. "But that," said
Mr. Clarkson, "was nothing unusual, for nobody missed
a pay day in those days, if he was well enough to call
for it." None of Porter's *Post* associates recall that

he wasted his money while he lived in Houston, though he spent freely when occasion called for it.

In Porter's column in the *Post*, Mr. Turner found the germs of two stories written in later years—one of them "A Poor Rule" (*Options*), a tale of relative unimportance, the other "The Enchanted Profile" (*Roads of Destiny*), O. Henry in his best vein. In one of his *Post* paragraphs, Porter told of a young Houston woman named Marian who decided to put the sincerity of her suitors to the test by reciting a poem and then asking their opinions of the performance. Marian and her story later developed into Ileen Hinkle of "A Poor Rule," the beautiful heroine who was not proof against flattery. The *Post* paragraph ended with this moral: "And what we discussed was whether it was better to lie to a woman or to tell her the truth. And as all of us were young then, we did not come to a decision."

"The Enchanted Profile" appeared in the *Metropolitan Magazine* for February, 1908, and presumably was written not earlier than a few months before, but its origin dates back to 1896 and the following paragraphs, entitled "A Universal Favorite":

The most popular and best loved young lady in the United States is Miss Annie Williams of Philadelphia. Her picture is possessed by more men, and is more eagerly sought after than that of Lillian Russell, Mrs. Langtry, or any other famous beauty. There is more demand for her pictures than for the counterfeit presentments of all the famous men and women in the world combined. And yet she is a modest, charming, and rather retiring young lady, with a face less beautiful than of a clear and classic profile.

Miss Williams is soon to be married, but it is expected that the struggle for her pictures will go on as usual.

She is the lady the profile of whose face served as the model for the head of Liberty on our silver dollar.

The net about Will Porter was tightening. In July, 1896, came the summons, long feared and expected, to go to Austin and stand trial for alleged embezzlement of funds while acting as paying and receiving teller of the First National Bank. The Federal authorities were pressing the case and had obtained indictments charging specifically that on October 10, 1894, he had misappropriated $554.48; on November 12, 1894, $299.60; and on November 12, 1895, $299.60. The obvious discrepancy will be discussed in the story of the trial.

When Will Porter said good-by to his family and bought a railway ticket from Houston to Austin he apparently had no thought of doing anything but return to face the situation. Probably it was in the course of the first few miles of the journey that the thought of flight and of Honduras entered his head. The newspapers of 1896 were filled with accounts of the great opportunities offered the enterprising and progressive young man in Honduras, the land of the little banana. In his column in the *Post*, Porter himself had made some humorous references to "Honduras, on the Mosquito Coast," and had presented as a typical Honduran menu: "Pale Ale, Chicken with Herbs, Rum, Fricassee of Young Monkey, Rye Whiskey, Green Turtle with Broth, Brandy and Soda, Oysters, Pale Ale." Also from his ranch days he had acquired a sound knowledge of Spanish. Honduras filled his imagination; it was a land of adventure and romance; once there, Athol and Margaret could join him.

The journey by rail from Houston to Austin is approximately one of one hundred and fifty miles. Fifty miles from Houston on the Houston and Texas Central Railroad, is the little town of Hempstead, the county seat of Waller County. There Porter left the train. When that night a train pulled out of Hempstead bound for New Orleans, Porter was on it. His days as Aladdin were at an end; his years as Sinbad the Sailor had begun.[1]

[1] Some years ago one of the authors of this book, spending a day with Mr. Rudyard Kipling at Batesmans, Burwash, asked Mr. Kipling how, in *Captains Courageous,* he had worked out the details of the record-breaking trip of the private car *Constance,* carrying Harvey Cheyne, Senior and Mrs. Cheyne from San Diego to the Eastern seaboard, to meet the son who had been given up as lost. "I didn't," was Mr. Kipling's reply. "I let the railroads do the work for me. I simply wrote them explaining the situation and asked them how they would have arranged to convey the *Constance* across the Continent in the fewest number of hours."

Following that method a letter was sent to the Houston offices of what is now the Texas and New Orleans Railroad Company asking coöperation to the extent of looking up the old time-tables with the idea of possibly throwing some light on W. S. Porter's flight. The following reply is due to the courtesy of Mr. L. B. McDonald, General Manager of the Southern Pacific Lines:

"Delay in making reply to your inquiry . . . concerning train schedules thro gh Hempstead . . . is the result of an effort to locate some old time-tables. We have, however, been unsuccessful, but some of our old employes located at Hempstead and operating out of that junction point recall approximate schedules which were in effect in 1896.

"A daylight train was operated from Hempstead to Austin leaving Hempstead between 10:00 and 11:00 A.M., shortly after passage of main line train operating between Houston and Dallas, this main line train leaving Houston about 9:00 A.M. A night mixed freight and passenger train was operated between Hempstead and Austin, leaving Hempstead around 2:00 o'clock in connection with main line train leaving Houston around 10:00 P.M. Companion runs were operated Austin to Hempstead, the mixed train arriving Hempstead about 5:00 A.M., connecting with the main line Dallas-Houston train scheduled to arrive Houston about 7:00 A.M. A daylight passenger train operated out of Austin about noon, arriving Hempstead about 5:00 P.M. and connecting with main line arriving Houston about 6:30 P.M.

"The night trains carried a through sleeper between Houston and Austin."

PART II

SINBAD

VI

LAND OF THE LOTUS-EATERS

There are yet tales of the Spanish Main. . . . The guns of the rovers are silenced; but the tintype man, the enlarged photograph brigand, the kodaking tourist, and the scouts of the gentle brigade of fakirs have found it out, and carry on the work. The hucksters of Germany, France, and Sicily now bag its small change across their counters. Gentlemen adventurers throng the waiting rooms of its rulers with proposals for railways and concessions. The little *opera-bouffe* nations play at government and intrigue until some day a big, silent gunboat glides into the offing and warns them not to break their toys.   *Cabbages and Kings*

VERY little exact information is available about what happened to William Sidney Porter in New Orleans when he stayed there in the course of his flight from Texas to Central America. Even the duration of his stay is a matter of surmise. In his later years, New Orleans was particularly emphasized in his scheme of autobiographical evasion. There is an airy gesture in his reference to the city as the place to which he went, when tired of Austin, to "take up literary work in earnest." Again, New Orleans figures prominently in his own accounts of how he came to adopt his pen name.

The probabilities are that the stay was a very short one, enforced rather than voluntary. He was no safer from legal pursuit in Louisiana than he would have been in Texas, in view of the fact that the offense with which he was charged was a Federal one. But when Porter reached the Crescent City he found himself practically without money. He was confronted by two problems, of obtaining funds to meet the immediate needs of existence, and further funds to pay for the passage to Honduras. To have applied for the kind of work for which he was fitted would have involved the presentation of credentials which he, as a fugitive from justice, was in no position to offer. He was obliged to turn to manual labor.

His life as Sinbad the Sailor began arduously. The Will Porter who had been so dapper in the Austin days was reduced to toiling on the levees as a stevedore, unloading bananas. There is the suggestion of nights spent on the benches in the city parks; of a furtive, down-and-out existence when, like the two adventurers of "The Shamrock and the Palm," he learned the meaning of Ordinance 5046, designed to deal summarily with the city's guests who were without visible means of support.

Hard as those New Orleans days were, the city came to mean much to him. It was the scene of a number of his stories, and an influence in many more. Caroline Francis Richardson in an article "O. Henry and New Orleans" which appeared in *The Bookman* in May, 1914, told of the appeal that down-town New Orleans made to O. Henry's story instinct and sympathy. "Like many other writers he found inspiration in the narrow, dingy, shadowy Quarter whose buildings and street names and traditions tell of many things that to-day are lost: riches and lives and causes." But O. Henry used his "copy" differently from other story-tellers who have found suggestion in New Orleans. In the O. Henry tales, no plot hinges on a mixture of blood; no hero or heroine is engulfed by flood or de-

voured by plague.   There is no use of Mardi Gras, All
Saints' Day, or Quatorze Juillet.

Miss Richardson has written:

As a setting, New Orleans can claim but a scant
share in the lives of some of O. Henry's knights of high
adventure.   This is the case with a certain grafter and
his partner, Caligula, who of their stay could remember only some drinks "invented by the creoles during
the period of Louey Cans, in which they are still served
at the side doors"; and an attempt "to make the French
Quarter pay up the back trading stamps due on the
Louisiana Purchase."

It is in that story, "Hostages to Momus," that the
Grafter explains the component parts of a perfect
breakfast: "There'll never be a perfect breakfast until
some man grows arms long enough to stretch down to
New Orleans for his coffee and over to Norfolk for his
rolls, and reaches up to Vermont and digs a slice of
butter out of a spring-house, and then turns over a
beehive close to a clover patch for the rest.   Then he'd
come pretty close to making a meal that the gods eat
on Mount Olympus.

Though the O. Henry stories touching New Orleans
or its vicinity are only eight in number—"Phoebe,"
"The Shamrock and the Palm," "Cherchez la Femme,"
"Blind Man's Holiday," "A Matter of Mean Elevation," "Helping the Other Fellow," "Whistling Dick's
Christmas Stocking," and "The Renaissance at Char-
leroi"—in them he established a definite claim.   Turn
to Lafayette Square for the bench where Clancy of
"The Shamrock and the Palm" brought about the
arrest of General De Vega.   In Ursulines Street, the
General was set to work filibustering with a rake and
shovel, while Clancy, with a memory of past wrongs,

made his headquarters just round the corner in a
saloon decorated with electric fans and cool merchan-
dise, and at fifteen-minute intervals strolled out to
watch the little man toiling in the heat, and remark,
"Fat, strong mans is needed in New Orleans. Yes. To
carry on the good work. Carrambos! Erin go bragh!"

It was near Congo Square that Captain Patricio
Malone, sitting over his cognac, told the story of
"Phoebe"; and Poydras Market was the scene of the
total eclipse of Badluck Kearney by the satellite in the
same tale. "Cherchez la Femme" introduced the café
of Madame Tibault in Dumaine Street, where a corner
of the wall was papered with the missing five-thousand-
dollar United States gold bonds that were supposed to
have been stolen by the wicked M'sieur Morin; and
told of L'Abeille, "the old French newspaper that had
buzzed for nearly a century." To a friendly stall-
keeper in the French Market, the tramp hero of "Whistling Dick's Christmas Stocking" owed his breakfast.
Grandemont Charles, of "The Renaissance of Char-
leroi," the little creole gentleman aged thirty-four, with
a bald spot on the top of his head and the manners of a
prince, was by day a clerk in a cotton broker's office
in one of "those cold, rancid mountains of oozy brick,
down near the Levee." By night, in the old French
Quarter, he was again the last male descendant of the
Charles family.

Something of the soul of New Orleans is in "Blind
Man's Holiday." There is also perhaps the suggestion
of an autobiographical touch. Lorison was an exile in
the quaint southern city, knowing but few people, living in a subjective world of shadows. To the girl

Norah he said: "I am an outcast from honest people; I am wrongly accused of one crime, and am, I believe, guilty of another." But in "Blind Man's Holiday" there are bits of description that remain in the memory long after the plot has been forgotten. For example:

The Rue Chartres, in New Orleans, is a street of ghosts. It lies in the quarter where the Frenchman, in his prime, set up his translated pomp and glory; where, also, the arrogant don had swaggered, and dreamed of gold and grants and ladies' gloves. Every flagstone has its grooves worn by footsteps going royally to the wooing and the fighting. Every house has a princely heartbreak; each doorway its untold tale of gallant promise and slow decay.

By night the Rue Chartres is now but a murky fissure, from which the groping wayfarer sees, flung against the sky, the tangled filigree of Moorish iron balconies. The old houses of monsieur stand yet, indomitable against the century, but their essence is gone. The street is one of ghosts to whoever can see them.

A faint heartbeat of the street's ancient glory still survives in a corner occupied by the Café Carabine d'Or. Once men gathered there to plot against kings, and to warn presidents. They do so yet, but they are not the same kind of men. A brass button will scatter these; those would have set their faces against an army.

As the story of Porter's stay in New Orleans is a matter of conjecture, to be filled out by reading between the lines of his tales, so also is the story of his journey to Honduras and his method of establishing himself there. At Trujillo, the Coralio of *Cabbages and Kings*, it is taken over for a time by Al Jennings, who has told it in his book, *Through the Shadows with O. Henry*. Jennings was a bank robber and train robber of the old West who, after a tempestuous career, recognized the truth of the adage, "you can't win"; mended his ways; became a respectable member of society; was elected to political office, and restored to full citizenship by President Roosevelt. But at the time of his first meeting with Porter he was still an outlaw. In company with his brother Frank he escaped from New Orleans, where the pursuit was closing in upon them, and on a tramp banana steamer that made a specialty of brandy smuggling, journeyed to Honduras, a land that beckoned particularly for the reason that it had no extradition treaty with the United States. The voyage was enlivened by the consumption of much of the contraband Three Star Hennessey.

Upon his arrival at Trujillo, Al Jennings sighted the American flag flying over a squat wooden bungalow, and with a morning-after thirst and a yearning for companionship approached the edifice. On the porch was seated an ample, dignified figure in immaculate white ducks. He had a large, nobly set head, with hair the color of new rope and a full, straight-glancing gray eye that noted without a sparkle of laughter every detail of the new arrival's makeup. But let Jennings tell the story:

He was already serene and comfortably situated with liquor, but he had about him an attitude of calm distinction. A rather pompous dignitary, he seemed to me, sitting there as if he owned the place. This, I thought, is indeed a man worthy to be the American consul.

I felt like a newsboy addressing a millionaire.

"Say, mister," I asked, "could you lead me to a

drink? Burnt out on Three Star Hennessey. Got a different brand?"

"We have a lotion here that is guaranteed to uplift the spirit," he answered in a hushed undertone that seemed to charge his words with vast importance.

"Are you the American consul?" I ventured also in a whisper.

"No, just anchored here," he smuggled back the information. Then his cool glance rested on the ragged edge of my coat.

"What caused you to leave in such a hurry?" he asked.

"Perhaps the same reason that routed yourself," I retorted.

The merest flicker of a smile touched his lips. He got up, took my arm, and together we helped each other down the street, that was as narrow as a burrow path, to the nearest cantina.

That, according to the story, was the first meeting of William Sidney Porter and Al Jennings. For years destiny was to lead them along the same dark roads, one of which Jennings likens to a tunnel, and then out again to the broader path which was the world's highway. "But to me," records Jennings, "in every detour of the road, he remained the same calm, whimsical Bill—baffling, reserved, lovable—who had led me to the Mexican doggery for my first drink in the paradise of fugitives."

To resume the Jennings story:

In the dingy adobe estanca I found the solution guaranteed to uplift the spirit. But it was not in the sweet, heavy concoction the dignitary from the consulate called for. It was in the droll, unsmiling waggery of the conversation that came forth in measured, hesitant, excessively pure English as we leaned on the rickety table and drank without counting our glasses.

Despite the air of distinction that was with him as a sort of birthmark, I felt at once drawn to him. I began to unfold my plan of settling in the country.

"This is an admirable location for a man who doesn't want much to do," he said.

"What line are you interested in?" I asked.

"I haven't given the matter much thought," he said, "I entertain the newcomers."

"You must be a hell of a busy man," I suggested.

"You're the first since my arrival."

He leaned over. "You probably wonder who I am and why I'm here."

In Honduras every American is a subject of suspicion.

"Oh, no," I put in quickly. "In my country nobody asks a man's name or his past. You're all right."

"Thanks, colonel." He drew in his upper lip in a manner that was characteristic. "You might call me Bill. I think I would like that."

Several hours we sat there, an ex-highwayman in a tattered dress suit and a fugitive in spotless white ducks, together planning a suitable investment for my stolen funds. Porter suggested a cocoanut plantation, a campaign for the presidency, an indigo concession.

In *Roads of Destiny* O. Henry wrote the story, "The Fourth in Salvador." The details of the ice plant and the $1,000 bonus from the government were pure invention. All the rest of the story was merely a whimsically colored account of an adventure which, according to Jennings, befell them the morning after the arrival of the tramp banana steamer in Trujillo. Frank Jennings had been smuggled ashore from the boat. Porter suggested that as the next day was the

Fourth of July it should be celebrated in an appropriate fashion.

To continue Al Jennings' account:

Long after midnight Porter took us to the consulate, where he made his home. He had a little cot in one corner of the main room. He took the blankets from it and spread them on the floor. The three of us stretched out.

About 11 o'clock in the morning the celebration of the Fourth opened. Porter, Frank, two Irishmen who owned an indigo concession, the American consul, myself and a negro brought along for the sake of democracy, made up the party. For a fitting observance of America's triumph Porter insisted that the English consul join us. We put the matter before her majesty's subject. He agreed that it would be "a devil of a fine joke."

There were but four life-sized houses in Trujillo. Under the shade of the governor's mansion we stood and sang "The Star Spangled Banner." Out of deference to our guest Porter suggested that we render one verse of "God Save the Queen." The Britisher objected. "Don't make a damn nonsense of this occasion," he demurred.

We started off to shoot up the town in true Texas style, prepared to wind up the fireworks with a barbecued goat in the lemon grove near the beach. We never got to the barbecue. A revolution intervened.

We had shot up two estancas. Glass was shattered everywhere. The Carib bartenders had fled. We were helping ourselves and scrupulously laying the money for every drink on the counter.

Suddenly a shot was fired from the outside. Porter had just finished smashing up a mirror with a bottle. He turned with a quiet that was as ludicrous as it was inimitable.

"Gentlemen," he said, "the natives are trying to steal our copyrighted Fourth."

We made a clattering dash for the street, shooting wildly in the air. A little man in a flaming red coat came galloping by. About thirty barefoot horsemen, all in red coats and very little else, tore up a mighty cloud of dust in his wake. They fired off their old-fashioned muzzle loaders as if they really meant murder.

As the leader whirled past on his diminutive gray pony Porter caught him by the waist and dragged him off. I sprang into the saddle, shooting and yelling like a maniac.

"Reinforcements, reinforcements!" Like a song of victory the shout thundered from the rear. I don't know where or how I rode.

But the next day the governor and two of his little tan Caribs called at the consulate. He wished to thank the American patriots for the magnificent aid they had given in quelling the revolution. They had saved the republic. With a lordly air he offered us the cocoanut plantations that grew wild all over the country. The incredible daring of the American riders had saved the nation.

We didn't even know there had been a revolution. And we didn't know whose side we had taken. Porter rose to the occasion.

"We appreciate the government's attitude," he answered with a touch of patronage in his tone. "So often patriots are forgotten."

It seems that in that moment when we rushed wildly to the door of the cantina we changed the tide of battle. The government troops were chasing the rebels and the rebels were winning. We had rallied the royal army and led it to victory. It was a bloodless battle.

Our triumph was short-lived. The government and the rebel leaders patched up their differences. The rebel general demanded amends for the insult to his troops. He demanded the lives of the outsiders who had impudently ended a revolution before it had decently begun.

Dates play little part in Al Jennings's free-hand narrative. There is nothing in the story of that first meeting on which to base even conjecture as to how long Porter had been established in Trujillo, or the number of months that had elapsed since his departure from Houston. The only clew to the early Honduran days comes from Texas. It was, according to Mrs. Maltby, two months after the flight that Athol received a letter from her husband, begging her to come to him, bringing Margaret. He expressed the belief that the change of climate would be beneficial to Athol's health, and said that he had been looking around for a school in which they could place Margaret, who had reached school age.

But that letter came too late. Though he did not know it, Athol was far too weak to undertake such a journey. Besides, had she been able to go she could hardly have done so without betraying his whereabouts. Mrs. Maltby writes: "I have been told that Athol said the hardest letter she ever wrote in her life was the one to Will Porter saying she could not come to him and realizing that he could not come to her. Nor could she tell him that the news that he had forfeited his bond had made her worse, much worse."

However, this exchange of letters must have long preceded the arrival in Honduras of the Jennings boys, and the Fourth of July prank. For that did not blow over as easily as the celebrators had hoped. The governor's first enthusiastic gratitude soon yielded to expediency. To conciliate the rebels he yielded to the demands that stern justice be meted out to the foreigners who had disturbed a day of pleasant revolution. The American consul, to whom an appeal for protection was made, advised immediate departure. Porter summed up the political aspect of the situation. "The State Department will refer our case to Mark Hanna. He will investigate our party affiliations. It will then be referred to the bureau of immigration, and by that time we will all be shot." The situation was later to be echoed in "Two Renegades."

There Barney O'Keefe, American soldier of fortune, caught red handed in arms against the government of the hour and sentenced to be shot, appeals to the United States consul to call up Uncle Sam on the cable.

"Have 'em send the *Kentucky* and the *Kearsage* and the *Oregon* down right away. That'll be about enough battleships; but it wouldn't hurt to have a couple of cruisers and a torpedo-boat destroyer, too. And—say, if Dewey isn't busy, better have him come along on the fastest one of the fleet."

But the consul demurs.

"Now what you want," he says consolingly, "is not to get excited. I'll send you over some chewing tobacco and some banana fritters when I go back. The United States can't interfere in this. You know you were caught insurging against the government, and you're subject to the laws of this country. Tell you the truth, I've had an intimation from the State Department—unofficially, of course—that whenever a soldier of fortune demands a fleet of gunboats in a case of revolutionary *katzenjammer*, I should cut the cable, give him all the tobacco he wants, and after he's shot take his clothes, if they fit me, for part payment of my salary."

The consul at Trujillo, according to Al Jennings, was equally unsympathetic. Immediate, undignified flight was the only way out of the predicament; so the Jennings boys and Porter scurried to the beach, found a small boat, and rowed out to the waiting *Helena*. Jennings tells of an interruption by a little Carib girl, an incident to which Porter was to refer in New York many years later: "Remember that little strip of brown muslin that fluttered down the street after us in Trujillo? I wonder what she was saying." "He didn't like 'unfinished stories,' " commented Jennings.

Bill, the new-found friend, had thrown in his lot with us. He didn't have a cent in the world. He didn't know where we were going or who we were. "What is your destination?" he asked quietly as the *Helena* steamed up. "I left America to avoid my destination," I told him. "How far can you go?" "As far as $30,-000 will take us." It took us farther than we reckoned.

In a general way the O. Henry stories, chronologically, follow the backgrounds against which he lived his own adventurous life. The earlier tales dealt with Texas; then he turned to New Orleans for his material; then to Central America; and finally he found his inspiration in his "Little Old Bagdad on the Subway," his "City of Too Many Caliphs," his "City of Chameleon Changes." It was with *Cabbages and Kings*, made up of the tales of Central America, that he invaded the Arabian Nights for the first time.

Analysis of the genesis and development of the writ-

ing of *Cabbages and Kings* properly belongs to a later
chapter dealing with "the story of the stories." But
the book calls imperatively for attention here. It reflects, where there is a dearth of personal evidence,
Porter's life and environment in the fugitive days in
Honduras, colored by the man's own whimsical
imagination and his flair for the extravagant. In one
of his letters to Athol he told of digging ditches and
subsisting on bananas. There we have the suggestion
of Clancy of "The Shamrock and the Palm," "filibustering" with pick and shovel and eating the tropical
fruit until it was "distasteful to the sight and an eye-
sore to the palate."

The American adventurers and the natives who
figure in the eighteen stories of *Cabbages and Kings*
must have been drawn from life. Perhaps at times
they were composites, but sheer invention was impossible. Was the American consul whose hospitality Porter was enjoying when Jennings first met him and who
a little later was to advise flight, the original of Willard
Geddes or of his successor John De Graffenreid Atwood? Who was "Beelzebub" Blythe, the fascinating
drunken beachcomber who as a last resort turned to
blackmail? Who were Billy Keogh, and Henry
Horsecollar, and Bob Englehart, and Bernard Bran-
nigan, and Homer P. Mellinger, and Dick, and Colonel
Falcon, and President Miraflores, and President
Losada? When, in "Shoes" and "Ships," Porter told
of a certain Pinkney Dawson, cornerer of the cocklebur
market and Johnny Atwood's rival in love, did his
mind go back a little maliciously to one Lee Zimple-

mann? These are questions. Certainly Anchuria was
Honduras and Coralio Trujillo.

Also, since O. Henry did not live to write the novel
which he planned, which was to have been the story of
a man born and "raised" in a somnolent little southern
town, *Cabbages and Kings* is the one work that offers
a basis for conjecture as to what he might have accomplished in protracted effort. It is not a novel, but
a number of short stories, some of them bearing not
the slightest relation to others, bound together by a
thin and synthetic, but highly ingenious plot that has
the characteristic O. Henry quality of surprise. Occasionally the very ingenuity of the plot has proved a
handicap. More than one reader, not particularly
puritanical or squeamish, has left the book unfinished,
resenting Goodwin's complaisant acceptance of a past
of the supposed Isabel Guilbert that was not only
tarnished but greedily sordid.

The late Harry Thurston Peck traced the origin of
the method of *Cabbages and Kings* back to the second
century, A.D., writing of it:

It represents a type of story which is nearly two
thousand years old—the second step in the evolution
of the novel. Mr. Porter finds his ancient prototype
in Apuleius of Madaura, that African novelist who
wrote in Latin as strange as some of Mr. Porter's
English, his romance entitled *The Golden Ass*. Apuleius at the very beginning of his book says: "I shall
weave together for you in this tale various stories in
the Milesian manner." This is precisely what Mr.
Porter has done about seventeen hundred years later.
Without knowing it he has constructed a series of
Milesian tales which have no relation to each other,

but which are artfully made to hang upon another
Milesian tale which serves as a thread to bind the whole
together. Thus in *Cabbages and Kings* there are told
the stories of "The Shamrock and the Palm," the plot
by which Billy Keogh and Johnny Atwood discomfit
the astute Pink Dawson, "The Flag Paramount," "The
Admiral," "Dicky," and "Rouge et Noir." These are
all Milesian stories—that is to say, short stories with
no immediate relation to the principal story, which
in itself is another Milesian, mechanically wedded to
them.

To revert to Al Jennings's story. Once on board the
ship in the harbor, the disturbers of revolution were
safe from pursuit. The narrative leads to South America. The voyage of the *Helena* was apparently one
of no definite purpose, the adventurers planning to loll
along, looking for a congenial place, where there would
be no extradition treaty to bother them, in which to
establish themselves. The ship's captain was evidently
either a kindred spirit, or else exceedingly obliging and
unsystematic. Buenos Ayres was visited and then Peru.
In time, according to the narrative, Porter and Al and
Frank Jennings found themselves in Mexico City.
There, in a hotel lobby, they ran into an old friend of
the Jennings brothers, a mining engineer named Rector, who had built the Isthmian railroad and was living
in a palace of white stone. Rector insisted that the
travelers be his guests.

At first, between Porter and Rector it was a case of
reciprocal Dr. Fell. Each regarded the other as an
object of suspicion. "Who is this friend of yours, this
Bill?" asked Rector. "Are you sure of him? He looks
to me like a detective." "I don't like your friend

Rector," Porter confided the same night. "He has a most unpleasant way of scrutinizing one." But this mutual mistrust was only temporary. At a grand ball at the hotel in Mexico City, Porter's indiscreet attentions to a señorita to whom he had not been introduced in the punctilious Mexican fashion, led to tragedy, Al Jennings shooting down a jealous don to save his friend's life. It was Rector who hurried Porter and the Jennings boys away in his carriage and pointed out the road of escape from Mexico. "We went," records Al Jennings, "to a little way station on the Tampico road, later caught a tramp steamer at Mazatlan and finally arrived at San Diego, striking out on a flying trip to San Francisco. We never got there."

The ill-gotten thirty thousand dollars with which the Jennings boys had landed in Honduras had dwindled to four hundred and seventeen dollars. Porter had no money at all. The hardened outlaws decided to rob a bank and with the proceeds buy a ranch fifty miles from San Antonio that had caught their fancy. The question was, what part was Porter to play in the affair? In the course of the flight from Honduras he had been forced repeatedly to borrow from his companions, and these loans humiliated him. The brothers did not want him to be under further obligation; they wanted him to earn his interest in the ranch. So they took him into their confidence. Al Jennings relates:

If you had seen Bill Porter's face and the helpless surprise that scooted across it, you would believe as I do that he was never guilty of the theft which sent him for nearly four years to the Ohio Penitentiary. He had neither the recklessness nor the sang froid of the lawbreaker. . . .

"Bill," I said, "we're going to buy the ranch for fifteen thousand dollars and we want you to come in with us on the deal." . . .

"Colonel," he said, "I would like nothing better than to settle in this magnificent country, and to live here unafraid and unmolested. But I have no funds."

"That's just it. Neither have we. We're about to get them. Down there in —— there's a bank with fifteen thousand dollars in its vaults. That money ought to be put in circulation." . . .

"Colonel," he said, "I think I would be a hindrance in this financial undertaking."

I wanted Porter to go with us. We didn't need him, but I had already grown very fond of the moody, reticent, cultured fellow. I didn't want him to be dependent on us and I wanted his company on the range.

"Well, you needn't take the gun. You just stay outside and hold the horses. We really need you for that."

He hesitated for a minute.

"I don't believe that I could even hold the horses," he answered.

That was the parting, though Al Jennings and William Sidney Porter were destined soon to meet again. The trail is not easy to follow. Where did Porter go after his separation from the Jennings brothers in California? How did he find his way back to Honduras and what was the manner of his reception there? Those are all matters of surmise. What is known is that one day in Honduras Porter received a letter from Austin. It was the letter accompanying the Christmas box. Into it Mrs. Roach had secretly slipped a note reading: "Will, you should come home. Athol packed this box running a temperature of 105." The summons was enough. Will Porter decided to return to face the music. He started at once, sailing from Honduras to New Orleans. He reached Austin, February 5, 1897.

VII

THE PERSISTING ENIGMA

Whither these roads led he knew not. Either way there seemed to lie a great world full of chance and peril.   Roads of Destiny

A FEW years ago a note was found in Austin throwing light on Porter's precarious financial condition in the months following his wife's death and preceding his trial. Dated September 1, 1897, it was a promise to pay the sum of $45.70, with interest at ten per cent, to Ph. Hatzfeld and Company. Hatzfeld had opened the first Parisian modiste shop in Texas. The shop, featuring the latest models, proved a decided attraction to the feminine population of Austin, drawing particularly girls about to be married and women planning for travel. For whose benefit Porter incurred the Hatzfeld debt is not known.

The note was never collected. Hatzfeld endorsed it "Pay to J. W. Maxwell without recourse on me." Apparently it was then turned over to a lawyer for collection. The lawyer, after following up the case, dismissed it as a bad debt, and scrawled across the bottom of the note: "In Illinois Penitentiary. She is dead." The "Illinois" was a slight error, but the meaning was obvious. "She is dead" was slang for the statement that it was uncollectable and a dead account, and had no reference to either Porter or his wife.

In those months Porter was also at work on his

earliest stories. That he sent several of them to New York is evident from the following letter:

New York, Dec. 2, 1897.

W. S Porter Esq.
  211 East 6th. St.
     Austin, Texas.
DEAR SIR:
Your story, "The Miracle of Lava Cañon," is excellent. It has the combination of human interest with dramatic incident, which in our opinion is the best kind of story. If you have more like this, we should be glad to read them. We have placed it in our syndicate of newspapers. The other stories we return herewith. They are not quite available.

Very truly yours,
THE S. S. McCLURE Co.

"The Miracle of Lava Cañon" was entered for copyright by the McClure Syndicate September 11, 1898, marked for publication September 18, 1898. It was to this story that the author referred many years later when he said: "My first story was paid for but I never saw it in print."

We now come to the enigma of Will Porter's life: the hazy events leading to his trial, conviction, and term in the Ohio Penitentiary. To-day there are many partisans who hotly refuse to admit even the possibility of his having been guilty of the crime for which he paid the penalty. That partisanship in itself may have no great significance. Where there has been an interesting personality involved, some of the most flagrant offenders have found champions. The Borgias have been whitewashed; Mary Queen of Scots

Pay to Geo C. Maxwell
Without Recourse on me
[signature]

$45.70

Austin, Texas, September 1st 189 7

Six months after date, for value received, I, we, or either of us promise to pay to the order of PH. HATZFELD & CO.

Forty-five and 70/100 Dollars, at their office in Austin, Texas,

with interest at the rate of ten feet centum per annum from Date until paid.

And in the event default is made in the payment of this note and interest at maturity, and it is placed in the hands of an attorney or agent for collection, or suit is brought on the same, then an additional amount of ten per cent on the principal and interest of this note shall be added to the same as collection fees,

Due

Address

[signatures]

PH. HATZFELD & CO.,
IMPORTERS,
500-502 Congress Ave., Austin, Texas.

EUGEN VON BOECKMANN PUBLISHING CO., PRINTER, BOOKBINDER AND STATIONER, AUSTIN, TEXAS.

WILL PORTER "PROMISES TO PAY"

A document illustrating the low state of his finances during his last months in Austin never plotted against Queen Elizabeth; Eve was quite guiltless in that little affair of the apple; it was all, as Thackeray has phrased it, a wicked fabrication of the serpent's.

But O. Henry's case is very different. It is not merely a matter of the posterity of a succeeding generation adapting its belief to its sympathies. The doubt of the justice of the verdict was not a development of years long after; it clouded the issue at the time, and troubled the consciences of many of those who were directly concerned in the case. According to Professor Smith, the foreman of the grand jury and the foreman of the trial jury are reported to have regretted afterward that they had voted to convict. "O. Henry was an innocent man," said the former, "and if I had known then what I know now, I should never have voted against him."

The writers of this book have received many letters from persons who assert their positive knowledge of Porter's innocence; but who for some reason or other have failed to support their contentions with the required evidence. Some of them offer merely theories. From time to time, the ancient and fantastic suggestion has been advanced that Porter's sacrifice was made "to save a woman's honor." That, however, is hardly tenable. Again his silence has been ascribed to a mistaken idea of friendship. Al Jennings, whose belief in Porter's innocence has already been cited, in March, 1912, wrote a letter to Robert H. Davis from which is quoted:

What would it be if I told the story of our meeting, the circumstances and surroundings, when and where,

plain and unvarnished? Now, this you cogitate upon.
What Bill really done that the world could know by
investigation is not all, but it is the worst. I once
asked him, after we had been together years, what he
"fell" for. "I was cashier, I bet that cotton would
go up, but cotton went down." The money was given
to him by another fellow associated in the same institution. This fellow had a charming wife and two
children; Porter was foot-loose. When the finger of
accusation was pointed at the other man, Bill Porter,
cold of face, stepped forward, saying easily, "You are
mistaken, it was I," the other fellow said: "O Bill,
don't do that." (You know Porter.) The expression
of his face never changed, and he said coldly, "I don't
believe we are on friendly terms."

It all reads like the story, "Friends in San Rosario."
But without questioning Mr. Jennings's sincerity or
memory, there are certain obvious flaws. Porter, with
Athol and Margaret, was hardly "foot-loose."

More than thirty-three years have passed since Will
Porter stood trial in Austin. The Judge and the
prosecuting attorney are dead. The writers of this
book would like nothing better than to remove forever
the last stigma, the last doubt, tarnishing O. Henry's
memory. But the clinching documentary evidence
necessary for that has not been forthcoming. Yet the
conceded facts are enough to justify posterity in ren-
dering the verdict "not guilty."

In the first place, the evidence counted little in a
trial that was naturally prejudged. When Porter
changed trains at Hempstead and fled to New Orleans
instead of returning to Austin to stand immediate
trial, he lost his case. The flight was interpreted as a

full confession of guilt. "Your Grand Jurors," so ran the charge, "further say that between the days of the sixth of July, A.D., 1896, and the fifth of February, A.D., 1897, the aforesaid W. S. Porter was a fugitive and fleeing from justice and seeking to avoid a prosecution in this court for the offense hereinbefore set out."

Perhaps a contributing factor in the verdict was also the very lenience with which he had been treated by the authorities, who, out of sympathy for his sick wife, had so long pretended to be unaware of his presence in the city. A full year passed between the time of his return and his trial. He had to pay for that as well as his flight. Moreover, there was his own attitude. There was no fight in him. He seemed absolutely indifferent to the outcome. He asked his friends as an especial favor to stay away from the courtroom. He gave his lawyer no help, no suggestion, and is quoted as having said that when he saw the jury he knew that he had no chance. It was composed of men who at that time "viewed all banks with suspicion and thought all bankers thieves." Will Porter remained silent and his attorney made no objection to the jurors.

Had there been no change of trains at Hempstead, the worst possible verdict would have been one corresponding to the Scotch "non proven." As it was, with all the weight of prejudice against the defendant, a shrewd, observant lawyer would have asked for and probably obtained a dismissal of the case on the grounds of a glaring inaccuracy in the indictment. The charge was that on October 10, 1894, Will Porter had misappropriated $554.48, on November 12, 1894, $299.60, and on November 12, 1895, $299.60. But

Will Porter had resigned and severed all connection with the bank in early December, 1894. In November, 1895, he was living in Houston, in the full swing of his work editing "Some Postscripts" for the Houston *Post*. It would have been a simple matter to bring dozens of witnesses to attest these facts. Yet both Porter and his attorney failed to notice, or else ignored the vital inconsistency.

Mrs. Maltby has written:

Today there seems to be an absolute unanimity of viewpoint in Austin regarding Will Porter. I fail to find a single man or woman who would entertain for a moment the thought that Will Porter was guilty. In talking, recently, to a prominent banker of Austin, who, like myself, had known Will Porter back in the Eighties, he said: "It might just as well have been me as Will Porter. I applied for that position in the First National Bank when Will Porter got it. He was older and had more experience, so they gave him the job. I thought he was fortunate and I was out of luck, but it was the other way round. Had I gotten the job, I would have been sent up. The Federal authorities were tired of that bank's methods and they had to make a killing. However, he just cinched things at Hempstead when he flew the coop."

Professor Smith has told that once, to a trusted friend in New York, O. Henry declared that Conrad's *Lord Jim* made an appeal to him made by no other book. "I am like Lord Jim," he added, "because we both made one fateful mistake at the supreme crisis of our lives, a mistake from which we could not recover."

And, like Lord Jim [Professor Smith comments], O. Henry was governed more by impulse than by

reason, more by temperament than by common sense.
The sails ruled the rudder in his disposition, not the
rudder the sails. When he changed trains at Hempstead it was not cowardice that motivated his action.
It was the lure of peace and quiet under Honduran
skies, the call of a new start in life, the challenge of a
novel and romantic career. The same faculties that
were to plot his stories were now plotting this futile
jaunt to Central America. The vision swept him along
till, like Lord Jim, he had time to reflect and still
longer time to repent.

Soon after his commitment, Will Porter wrote to his
mother-in-law, Mrs. Roach, protesting his innocence.
On February 17, 1898, the jury brought in its verdict
of guilty; and on March 25th, Porter was sentenced to
a five-year term of imprisonment in the Ohio Penitentiary. From the jail in Austin he wrote another letter
to Mrs. Roach:

I feel very deeply the forbearance and long-suf-
fering kindness shown by your note, and thank you
much for sending the things. Right here I want to
state solemnly to you that in spite of the jury's verdict
I am absolutely innocent of wrong doing in that bank
matter, except so far as foolishly keeping a position
that I could not successfully fill. Any intelligent person who heard the evidence presented knows that I
should have been acquitted. After I saw the jury I had
very little hopes of their understanding enough of the
technical matters presented to be fair. I naturally
am crushed by the result, but it is not on my own
account. I care not so much for the opinion of the
general public, but I would have a few of my friends
still believe that there is some good in me.

Just a month after his sentence, on April 25, 1898, Will Porter entered the penitentiary at Columbus. He was to remain there for three years and three months, lacking a day. The presumption is that when he passed through the prison gates, an innocent man went to punishment.

VIII

MARGARET

The real sort, that open chrysanthemum shows and christen battleships.   *Cabbages and Kings*

FOR the thirty-nine months following May, 1898, the material body of William Sidney Porter was in Columbus; his heart was in Austin. Athol was in her grave, but Margaret was still there to fill the yearning of his dreams.

She was eight years old when her father went away. With the acuteness of the child for suffering she mourned his absence and wondered at it. That she never realized its significance is almost a miracle. Of course her grandparents shielded her from the knowledge in every way, inventing explanations to meet her inquiries. But the wonder is that some playmate of her own age, with the perverse cruelty of childhood and of those who go through life retaining childhood's worst qualities, did not blurt out the real reason for her father's absence. Margaret Porter was a woman nearly thirty years of age before she learned the truth about those years.

From the earliest days, the relations between father and daughter had been particularly close. She was an only child and perhaps she unconsciously shared his worry over her mother's health. When Athol died, Will Porter turned instinctively to Margaret as his charge and refuge. He seemed to realize her need for

119

comfort and solace and rallied to the claim. Mrs. Maltby has told how when no one else could soothe the child on the day of her mother's death he took her in his arms and away from the house. It was a hot, sultry night.

With old Charley and the buggy he drove Margaret out in the country where they could be alone with God and the stars. After a while her sobs ceased and she slept. Back to the Roach home he came with Margaret. Lifting the sleeping child, he started in the house. But Margaret woke and wept again. Another hour was spent in driving aimlessly about. Each time he would return and start with the child into the house her tears would start afresh. It was almost midnight before he finally put her to sleep. The rest of the night he spent on the porch beside the hammock, swinging Margaret gently to keep her soothed and asleep.

The second night was a repetition of the first. They drove until almost midnight. Margaret was frantic with fear if he left her for a moment, fearful that he, too, would "go away for good." When it came time for the funeral he would not go to the cemetery with the family, but requested that he be allowed to go alone with Margaret and drive old Charley. During the services at the grave they sat apart until all the others had left, then he and Margaret went over to the new-made grave and arranged the flowers, remaining there for hours.

In 1923, when she was Mrs. Cesare, Margaret wrote[1] of her own early memories, recalling that when she

[1] "My O. Henry," *Mentor*, February, 1923.

first met her father he was not O. Henry—just Bill
Porter. Her mother accomplished the introduction.
His first remark was an aside to her: " 'Do you think
she'll ever develop an intelligent, human expression?'
He laughed when he said it, and although it was *at*
instead of *with*, his laughter held no sting. It never
did."

We were inseparable playmates and companions
until my eighth year and the death of my mother.
After that we were much apart, meeting, after long
intervals, during summer vacations. On these occasions he would just begin to emerge from an ever-
increasing reserve that seemed to beset us both, and
begin to be companions again when the time would come
to pack off for school.

But the early days were untinged with the quite natural reserve of maturity. Uncle Remus was a strong
bond between us. These stories were read and read until
he would find himself prompted for the slightest variation from the text. It was his delight to test the
drowsiness of his audience by opening both volumes
and reading straight across the four pages. If he
crossed the second page undetected he knew he was
free for the evening.

Another popular means of entertainment was drumming the rhythm of a melody with the finger tips
against the wooden headboard of the bed, we guessing
the tune in turn. Frequently he found himself receiving too enthusiastic applause when he desired to
be relieved by Morpheus. On such occasions he was
forced to resort to trickery. Usually one of his thumbs
was grasped tightly against such contingency. When
this grip became slack from conquering sleep he found
that it was sometimes safe to substitute, for thumb, the
nose of a carnival mask—and then *exit*.

Throughout the mesh of early memories runs a silver

thread of laughter. He seemed always to be highly amused by something. Almost always his laughter was silent. Sitting on his knee I would feel him shaking, and look around to find him breathless with laughter. Sometimes the softest of chuckles would reveal him ruddy with suppressed mirth. Usually, I was the object of his amusement; often it was the result of some joke or trick of his own invention.

The intimate and perfect understanding of early days continued, though less often expressed; for I had inherited the reserve that later was so marked a part of his personality. This characteristic has been explained and analysed in various ways. A popular conception is that it was shyness. That I do not accept as the true interpretation. It was, rather, the outward manifestation of a passionate desire to be wholly and only himself. Against the intrusion of more aggressive personalities an invisible barrier was erected. It was a polite "No Trespassing" sign. Sometimes the barrier took the form of words—a barrage of sound protecting the innermost silences of self. When once asked what he thought of the hereafter he replied lightly:

> I had a little dog and his name was Rover,
> And when he died he died all over.

There is much to be read between the lines in these quoted memories. Naturally, after the mother's death they were much apart, and it was a changed Bill Porter, lacking something of the old spontaneity and light joy of life, that she found when they were reunited. There is also much revealed in the letters that from time to time he wrote to her in those years. In these letters she was still "Margaret"; in later life she became "Bill," or "Jim," or "Pete."

HELLO, MARGARET:

Don't you remember me? I'm a Brownie, and my name is Aldibirontiphornikophokos. If you see a star shoot and say my name seventeen times before it goes out, you will find a diamond ring in the track of the first cow's foot you see go down the road in a snow-storm while the red roses are blooming on the tomato vines. Try it some time. . . . Well, good-bye. I've got to take a ride on a grasshopper. I'll just sign my first letter—"A."

July 8, 1898.

MY DEAR MARGARET:

You don't know how glad I was to get your nice little letter to-day. I am so sorry I couldn't come to tell you good-bye when I left Austin.

Well, I think it's a shame some men folks have to go away from home to work and stay away so long—don't you? But I tell you what's a fact. When I come home next time I'm going to stay there. You bet your boots I'm getting tired of staying away so long.

I'm so glad you and Munny [the family name for Athol's mother, Mrs. Roach] are going to Nashville. I know you'll have a fine ride on the cars and a good time when you get to Uncle Bud's. Now you must have just the finest time you can with Anna and the boys and tumble around in the woods and go fishing and have lots of fun. Now, Margaret, don't you worry any about me, for I'm well and fat as a pig and I'll have to be away from home a while yet and while I'm away you can just run up to Nashville and see the folks there.

And not long after you come back home I'll be ready to come and I won't ever have to leave again.

So you just be as happy as you can, and it won't be long till we'll be reading Uncle Remus again of nights.

I'll see if I can find another of Uncle Remus's books when I come back. You didn't tell me in your letter about your going to Nashville. When you get there you must write me a long letter and tell me what you saw on the cars and how you like Uncle Bud's stock farm.

When you get there I'll write you a letter every week, for you will be much nearer to the town I am in than Austin is.

I do hope you will have a nice visit and a good time. Look out pretty soon for another letter from me.

I think about you every day and wonder what you are doing. Well, I will see you again before very long.

Your loving
PAPA

August 16, 1898.

MY DEAR MARGARET:

I got your letter yesterday, and was mighty glad to hear from you. I think you must have forgotten where you were when you wrote it, for you wrote "Austin, Texas" at the top of it. Did you forget you had gone to Tennessee?

The reason why I have not written you a letter in so long is that I didn't know the name of the post-office where you and Munny were going until I got her letter and yours yesterday. Now that I know how to write I will write you a letter every Sunday and you will know just when you are going to get one every week. Are you having a nice time at Aunt Lilly's?

Munny tells me you are fat and sassy and I am glad of it. You always said you wanted to be on a farm. You must write and tell me next time what kind of times you have and what you do to have fun.

I'd have liked to see the two fish you caught. Guess they were most as long as your little finger, weren't they? You must make Munny keep you up there till the hot weather is over before you go back to Austin. I want you to have as good times as you can, and get well and strong and big but don't get as big as Munny because I'm afraid you'd lick me when I come home.

February 14, 1900.

DEAR MARGARET:

It has been quite a long time since I heard from you. I got a letter from you in the last century, and a letter once every hundred years is not very often. I have been waiting from day to day, putting off writing to you, as I have been expecting to have something to send you, but it hasn't come yet, and I thought I would write anyhow.

I am pretty certain I will have it in three or four days, and then I will write to you again and send it to you.

I hope your watch runs all right. When you write again be sure to look at it and tell me what time it is, so as I won't have to get up and look at the clock.

With much love,
PAPA

May 17, 1900.

DEAR MARGARET:

It has been so long since I heard from you that I'm getting real anxious to know what is the matter. Whenever you don't answer my letters I am afraid you are sick, so please write right away when you get this. Tell me something about Pittsburg and what you have seen of it. Have they any nice parks where you can go or is it all made of houses and bricks? I send you twenty nickels to spend for anything you want.

Now, if you will write me a nice letter real soon I will promise to answer it the same day and put another dollar in it. I am very well and so anxious to be with you again, which I hope won't be very long now.

With much love, as ever,

PAPA

October 1, 1900.

DEAR MARGARET:

I got your very nice, long letter a good many days ago. It didn't come straight to me, but went to a wrong address first. I was very glad indeed to hear from you, and very, very sorry to learn of your getting your finger so badly hurt. I don't think you were to blame at all, as you couldn't know just how that villainous old "hoss" was going to bite. I do hope that it will heal up nicely and leave your finger strong. I am learning to play the mandolin, and we must get a guitar, and we will learn a lot of duets together when I come home, which will certainly not be later than next summer, and maybe earlier.

I suppose you have started to school again some time ago. I hope you like to go, and don't have to study too hard. When one grows up, a thing they never regret is that they went to school long enough to learn all they could. It makes everything easier for them, and if they like books and study they can always content and amuse themselves that way even if other people are cross and tiresome, and the world doesn't go to suit them.

You mustn't think that I've forgotten somebody's birthday. I couldn't find just the thing I wanted to send, but I know where it can be had, and it will reach you in a few days. So, when it comes you'll know it for a birthday remembrance.

I think you write the prettiest hand of any little girl (or big one, either) I ever knew. The letters you make are as even and regular as printed ones. The next time you write, tell me how far you have to go to school and whether you go alone or not.

I am busy all the time writing for the papers and magazines all over the country, so I don't have a chance to come home, but I'm going to try to come this winter. If I don't I will by summer sure, and then you'll have somebody to boss and make trot around with you.

Write me a letter whenever you have some time to spare, for I am always glad and anxious to hear from you. Be careful when you are on the streets not to feed shucks to strange dogs, or pat snakes on the head or shake hands with cats you haven't been introduced to, or stroke the noses of electric car horses.

Hoping you are well and your finger is getting all right, I am, with much love, as ever,

PAPA

DEAR MARGARET:

Here are two or three more pictures, but they are not very good. Munny says you are learning very fast at school. I'm sure you're going to be a very smart girl, and I guess I'd better study a lot more myself or you will know more than I will. I was reading today about a cat a lady had that was about the smartest cat I ever heard of. One day the cat was asleep and woke up. He couldn't see his mistress, so he ran to a bandbox where she kept the hat she wore when she went out, and knocked the top off to see if it was there. When he found it was there he seemed to be contented and lay down and went to sleep again. Wasn't that pretty bright for a cat? Do you think Nig would do anything that smart?

You must plant some seeds and have them growing so you can water them as soon as it gets warm enough. Well, I'll write you another letter in a day or so. So good-bye till then.

Your loving
PAPA

My dear Margaret:

I ought to have answered your last letter sooner, but I haven't had a chance. It's getting mighty cool now. It won't be long before persimmons are ripe in Tennessee. I don't think you ever ate any persimmons, did you? I think persimmon pudden (not pudding) is better than cantaloupe or watermelon either. If you stay until they get ripe you must get somebody to make you one.

If it snows while you are there you must try some fried snowballs, too. They are mighty good with Jack Frost gravy.

You must see how big and fat you can get before you go back to Austin.

When I come home I want to find you big and strong enough to pull me all about town on a sled when we have a snow storm. Won't that be nice? I just thought I'd write this little letter in a hurry so the postman would get it and when I'm in a hurry I can never think of anything to write about. You and Munny must have a good time, and keep a good lookout and don't let tramps or yellowjackets get you. I'll try to write something better next time. Write soon.

Your loving
Papa

November 12.

My dear Margaret:

Did you ever have a pain right in the middle of your back between your shoulders? Well, I did just then when I wrote your name, and had to stop a while and grunt and twist around in my chair before I could write any more. Guess I must have caught cold. I haven't had a letter from you in a long time. You must stir Munny up every week or two and make her send me your letter. I guess you'd rather *ride* the pony than *write* about him, wouldn't you? But you know I'm always so glad to get a letter from you even if it's only a teentsy weentsy one, so I'll know you are well and what you are doing.

You don't want to go to work and forget your old Pop just because you don't see much of him just now, for he'll come in mighty handy some day to read Uncle Remus to you again and make kites that a cyclone wouldn't raise off the ground. So write soon.

With love as ever,
PAPA

MY DEAR MARGARET:

I ought to have answered your letter some time ago, but you know how lazy I am. I'm very glad to hear that you are having a good time, and I wish I was with you to help you have fun. I read in the paper that it is colder in Austin than it has been in many years, and they've had lots of snow there, too. Do you remember the big snow that we had there once? I guess everybody can get snow this winter to fry. Why don't you send me some fried snow in a letter? Do you like Tennessee as well as you did Texas? Tell me next time you write. Well, old Christmas is about to come around again. I wish I could come and light up the candles on the Christmas tree like we used to. I wouldn't be surprised if you haven't gotten bigger than I am by now, and when I come back and don't want to read Uncle Remus of nights, you can get a stick and make me do it. I saw some new Uncle Remus books a few days ago and when I come back I'll bring a new one, and you can say "thankydoo, thankydoo." I'm getting mighty anxious to see you again, and for us to have some more fun like we used to. I guess it won't be much longer now till I do, and I want to hear you tell about all the times you've had. I'll bet you haven't learned to button your own dress in the back yet, have you?

I hope you'll have a jolly Christmas and lots of fun— Geeminy, don't I wish I could eat Christmas dinner with you! Well, I hope it won't be long till we all get home again. Write soon and don't forget your loving

PAPA

MY DEAR MARGARET:

Here it is summertime, and the bees are blooming and the flowers are singing and the birds making honey, and we haven't been fishing yet. Well, there's only one month more till July, and then we'll go, and no mistake. I thought you would write and tell me about the high water around Pittsburg some time ago, and whether it came up to where you live, or not. And I haven't heard a thing about Easter, and about the rabbit's eggs—but I suppose you have learned by this time that eggs grow on egg plants and are not laid by rabbits.

I would like very much to hear from you oftener; it has been more than a month since you wrote. Write soon and tell me how you are, and when school will be out, for we want plenty of holidays in July, so we can have a good time. I am going to send you something nice the last of this week. What do you guess it will be?

Lovingly,
PAPA

Throughout these letters, with references to expected home-comings, there is evident the constant thought of the pardon for which Porter was always hoping but which never came. The dreams in which he indulged, of a reunion with his only child and of long years of close companionship, were never to be quite realized.

The affection between father and daughter never waned; never wavered. But destiny was to keep the two much apart during the nine years of Will Porter's life after the release from the Columbus Penitentiary. Perhaps he had a share in helping to mold destiny.

It is natural to wonder why, after he had established himself in New York, and before his second marriage, with an income sufficient to provide for their needs assured, his first thought was not to make a home for Margaret and himself. Probably it was the persistent fear of the chance encounter, the thought of the man out of the past who might be lurking round the corner. The burden of the Old Man of the Sea was heavy enough when it meant merely the embittering of his own life. Far more to be dreaded was the possibility that a life of intimacy such as the two would neces-sarily have shared, might bring to Margaret the realization, or even the suspicion of the secret which he thought to keep from all the world.

In the last few years, however, they were at times together. After Porter's second marriage, to Sara Lindsay Coleman at Asheville, November 27, 1907, Margaret lived with the newly wedded pair at their Long Island home. She was also in Asheville, North Carolina, when her father went there in his belated search for health. She herself has left a record of those later days, telling of memories of moments

when he seemed miraculously freed from the hovering shadow of ill health that clouded the last few years. I have known him to sit at the piano and strum the accompaniment to a gay darky song, singing in dialect, with only me as audience. The intrusion of another

person would precipitate a hollow silence. In one of
these lighter moods he brought a mandolin and a
guitar home. He had taught me guitar accompani-
ments, so we spent many an hour reviving half-forgot-
ten tunes. But upon the lightness of such moods a
shadow would descend and he would be plunged into
silence, black silences, the portent of which he alone
could know; for, although there is understanding, it
is not humanly possible to accompany one of those dark
journeyings.

Here are some more of Margaret's memories:

Toward the close of the last year, spent in seeking
health in southern mountains, he had been particularly
gay during dinner one evening, and afterward had
entertained the household with impersonations of well
known people. From the elevation of the first landing of the stairs in the great living room he called
out celebrities: "Buffalo Bill." His make-up for this
was the index finger of one hand held across his upper
lip, the forefinger of the other meeting it at right
angles, bisecting his chin. Down the list he went.
Never was his mood lighter.

Then, suddenly, someone entered or left the room,
attention was momentarily taken from him, and when
it returned again he was not there. I found him sitting in the far corner of the dark porch overlooking
the mountains. There was no moon and the night was
black. I felt that it was no less dark than the sudden depression that had seized him. A strong wind
blew steadily from the mountains. The night seemed
filled with premonition. I felt that he sensed it too.
I could not—and knew that he would not have me—
speak. I sat on the steps near him. After a long
time, still without words, we got up and went together
into the house.

Through the riotous carnival of colors of the autumn

MARGARET

woods we had many a long tramp, each with a gun, which we shot, somehow, only at inanimate targets, though troops of rabbits scurried through the dry leaves, and squirrels were busy storing away nuts. It was almost as though he felt that life was too precious a thing to steal from any creature. He had never joined in the so-called sports that involve killing.

It was late winter when I met him coming in at dusk from a tramp alone, with something held in his gun-free hand. It was a dead bird, warm and limp. His expression was rueful, and his laugh short and not quite steady as he said that he had aimed at a cornstalk and killed a songbird. We were near the house. He stooped quickly, made a hollow in the moist earth, laid the bird on a bed of leaves, covered it with earth and leaves. To the other member of the household who joined us he replied that he had had "a fine walk." But I knew that the joy of the day, for him, was buried beneath the leaves at his feet.

Not long after that he returned to New York. For a few short minutes on the day of his departure we found ourselves unexpectedly alone. "Bill," he began —he had always called me "Bill," "Jim," or "Pete," seldom Margaret—"Bill." It was an attempt to put into words all the unspoken things of the past. In it I sensed his realization of the futility of attempting to express the emotions that crowd the moment of parting. Also I felt, as I believe he did, that this parting was going to be different from all the others. Words are such impotent things in the face of parting. "I have seen," I managed to tell him, "and understood." There flashed across his face an expression of inestimable relief and one of his rare smiles. We did not meet again.

Margaret's story belongs here—all of it. It is little happier than the stories of her father and mother.

From both sides she inherited the scourge of phthisis. Like both her parents, she died young. But there was a brief hour of a little fame, that was largely reflected. Naturally she had wanted to write, and to that end had diligently read her father's stories, and had taken a course at Columbia. As "Miss O. Henry" she was launched. But she never went far.

Margaret married first Oscar Cesare, the cartoonist. But it was not a happy marriage and after a time the two parted. She was struggling along, hoping to do something worth while with her pen, when her fatal inheritance became her chief problem. Doctors told her that she must go to the desert, to a land of dry winds and warm sunshine. She left New York for the Pacific Coast, staying at Reno a sufficient time to obtain a divorce from Cesare. Then she proceeded to California. In Hollywood, where she was negotiating with the producers over the motion picture rights of her father's stories, her illness took a highly serious turn.

Friends urged her to go at once to the desert to fight her battle. There was one of these friends, a comparatively new acquaintance, named Guy Sartin. He was a young Englishman and a writer. He offered to find a house for her in the desert and to look after her welfare. He used the excuse that he could write just as well in the desert as in Hollywood. After much exploration he found the spot desired. It was in the town of Banning, nestling between Mount San Jacinto and Mount San Gorgonio Pass, at an altitude of 2,315 feet. At one side towered Old Grayback to an elevation of 11,485 feet, and all about were rugged snow-capped peaks. The almond orchards in the valley below extended for miles to the rim of the desert.

It was there that Margaret Porter spent her last days. In a motor car, with her baggage, she made the ninety-mile journey to Banning. On the hillside she bought a small plot of ground. Sartin superintended the construction of a bungalow. Most of the time in those two and a half years Margaret spent in bed, growing steadily weaker. Nearly every day Sartin strolled over from his own quarters to devote long hours to reading to her. Finally one spring night she had an attack in her lungs which left her exhausted. She realized that the end was near.

Like an O. Henry story were the last hours of her life. She sent for a lawyer, made her will, and asked that a pretty new jacket be made for her as a wedding gown. "I guess it's about over, Guy," she said to Sartin. "And now we'll be married." A clergyman was summoned and a marriage license secured. Sartin gathered roses from the gardens and two or three neighbors were invited in. In the afternoon sunlight the wedding ceremony was solemnized. Margaret lying on her bed, dressed in her new jacket; Sartin standing beside the bed. When the ring was placed on her finger she had to hold it there with her thumb because it had been selected to fit her husband's finger and not her own. She knew she could not wear it long.

For three days after the wedding she lingered on. Then the curtain fell. To her husband of those three days she left everything—her share in the royalties from O. Henry's books, her hillside home and all its belongings, her unfinished manuscripts, one of them being half a volume of a memoir dealing with her father, and her wedding gown, the one of black lace over pink chiffon which she wore only on her deathbed. So no more of Margaret.

IX

THE DARK HOUR

They shut the world out and bolted the doors.
The World and the Door

MANY strange suggestions have come out of Texas; none stranger than the one not long ago offered in all seriousness and with the kindliest intentions that the Austin jail, where William Sidney Porter was imprisoned for ten weeks after his conviction, be preserved as a monument to O. Henry. Porter entered the jail on February 17, 1898, the day that the jury brought in its verdict; on March 25th he was sentenced; and on April 25th he left the Austin jail to be taken to Columbus. Probably the darkest hour of his life was when, under guard, he made that journey from Texas to Ohio.

Edmund Travis, in an article in *Bunker's Monthly* for June, 1928, expressed the opinion that because he was sensitive and imaginative, Porter went through his greatest suffering before he entered a place of punishment. He did not need to be actually behind stone walls and iron bars to feel the terror and shame of imprisonment. When he reached Columbus the worst was over for him; and, no doubt, after the first shock he experienced a sense of relief. The impulse to despair, evident in some of his early letters, passed. He was buoyed first by hope for a successful appeal, and later by the hope of pardon.

Mr. Travis takes issue with "the average biographer" who holds that while they were of great importance in the formation of O. Henry's cast of thought, the prison years were otherwise "lost years," in which the prisoner did little more than suffer. Mr. Travis writes:

The real importance of his prison life is due to these circumstances: First, that his personal economic problem had been taken out of his hands; whether he did little or much, he was certain to be lodged, fed, and clothed for a term of years. Second, that there was no one dependent upon him; his daughter was well cared for by her grandparents. Third, that he had long hours in which no labor was required of him, but which he must spend in confinement. And finally, that he knew he could write short stories, and this was at once the most logical and most congenial thing for him to do.

Throughout life, procrastination was Porter's worst enemy. The amount of work that he accomplished showed that there was no lack of industry and energy. But before Columbus there was always the excuse to put off the story on which he was at work in order to seek employment more immediately profitable. In the prison, there was no job hunting plea. To plan and write stories, or gather story material, when there was time from prison duties, was to follow the line of least resistance and most promise. To Mr. Travis, the prison years were far from "lost." In prison he gathered the material for many of his tales; and there he actually wrote such tales as "The Duplicity of Hargraves," "A Fog in Santone," "Georgia's Ruling," "A

Blackjack Bargainer," "The Marionettes," and "Whistling Dick's Christmas Stocking."

When Porter entered the Columbus Penitentiary the first question asked him was as to the nature of his trade or profession. He replied that he was a newspaper reporter. As that occupation did not suggest any practical application, he was questioned further as to what he could do. Almost as an afterthought was his reply that he was a registered pharmacist.

The profession that he loathed in Greensboro because it meant confinement [comments Professor Smith] was now, strangely enough, to prove the stepping-stone to comparative freedom. His career as a drug clerk in the prison, his fidelity to duty, the new friendships formed, the opportunity afforded him to write, and his quick assimilation of short-story material from the life about him are best set forth in the testimony of those who knew him during these years of seeming eclipse.

Dr. John M. Thomas was then chief physician at the prison. His letter is especially interesting for the light that it throws on the origin of the stories contained in *The Gentle Grafter*:

Druggists were scarce and I felt I was fortunate in securing the services of Sydney Porter, for he was a registered pharmacist and unusually competent. In fact, he could do anything in the drug line. Previous to his banking career in Texas he had worked in a drug store in North Carolina, so he told me. While Porter was drug clerk, Jimmie Consedine [*sic*] one time proprietor of the old Metropole Hotel in New York, was also a prisoner. Consedine spent all his time painting. Out of this came a falling out with O. Henry. Consedine painted a cow with its tail

touching the ground. Porter gave a Texas cowman's explanation of the absurdity of such a thing and won Consedine's undying hatred.

After serving some time as drug clerk, O. Henry came to me and said: "I have never asked a favor of you before but there is one I should like to ask now. I can be private secretary to the steward outside (meaning that he would be outside the walls and trusted). It depends on your recommendation." I asked him if he wanted to go. When he said he did, I called up the steward, Mr. C. N. Wilcox, and in twenty minutes O. Henry was outside.

He did not associate very much with any of the other inmates of the prison except the western outlaws. Very few of the officers or attendants at the prison ever saw him. Most convicts would tell me frankly how they got into jail. They did not seem to suffer much from mortification. O. Henry, on the other hand, was very much weighed down by his imprisonment. In my experience of handling over ten thousand prisoners in the eight years I was physician at the prison, I have never known a man who was so deeply humiliated by his prison experience as O. Henry. He was a model prisoner, willing, obedient, faithful. His record is clear in every respect.

It was very seldom that he mentioned his imprisonment or in any way discussed the subject. One time we had a little misunderstanding about some alcohol which was disappearing too rapidly for the ordinary uses to which it was put. I requested that he wait for me one morning so that I could find out how much alcohol he was using in his night rounds, and after asking him a few questions he became excited when he thought I might be suspecting him. "I am not a thief," he said, "and I never stole a thing in my life. I was sent here for embezzling bank funds, not one

cent of which I ever got. Some one else got it all,
and I am doing time for it."

You can tell when a prisoner is lying as well as
you can in the case of anybody else. I believed
O. Henry implicitly. I soon discovered that he was
not the offender in the matter of the alcohol. But
the question disturbed him and he asked me once or
twice afterward if I really thought that he ever stole
anything.

Once in a while he would talk about his supposed
crime and the great mistake he made in going to Central America as soon as there was any suspicion cast
on him. When he disappeared suspicion became conviction. After his return from Central America, when
he was tried, he never told anything that would clear
himself. While he was in Central America he met Al
Jennings, who was also a fugitive from justice. After
they returned to the States they renewed their friendship at the prison, where both eventually landed. Jennings was also one of the trusted prisoners and in the
afternoon they would often come into my office and tell
stories.

O. Henry liked the western prisoners, those from
Arizona, Texas, and Indian Territory, and he got
stories from them all and retold them in the office.
Since reading his books I recognize many of the stories
I heard there. As I mentioned before, he was an unusually good pharmacist and for this reason was permitted to look after the minor ailments of the prisoners
at night. He would spend two or three hours on the
range or tiers of cells every night and knew most of the
prisoners and their life stories.

The Gentle Grafter portrays the stories told him
on his night rounds. I remember having heard him
recount many of them. He wrote quite a number of
short stories while in prison and it was a frequent thing
for me to find a story written on scrap paper on my

desk in the morning, with a note telling me to read it
before he sent it out. We would often joke about the
price the story would bring, anything from twenty-
five to fifty dollars. He wrote them at night, in from
one to three hours, he told me.

The question of the original of the Jimmy Valentine
of "A Retrieved Reformation" is likely always to remain a matter of controversy. According to Dr.
George W. Williard, who was the night doctor at the
penitentiary, the original Jimmy was one Jimmy Connors. Dr. Williard, who was a friend and admirer of
Porter, has contributed the following reminiscences:

He was the last man you would ever pick for a
crook. Toward every one he was quiet, reserved, almost taciturn. He seldom spoke except in answer.
He never told me of his hopes, his aims, his family,
his crime, his views of life, his writing—in fact, he
spoke of little save the details of his pharmaceutical
work in which he was exceptionally careful and pro-
ficient. The chief means by which I judged his character was by the way he acted and by one or two
little incidents which brought out the man's courage
and faithfulness.

I respected him for his strict attention to business,
his blameless conduct, and his refusal to mix in the
affairs of other prisoners. He seemed to like me personally because I did not ask him personal questions
and because I showed the consideration that one intelligent man must feel toward another under such
circumstances. So we grew to be friends.

He was as careful and conscientious as if the drug
store at the prison had been his own property. His
hours were from six in the evening to six in the morning. Often I left at midnight with Porter in charge
and I knew things would run as regularly and effec-

tively until morning as if I had remained. Porter was almost as free from prison life as any one on the outside. He received all the magazines and did a lot of reading. He did not sleep in a cell but on a cot in the hospital during the day time. His ability and conduct were such that, once he had demonstrated them, there was never any danger that he would have to eat and sleep and work in the shops with the other prisoners.

Convicts who were ill or who claimed to be ill would be brought into the hospital in charge of a guard and, ranging themselves along the front of the drug counter, would be given medicines by the drug clerk according to my instructions. It was part of Porter's duties to know a couple of hundred drugs by number as well as by name and to be able to hand them out without mistake quickly. Constant desire of prisoners to escape work by feigning illness necessitated the physician and his clerk being always on their guard against shams. Often some violent convict, when refused medicine, would rebel.

One night a huge Negro to whom I refused a drug became abusive. The guard who had brought him in had stepped away for a moment and the prisoner directed at me a fearful torrent of profanity. I was looking around for the guard when Sydney Porter, my drug clerk, went over his counter like a panther. All of his hundred and seventy or eighty pounds were behind the blow he sent into the Negro's jaw. The Negro came down on the floor like a ton of brick. He did not utter a word.

Another time a certain piece of equipment was stolen from the penitentiary hospital. There had been a good deal of stealing going on and I was responsible when it happened during my "trick." I mentioned this to Porter and he gave me the name of a certain official who, he said, had stolen the property. I told the warden who had taken the property and said it would have to come back at once. In twelve hours it was back. Porter said in his quiet way: "Well, I see you got in your work." It was the only time he ever told on any one and he did it merely out of loyalty to me. Although nearly every drug clerk at the prison was at some time or other guilty of petty trafficking in drugs or whisky, Porter was always above reproach. He always had the keys to the whisky cabinet, yet I never heard of his taking a drink.

The moment I read O. Henry's description and character delineation of Jimmy Valentine in "A Retrieved Reformation," I said, "That's Jimmy Connors through and through." Connors was in for blowing a post-office safe. He was day drug clerk in the prison hospital at the same time that Porter was night clerk. The men were friendly and often, early in the evening, before Connors went to bed, he would come and talk to Porter and tell him of his experiences.

Although Connors admitted himself guilty of many other jobs he claimed not to be guilty of the one for which he was serving time. Another man who resembled Connors had blown a safe and Connors was arrested and sent to prison for it. Because of fear of implicating himself in other jobs of which he was guilty, he said, he never told on the other man and went to prison innocent. This statement was borne out early in his term in the penitentiary by the arrival of the sheriff who had sent him up and who, in the meantime, had arrested the real culprit and secured from him a confession. To right his wrong the sheriff went to Washington, but the inspectors knew Jimmy Connors and said he doubtless was guilty of some other jobs and had best stay in prison for safe-keeping. He did stay, giving O. Henry the chance to meet him and find inspiration for "A Retrieved Reformation."

Porter never said a word to me about his own crime,

but another man once told me that Porter had told him that he had been "railroaded" to prison, so I think he secretly held himself unjustly dealt with. The fact that he and Jimmy Connors agreed on this point in their respective cases doubtless drew them together.

Poor Jimmy! He never lived to try any sort of reformation on the outside. He died of kidney trouble in the penitentiary hospital, May 19, 1902, which was after Porter left and before Jimmy Valentine became famous in story, play, and song. He was a wonderful chemist and I still, in my daily practice, use one formula he gave me. It is not saying too much, I am sure, to state that the recent craze for "crook" plays in the theatrical world may be traced directly to this dead prisoner, for from him O. Henry drew the character which made the story famous, and from the story came the first "crook" play which won wide success, leading the way to the production of many similar plays. You would recognize instantly, if you knew customs and conditions, that the prison atmosphere at the beginning of the story was gathered bodily from Ohio penitentiary life as Porter knew it.

Of all the characters that figure in the O. Henry stories Jimmy Valentine is by far the most widely known; in fact, he is the only character who by name stands out conspicuously in the long roster. Probably that is largely due to the popularity of the play and the association of Jimmy's name with the play title. It is a peculiarity of the stories that the names of the men and women who figure in them mean nothing or little. Much the same may be said of the short stories of Guy de Maupassant, with whom O. Henry has so often been compared. In O. Henry's case the exceptions to this rule are few. The name of Frank

Goodwin, who is the outstanding figure through the stories of *Cabbages and Kings*, is relatively well remembered, and in the same book the name of "Beelzebub" Blythe has been preserved through sheer force of alliteration. Della of "The Gift of the Magi"; Dulcie of "An Unfinished Story"; Hetty of "The Third Ingredient"; and Nancy of "The Trimmed Lamp" are not entirely forgotten names. But of the hundreds of thousands who have read and reread the O. Henry tales, how many can recall without reference to the printed page the name of the heroine of "A Municipal Report," the heroine of "The Enchanted Profile," the hero of "Mammon and the Archer," or the hero of "The Defeat of the City"?

Dr. Williard's opinion about the original of Jimmy Valentine is not shared by Al Jennings, who believes that Porter drew the suggestion of his story, not from Connors, but from a convict at the Ohio Penitentiary by the name of Dick Price. On one occasion the combination of the safe in a publishing house near the prison had been lost. As it was necessary to reach the contents of the safe without delay, the prison warden was approached with the suggestion that among the inmates there might be some deft cracksman who could deal with the situation. Price was the immediate selection, and he justified the warden's confidence. Ten seconds after he began operations the safe was open. The warden and the convict had just returned to the post office after the feat when Porter entered. "Dick Price," says Al Jennings, "is the original of the immortal Jimmy Valentine. . . . Bill Porter took but one incident out of that tragic life for his story 'A

Retrieved Reformation.' " Like the Jimmy Connors
of Dr. Williard's suggestion, Price never had a chance
for any sort of reformation on the outside. He too
died within prison walls.

The history of the real Jimmy Valentine [says Jen-
nings] shadowed, embittered, done to death in the stir,
was just another of the tragedies that ripped through
the film and showed Bill Porter the raw, cruel soul of
the "upper crust." Dick Price was one of the unfor-
tunates who really never have a chance in life. His
father, who had been a soldier in the Union army, died
of delirium tremens when the boy was a child, and his
mother, by taking in washing, sometimes managed to
provide enough for them to eat. At other times Dick
fed himself from the garbage cans. One day when
he was eleven years old, ravenous with hunger, he stole
a ten-cent box of crackers from a box car. "And for
that," he afterwards related, "they sent me to hell for
the rest of my life."

The reformatory held him for seven years and then
turned him out a master mechanic. He tried to go
straight, but it was no use. No sooner had he found a
job when some one learned of his reform school record
and he was discharged. He had to steal to live. He
cracked a safe, took a few hundred dollars, was caught
and sent to prison. After his release his situation was
again desperate. He cracked another safe, and as it
was his third offense under the "habitual criminal act,"
which then prevailed in Ohio, was sentenced to prison
for life. He was then twenty. He remained in the
penitentiary for the remaining sixteen years of his
existence. The sentence involved the denial of all
privileges. He could not have a book or paper. He

could neither write a letter nor receive one. Naturally he became morose and brooding, what the convicts called a "stir bug."

For his legal safe opening exploit he was promised a pardon. The story deserves detailed telling both for the reason of its association with "A Retrieved Reformation," and because it was a service of great value to the state. In connection with the placing of the Press-Post Publishing Company in the hands of a receiver there was a scandal with which Columbus rang. There were wholesale charges of theft. The stockholders, believing themselves to have been robbed, blamed the directors; the directors pointed to the treasurer and obtained a warrant for his arrest. He locked the safe and fled. Some of the most prominent men in Columbus were implicated. The court had to get the papers out of the safe. Then some one suggested applying to Warden Darby of the penitentiary for the services of a clever cracksman who might help them out of the difficulty.

The warden first thought of the use of nitroglycerin, but that was considered too risky as it was necessary to recover the papers intact. Jennings, then a privileged convict, recommended the particular talents of Dick Price for the task, and Price was selected, the warden promising to do everything in his power to secure a pardon in case of success. In a closed carriage the warden, Price, and Jennings were taken from the prison to the office of the publishing company. Various state officials were already there. Filing his nails to the quick, Price went to work. His sensitized fingers found the combination, there was a turn of the

dial, a pull at the knob, and the safe was open.   There
were the papers necessary to serve the ends of justice.
The next morning every newspaper in Columbus was
full of the sensational story.   All sorts of explanations
were given, one account ascribing the feat to the use of
a steel wire, and another to the use of a paper cutter.
Price's premonition that he would not receive the
promised pardon proved right.   He was already dying
when the news came that the application had been
denied.

Jennings relates that he told Porter the details of
the safe opening, but that the latter revolted at the
thought of a man filing his nails to the quick and then
filing until the nerves were exposed.   "Colonel, this is
a wonderful episode.   It will make a great story."
Even then he was storing it away for future use.   "Bill
took no notes," says Jennings.   "Once in a while he
would jot down a word or two on a scrap of paper, a
corner of a napkin, but in all our rambles together I
never noticed the pencil much in evidence.   He preferred to work his unfailing memory."

"A Retrieved Reformation" was published in the
spring of 1903.   Jennings asked Porter why he had
not used the story before, and the reported reply was:
"I've had it in mind, Colonel, ever since you told me
of it.   But I was afraid it would not go.   Convicts, you
know, are not accepted in the best society even in fiction."   Asked further why he had departed from Dick
Price's method of safe opening, he explained:

Colonel, it chills my teeth to think of that gritting
operation.   I prefer a set of tools.   I don't like to make

my victims suffer. And then, you see, the tools enable
Jimmy to make a present to a friend. That gift illustrates the toleration of the man who has been in prison.
Jimmy decided to quit the game himself, but he does
not expect the whole world to share his fervor of reform. Instead of burying the instruments of his
former profession, as your reformed citizen would have
done, he straightway sends them to a former pal. I
like that spirit in my character. The ordinary man
who makes a New Year's resolution immediately sends
down censure on the fellow who isn't perched on the
wagon with him. Jimmy does no such thing. That's
one of the advantages of spending a few vacations in
prison. You grow mellow in your judgments.

There are two letters written by Porter soon after
he entered the penitentiary that throw light upon his
impressions of and reactions to the life. The first
under the date of May 18, 1898, was to Mr. Roach.

DEAR MR. ROACH:
I wrote you about ten days ago a letter which I
sent through the office of this place. I could not say
in it what I wanted to as the letters are all read here
and they are very strict about what is in them. I now
have the opportunity to send an occasional letter by a
private way, and to receive them by the same means.
I want to give you some idea of the conditions here.
I accidentally fell into a place on the day I arrived
that is a light one in comparison with others. I am
the night druggist in the hospital, and as far as work
is concerned it is light enough, and all the men stationed in the hospital live a hundred percent. better
than the rest of the 2500 men here. There are four
doctors and about twenty-five other men in the hospital force. The hospital is a separate building and
is one of the finest equipped institutions in the country.

It is large and finely furnished and has every appliance of medicine and surgery.

We men who are on the hospital detail fare very well comparatively. We have good food, well-cooked and in unlimited abundance, and large clean sleeping apartments. We go about where we please over the place, and are not bound by strict rules as the others are. I go on duty at five o'clock P.M. and off at five A.M. The work is about the same as in any drug store, filling prescriptions, etc. and is pretty lively up to about ten o'clock. At seven P.M. I take a medicine case and go the rounds with the night physician to see the ones over in the main building who have become sick during the day.

The doctor goes to bed about ten o'clock and from then on during the night I prescribe for the patients myself and go out and attend calls that come in. If I find any one seriously ill I have them brought to the hospital and attended to by the doctor. I never imagined human life was held as cheap as it is here. The men are regarded as animals without soul or feeling. They carry on all kinds of work here; there are foundries and all kinds of manufacturing is done, and everybody works and works twice as hard as men in the same employment outside do. They work thirteen hours a day and each man must do a certain amount of work or be punished. Some few strong ones stand the work, but it is simply slow death to the majority. If a man gets sick and can't work they take him into a cellar and turn a powerful stream of water on him from a hose that knocks the breath out of him. Then a doctor revives him and they hang him up by his hands with his feet off the floor for an hour or two. This generally makes him go to work again, and when he gives out and can't stand up they bring him on a stretcher to the hospital to get well or die as the case may be.

The hospital wards have from one hundred to two

hundred patients in them all the time. They have all
kinds of diseases—at present typhus fever and measles
are the fashion. Consumption here is more common
than bad colds are at home. There are about thirty
hopeless cases of it in the hospital just now and nearly
all the nurses and attendants are contracting it. There
are hundreds of other cases of it among the men who
are working in the shops and foundries. Twice a day
they have a sick call at the hospital, and from two
hundred to three hundred men are marched in each
day suffering from various disorders. They march in
single file past the doctor and he prescribes for each
one "on the fly." The procession passes the drug counter and the medicines are handed out to each one as
they march without stopping the line.

I have tried to reconcile myself to remaining here
for a time, but am about at the end of my endurance.
There is absolutely not one thing in life at present or
in prospect that makes it of value. I have decided to
wait until the court decides the appeal, provided it is
heard within a reasonable time, and see what chance
there comes out of it.

I can stand any kind of hardship or privation on
the outside, but am utterly unable to continue the life
I lead here. I know all the arguments that could be
advanced as to why I should endure it, but I have
reached the limit of endurance. It will be better for
every one else and a thousand times better for me to
end the trouble instead of dragging it out longer.

Perhaps the end of the foregoing letter, with its
hint of "ending the trouble" represents the darkest
hour, when William Sidney Porter's despair was
deepest.

Still gloomy, but with a suggestion of lightness was
his letter of seven weeks later to Mrs. Roach:

Dear Mrs. R.

I have little to say about myself, except that as far as physical comfort goes I am as well situated as any one here. I attend to my business (that of night druggist) and no one interferes with me, as the doctor leaves everything in my hands at night. I attend to sick calls and administer whatever I think proper unless it happens to be a severe case and then I wake up the doctor. I am treated with plentiful consideration by all the officials, have a large, airy, clean sleeping room and the range of the whole place, and big, well kept yard full of trees, flowers and grass. The hospital here is a fine new building, fully as large as the City Hall in Austin, and the office and drug store is as fine and up-to-date as a first class hotel. I have my desk and office chair inside the drug store railings, gas lights, all kinds of books, the latest novels, etc. brought in every day or two, three or four daily papers, and good meals, sent down the dumbwaiter from the kitchen at ten o'clock and three P.M. There are five wards in the hospital and they generally have from fifty to two hundred patients in them all the time.

The guards bring in men who are sick at all hours of the night to the hospital which is detached some one hundred yards from the main buildings. I have gotten quite expert at practising medicine. It's a melancholy place, however—misery and death and all kinds of suffering around one all the time. We sometimes have a death every night for a week or two. Very little time is wasted on such an occasion. One of the nurses will come from a ward and say—"Well, So and So has croaked." Ten minutes later they tramp out with So and So on a stretcher and take him to the dead house. If he has no friends to claim him—which is generally the case—the next day the doctors have a dissecting bee and that ends it. Suicides are as common as picnics here. Every few nights the doctor and

I have to strike out at a trot to see some unfortunate who has tried to get rid of his troubles. They cut their throats and hang themselves and stop up their cells and turn the gas on and try all sorts of ways. Most of them plan it well enough to succeed. Night before last a professional pugilist went crazy in his cell and the doctor and I, of course, were sent for. The man was in good training and it took eight of us to tie him. Seven held him down while the doctor climbed on top and got his hypodermic syringe into him. These little things are our only amusements. I often get as blue as any one can get and I feel as thoroughly miserable as it is possible to feel, but I consider that my future efforts belong to others and I have no right to give way to my own troubles and feelings.

X

RESIGNATION

I went here and there at my own dear will, bound by no limits of space, time, or deportment.   *A Ramble in Aphasia*

WITH the exception of the correspondence with Mr. and Mrs. Roach and Margaret, Will Porter wrote few letters from the Ohio Penitentiary. Greensboro, for example, seems never to have heard from him at all; and probably his native town was the last to learn the complete story of the life of her most distinguished son. Porter did not write to his Texas friends for various reasons. Many of them, those associated with the ranch days, for example, did not know of his suffering and humiliation, or at least he thought that they did not know, and he wished them to remain in ignorance. There were others who, according to his way of thinking, knew entirely too much, and who, in not coming forward at the time of his trial had failed him in his hour of need. The thought of these false friends in his earlier prison days did much to add to his bitterness and depression.

But as time passed resentment gave way to a certain resignation. Once he had given up all hope of a quick pardon or a repeal of his case he began to adapt himself to the material conditions of prison life, hard as they were, and to find a philosophical consolation in the comparison of his own situation with that of the less favored inmates of the institution. His growing interest in his writing did much to lighten the burden. On this subject Professor Smith has quoted J. B. Rumer, a night guard in the penitentiary, who was thrown with Porter during the latter's working hours from midnight to dawn. The two talked but little, Porter being absorbed with his stories:

After most of his work was finished and we had eaten our midnight supper, he would begin to write. He always wrote with pen and ink and would often work for two hours continuously without rising. He seemed oblivious to the world of sleeping convicts about him, hearing not even the occasional sigh or groan from the beds which were stretched before him in the hospital ward or the tramp of the passing guards. After he had written for perhaps two hours he would rise, make a round of the hospital, and then come back to his work again. He got checks at different times and once told me that he had had only two stories rejected while he was in prison.

These stories were mailed to New Orleans and from there forwarded to the various magazines in New York for which they were intended. The obliging intermediary was a person whom Porter never met, a sister of a New Orleans banker who was serving a term in Columbus, and who plays a conspicuous part in the story of the prison days. One of the stories was "Whistling Dick's Christmas Stocking," published in *McClure's Magazine* for December, 1899. Another was "Georgia's Ruling," which the *Outlook* printed in its issue of June 30, 1900. The acceptance of the latter story was particularly pleasing to Porter. The idea that the *Outlook*, then a strictly religious publication, was giving publicity to the work of a jailbird, then doing time in the "stir," was highly tickling to his sense of humor.

Al Jennings has told the story of one of the tales that did not find immediate acceptance. That was "A Christmas Chaparral Gift," which was first sent out from Columbus, and eventually published in *Ainslee's* for December, 1903. Jennings calls it "The Christmas Chaparral," which may be an error, and again may have been the original title. Porter, immediately after finishing the tale, read it to Jennings and to a certain Billy Raidler, a famous train-robber and the terror of the Indian Territory in his outlaw days. Raidler was chief post-office clerk in the Columbus Penitentiary. Jennings himself was beginning his literary work, having started to write the memoirs of his bandit years. He called it *The Long Riders*, and in it there were chapters with forty thousand words and not one climax, and other chapters with but seven sentences and as many killings as there were words. "Every man in prison is writing a story," says Jennings. "Each man considers his life a tragedy— an adventure of the most absorbing interest."

Raidler was Jennings's particular audience and critic, and after the reading of one installment of *The Long Riders* and the consequent discussion, suggested that the manuscript be shown to Bill Porter, who "was also writing a story." Two weeks later Porter read his own story, which he described as a "little scrap." Sitting on a high stool near his desk in the prison drug store he drew from his pocket a roll of brown paper. Jennings has pictured the scene:

From the moment that Porter's rich, low, hesitant voice began there was a breathless suspense until suddenly Billy Raidler gulped, and Porter looked up as one aroused from a dream. Raidler grinned and jabbed his maimed hand onto his eye.

"Damn you, Porter, I never did it in my life before. By God, I didn't know what a tear looked like."

It was a funny thing to see two train robbers blubbering over the simple story. Perhaps the criminal is oversentimental, but the queer twist in Porter's story just seemed to sneak into the heart with a kind of overflowing warmth.

It was "The Christmas Chaparral" he read to us. Both Billy and I could understand the feelings of the cowpuncher who had lost out in the wooing of the girl. We could feel his hot jealousy toward the peeler who won the bride. We knew that he would keep his promise—we knew he would return to kill his rival.

And when he comes back on Christmas Eve, dressed as a Santa Claus, armed to bring tragedy to the happy ranch house, we could sympathize with his mood. He overhears the wife say a word in his defense—he hears her praise the early kindness of his life. He walks up to her—"There's a Christmas present in the next room for you," he says, and leaves the house without firing the shot that was to have ended the husband's life.

It was a little moment of triumph for Porter as he sat there aglow with the satisfaction of appreciated authorship. He rolled up the manuscript and climbed down from the stool.

"Gentlemen, many thanks. I never expected to win tears from experts of your profession." And then we all fell into speculation as to what the story should bring and where we ought to send it. We felt an interest in its fate. *The Long Riders* and its many

buckets of blood were forgotten in the wizardry of
"The Christmas Chaparral." With the fervor of hero-
worshippers, Raidler and I acknowledged Bill Porter,
the genius.

We decided to send the story to the *Black Cat*.
There was in the prison at this time a cultured Frenchman, a banker from New Orleans. Through his sister,
Porter's stories, bearing the New Orleans address, were
sent to the editor.

When "The Christmas Chaparral" was sent out,
Billy and I could hardly wait for the weeks to go by.
We were sure it would be accepted at once. At least
$75 was the price we thought it ought to bring. It
came back.

There are many conflicting accounts as to when,
where, and why Porter adopted his pen name of O.
Henry. There was a Captain Orrin Henry connected
with the penitentiary. His name may have played a
suggestive part. Porter himself, with his Old Man of
the Sea complex, added to the mystification with the
idea of covering up his trail. His own specious explanation was that he picked the name out of a newspaper when he was in New Orleans, and that as it was
a city of many French names he had surmised that the
O. stood for Olivier. As a matter of fact, Porter was,
as has already been told, in New Orleans in the summer
of 1896, on his way to Central America, and again, the
following winter, on his way back to Austin. How
long he stayed on these occasions is a matter of conjecture. Certainly the stays were brief. He can
scarcely have spent his time there at writing, so if he
did pick up the name of O. Henry at one of these times,
it was not to mask his identity as an author. His

first work of fiction, "The Miracle of Lava Cañon," was not written till the autumn of 1897. Yet the tradition that he began his career as a short story writer in New Orleans has persisted, and the Crescent City has claimed him as a fellow townsman.

It is practically certain that the name O. Henry, as a pseudonym, was born in the Columbus Penitentiary. Jennings, in *Through the Shadows with O. Henry*, naturally is frank and unreserved in his references to Porter and his story. In an earlier book, *Beating Back*, written in collaboration with Will Irwin, he was far more reticent. At the time that *Beating Back* was written, the story of O. Henry's prison years was still a *secret de Polichinelle*, that is, a supposed secret that is really known to all the world. Therefore Jennings's introductory words: "He whom I am going to call Bart." Bart was O. Henry.

Another version of the origin of the pen name comes from Al Jennings, sifted through Will Irwin. Mr. Irwin recently retold it to the authors of this book in the form that seems most reasonable to him. It had to do with the festivities of a prison club of which more will be told later. Subsequent events have gone far to justify Jennings's picture of prison conditions at Columbus at the beginning of the century. The penitentiary was run ostensibly by incompetents, who owed their positions to political patronage. Actually the management was in the hands of a group of clever convicts. They did the work. In return they received many privileges and considerable freedom. Jennings was one of these men; Porter was another.

ORRIN HENRY

*Captain of the Guard in the Ohio Penitentiary. He is re-
garded by many as the source of the pseudonym "O. Henry."*

Out of these conditions the club came into being. It was primarily a Sunday dining club.

Sunday afternoon [records *Beating Back*] was an off time. The others must stay in their cells after chapel; but we, on the theory that our work demanded it, had the run of the institution. The guards winked at any of our infractions which did not bump into the letter of the law. They had to; we knew all about the workings of the Ohio Penitentiary. I believe it was a burglar, gone out before I joined the first class, who sprang the idea of Sunday dinners. The boys worked like beavers on his plan.

The highest professional talent was requisitioned. Some of the expert burglars and counterfeiters—all fine mechanics—cut a cupboard in the loft above the construction office. Over this a secret panel was fitted. These same mechanics made a gas stove, and connected it with the prison mains. It stood on a shelf, which swung out and back into the wall like a shelf of drawings. Piece by piece the boys picked up from the kitchen, pantries and dining rooms a complete set of dishes, knives, forks, spoons and pots.

The club was formally opened. Every Sunday at the regular meeting the president appointed a dinner committee, whose duty it was to find what supplies were needed for the following Sunday banquet and supply them. Every trick and device, including theft when necessary, was used. The guards were wheedled. Personal economies were practiced.

Yet often, as the week went on, we'd still find ourselves short of some little thing, like salad oil, or cloves, or garlic. The whole committee would start out as

though this was their one object in life; and their
adventures brought many a laugh next Sunday. No
one can know how much this little interest did to lighten
our lives. When news went about that we'd secured
a roast, a turkey, or some other special delicacy for
next Sunday our mouths watered for two days ahead.

Bart, from the beginning, was the prince of forag-
ers, as later he became the prince of cooks. He could
get more provisions in a day than all the rest in a
week. He had made slits in the lining of his coat, and
there he carried his plunder. His coat bulged with a
Mother Hubbard effect. As he passed the patrol
guard, he would cast one quiet glance, and the guard
would look in the opposite direction. Had the gate
closed on him suddenly, his coat would have resembled
the wreck of a grocery wagon. Once he even brought
in six bottles of wine.

As cook Bart shared honors with the man called
Jean, in reality a certain G——, a Louisianian of
French descent, a defaulting cashier from New Orleans.
At first Bart was the pupil. Cooking by instinct, he
learned much from G——, who was largely book
taught, and relied on weight and measure. The two
were forever amiably quarreling. "There's no taste to
it," G—— would argue. "All right," Bart would
answer, "wait until our guests object."

According to Will Irwin's belief, to these battles
over seasoning, the real origin of the pen name of O.
Henry is to be traced. G—— was on one point mentally defective. He suffered from curious lapses of
memory that caused him to forget the names of his
closest companions. In prison, as throughout life,

WHAT THE "O" MIGHT HAVE MEANT
A facetious explanation from O. Henry to an inquirer

nearly everybody called O. Henry "Bill." But there
were times in the course of the wrangling incidental
to the preparation of dinner for the club when G——
could not recall the name. He would grope helplessly,
stutter, and then call out to his aide: "Oh, Henry, mix
a little more of the salad dressing."

There are still other stories of the origin of the pen
name; that for some reason not quite clear the O stood
for Orrin, the name of an old deaf man whom Porter
knew back in the Greensboro days; that the jailer at
the Austin prison where Porter spent the weeks between
his conviction and his transference to Columbus was
named Henry, that when he was wanted in the office or
for meals, his wife would call: "Oh, Henry." At first
Porter probably attached little importance to his pen
name. Adopted in the mood of a moment, it was principally useful in hiding from the world the identity of
the man behind it. In his early New York days, he
signed various names that popped into his head. The

significances of O. Henry to him began when, through growing success, it became a trade-mark that carried a story at once to an editor's desk, and, what was more, meant a boosting of the story's price.

In *Beating Back*, Al Jennings ascribed the establishment of the prison club to a nameless burglar who had departed from Columbus before his own arrival. In *Through the Shadows with O. Henry*, he says that it was Porter who founded the club, and, inferentially, gave it the name of the Recluse Club. According to the latter version the membership was limited to six; three bank robbers, or three men who were doing time on charges of having robbed banks, one forger, and two train-robbers. The train-robbers were Jennings and Billy Raidler. "We met on Sunday in the construction office," records Jennings. "And never a club in the highest strata of society had graver, brighter, happier discussion—never an epicure's retreat served a more delicious menu than our Sunday repasts." Of that exclusive club Bill Porter was king.

Jennings, in *Through the Shadows with O. Henry*, called the bankers Carnot, Ikey, and Louisa. Louisa was obviously the G—— of *Beating Back*. As G——, his memory may have been subject to lapses; but as Louisa he is presented as a culinary artist and a marvel of resourcefulness. An architect and a draftsman as well as a banker, he had superintended the building of the false wall, with the kitchenette with full equipment behind it. More important, he was the official chef of the Recluse Club. The supreme manifestations of his art were his preparation of tomato soup, and his cold bread pudding made with raisins and currants.

Says Jennings: "I've given that recipe of Louisa's to every woman I ever met. Not one of them could turn out the delicacy as the chef of the Recluse Club did it."

One wonders if the haze of memory has not somewhat colored Jennings's recollection of the improvised banquet room, with its "fairy table, decorated with flowers and set for six, and laden with all manner of delicacies—olives, radishes, sugar, cream, white bread, lettuce, tomatoes." There were even place cards, which provided Porter with an opportunity to display his literary turn and his talent as an artist. Of the club members, only Jennings and Raidler acknowledged that they were guilty. The bankers, like Porter, maintained their entire innocence of the crimes for which they were being punished, and resented the idea that any one should think of them as convicts. So Porter's whimsical humor moved him in drawing the place cards to depict the bankers as cherubs, friars, or unstained lilies.

Jennings has pictured a typical dinner of the Recluse Club:

The club and its layout was distinctly against prison rules. At a moment's signal, gas stove and its range could be hidden out of sight. A false wall had been built and the kitchenette was hidden like a long telephone booth behind it. It was stocked with silverware, napkins, flavoring extracts, flour and every necessity, enough, in fact, for a small hotel. All had been stolen or bargained from the head clerks in other shops and from the chief cook in the kitchen. Louisa dodged from behind the door, a great dish cloth tied about his waist. "Dinner is served, gentlemen. Make yourselves at home."

Here is a record of the Porter of the Columbus days from an entirely different source. Alexander Hobbs, who later became the political boss of the colored voters of Columbus, was a Negro prisoner who served as valet to one of the prison physicians. He has written:

Mr. Porter was from the South and he always called colored men niggers. I never got fresh with him. I treated him with respect but let him alone. One day he asked me about it and I said: "Mr. Porter, I know you don't want nothing to do with no black folks." He laughed and after that we always got along fine.

Mr. Porter was a nurse over in the hospital and he hadn't been long when by mistake one day Warden E. G. Coffin was given an overdose of Fowler's solution of arsenic. The right antidote couldn't be found and the day physician, the nurses, and all the prison officers were crowded around the bed on which the warden was lying, in great fright. Everybody was panic-stricken and it looked like the warden, who was unconscious, was going to die with doctors and a drug store right there beside him.

Then Mr. Porter, who had been upstairs nursing a sick prisoner, came walking down. He had learned what was the matter. I can just see him yet, as he came down them stairs, as quiet and composed as a free citizen out for a walk. "Be quiet, gentlemen," he says, and walks over to the drugstore and takes charge, just as easy as if he owned the prison. Then he mixes a little drink, just like mixing a soda water. In an hour the warden was out of danger and the next day Mr. Porter was made night drug clerk.

Porter's last promotion within prison walls came in October, 1900, nine months before his release. Then he was made a bookkeeper in the office of the prison steward. This office was in a two-story building

some distance from the prison proper, and upon entering it Porter felt almost free. So far as appearance
went, he was as free as any salaried bookkeeper. He
worked without other supervision than that of the
steward and storekeeper and could leave the building
whenever he liked. He ate and slept in the office building, and, after working hours, his time was his own.
Often he would take long walks by the river at night or
ramble through the streets of Columbus, meeting people
who had no idea that he was an inmate of the
penitentiary.

On July 24, 1901, William Sidney Porter, like
Jimmy Valentine, received his suit of villainously fitting, ready-made clothes, his pair of stiff squeaky
shoes, his railroad ticket, his five-dollar bill, and the
Warden's handshake and admonition as to his conduct
in the future, and passed out of the prison walls.
According to Jennings, Porter did not wear the ready-
made suit provided by the state, but managed to secure
a better one, which led to the ironic comment: "Porter's going on his honeymoon"; and in addition to the
state five-dollar subsidy, he had in his pocket between
sixty and seventy dollars, the unspent earnings from
his recent stories.

He went immediately to Pittsburgh, where Mr. and
Mrs. Roach were living. Soon after Porter's enforced
departure from Austin the Roaches had also left the
city, taking Margaret with them. For a time they
had lived in middle Tennessee, thence moving to Pittsburgh, where Mr. Roach was managing the Iron Front
Hotel. There are stories that conflict. One of them is
that Porter was made welcome and a room in the hotel

was fitted up for him as an office where he spent the greater part of his time writing stories.

Another flashlight on Will Porter's Pittsburgh days is furnished by a sketch called "Pittsburghesque" in the Pittsburgh *Post-Gazette* for March 28, 1930. In that sketch Charles F. Danver told of a second-floor room at the corner of Wylie and Fullerton Streets, in the heart of the Smoky City's Little Harlem, that Porter, in those restless days, once called "home." For three months he lived there, in what is now described as an ancient gray brick structure.

The second floor is now unoccupied. On the first floor there is a pawnshop. And below that, in the basement, one of the Hill District's hottest night spots. . . . We stood there the other night in the driving snow [wrote Mr. Danver] wondering what O. Henry would think were he alive and back. Jazz tunes drifted from a dozen radios, and the odor of sizzling hamburger came from Negro hot-dog shops. A little white girl passed with a basket of artificial flowers, peddling them from door to door.

The environment was different in the months of late 1901 and early 1902 when Porter was struggling with his short stories and doing occasional work for the Pittsburgh *Dispatch*. Fullerton Street was then called Fulton, and at the corner of Wylie there was Emil G. Stucky's drug store. Samuel C. Jamison, later to become coroner of Allegheny County and an important political figure, was a clerk in the drug store. To him Porter came with a letter of introduction from one Bill Smith, a distant relative of Jamison. Porter was broke, and Mr. Jamison suggested that he move into

the room above the drug store. Porter accepted the
invitation and lived there for three months.

He was a mighty fine fellow [Mr. Danver quotes
Mr. Jamison as saying]. I was then in my last year
in the Pittsburgh College of Pharmacy. I had lots
of room and didn't mind sharing it with Bill. We
occupied the same bed—one of those old high walnut
fellows—and together, when necessary, fought the in-
sect life. Bill never rolled in before 3 o'clock in the
morning. His work at the paper kept him that long.
He didn't do much but work and play cards occasionally. He played a good game of poker, but as we
played five-cent limit, he never won very much.

At that time there was a saloon at 79 Fulton Street,
known as Angloch's, and there one could get a fine
sandwich for five cents. Beer was also a nickel and
they threw in a bowl of soup. That's where O. Henry
ate most of the time he was here. He was fastidious
about his dress and tried to look as English as possible. He liked yellow kid gloves, carried a cane and
wore spats, which in those days were somewhat of a
rarity. We used to kid him about his clothes, but he
didn't mind.

According to Mr. Danver, the coroner contributed
to O. Henry's career by helping him to make his way
to New York. At that time political influence still
meant something in obtaining railroad passes. Porter,
as usual, was broke, and Mr. Jamison, through Select
Councilman John Landie, got him a pass for the journey. Porter's last gift from his roommate was one
dollar to buy the favorite yellow gloves. It had been
the reporter's habit to borrow Mr. Jamison's on occasion, as he never seemed happy unless he wore them.
On receiving the dollar bill Porter asked: "But why

the dollar? They cost only fifty cents a pair." "Yes, I know," was the reply. "But you'd better buy two pairs so that you can have clean ones when you hit New York."

From first to last Porter was always dissatisfied in Pittsburgh. He never liked the city. From time to time in his stories he showed his distaste for it; and in a letter to Jennings in the penitentiary he wrote:

I want to say that Pittsburgh is the "low-downedest" hole on the surface of the earth. The people here are the most ignorant, ill-bred, contemptible, boorish, degraded, insulting, sordid, vile, foul-mouthed, indecent, profane, drunken, dirty, mean, depraved curs that I ever imagined could exist. Columbus people are models of chivalry compared to them. I shall linger here no longer than necessary.

Yet he lingered in Pittsburgh through the autumn of 1901 and the following winter. Then the call to New York came. With his departure from Pittsburgh, his life as Sinbad the Sailor came to an end. Unhappily, entering upon the new life, he carried with him his Old Man of the Sea. That burden was long to weigh heavily upon his shoulders.

PART III
HAROUN

XI

THE DISCOVERY OF BAGDAD

The true adventurer goes forth aimless and uncalculating to meet and greet unknown fate. A fine example was the Prodigal Son—when he started back home.   *The Green Door*

ONE day in the spring of 1902, William Sidney Porter trod for the first time the cobblestones of the city that he was destined to rechristen his "Little Old Bagdad on the Subway," his "Noisyville on the Hudson," his "City of Chameleon Changes," his "City of Too Many Caliphs." He spent a night or two in one of the decidedly plebeian hotels that lined the water front, and then moved eastward and northward to establish himself in more congenial and comfortable quarters. In those first two days he made no known contacts.

It is the fashion nowadays to picture a bygone period by the elaboration of details; by the flashing of the names of plays and pugilists, of vaudeville performers and their popular turns, or topical songs, of ladies conspicuous in the chorus and celebrities of the underworld, of eccentrics and police captains and racehorses. Often this method is a mere flourish, a filling in of space. In the case of O. Henry it is not only legitimate, it is the only way to the full understanding and interpretation of tales in which the fad, the personality, the haunting air of the hour was in the very warp and woof.

To impinge the Robinson Crusoe *motif* upon the

173

Arabian Nights *motif*, suppose we indulge in the fancy of a modern Alexander Selkirk, originally a New Yorker of the age of innocence, which for the purpose may be assigned to somewhere in the 1880's. For long years he has been a castaway on an island in a remote and lonely sea. As in the case of Crusoe, or of Rip van Winkle during his twenty years' sleep, or Edmond Dantes when a prisoner in his dungeon in the Château d'If, the march of history and the conflicts and upheavals of the world of men mean nothing to him. Then to carry on the whimsical fancy, one day the tides wash up on the shore of his island an iron-bound chest which, being opened, is found to contain the works of a certain O. Henry, an author to him of course entirely unknown. Imagine his mental reactions in trying to visualize and understand the world and his own land and city in particular, from a study of these books. Imagine the queer interpretations, the odd surmises, the humorous yet natural misconceptions.

To meet such a supposed situation by an attempt to reconstruct from memory, from old newspaper files and old advertisements, the spirit and flavor of that age when the century was in its infancy is here far from being a mere rhetorical flourish. It reflects the life of O. Henry and the stories of O. Henry. Were all other records lost, from the forty-odd tales against the definite New York background, a future historian might rebuild a grotesque and alluring city that would somehow be the city of that decade from 1900 to 1910, echoing its voice, expressing the moods of its four million, and illuminating its caliphs and its *cadis*, its Little Humpback; in short, as O. Henry himself

worded it, the city of Fitbad the Tailor, and of Ali
Baba and the Forty Thieves on every block. From the
other stories a picture might be drawn of the vast
hinterland of New Arabia that stretched away to the
westward of Bagdad.

To illustrate by reference to one dominating personality of the age. The imaginary historian, recon-
structing from the O. Henry pages, would first find
himself confronted and puzzled by a man of might, a
strange superman, who apparently reigned over a
country that was feverish, turbulent, and highly
charged with electricity. This powerful being, this
"Theodore, by the Grace of God, Autocrat of all the
Americas," was at times swayed by benevolent eccentricities. His activities were many and varied. There
was a popular rhyme of the day [7] which thus described them:

> At 4 A.M. he shoots a bear,
> At 6 subdues a restive horse;
> From 9 to 4 he takes the air,
> He doesn't take it all, of course.
> And then, at 5 o'clock, maybe,
> Some colored man drops in to tea.

In other aspects he would seem to have been a kind
of St. George, battling with many dragons. These
dragons, in the quaint phraseology of the age were
known as "malefactors of great wealth." Other impish
objects of his righteous wrath were called "nature
fakirs"; and still others "muck-rakers." Linked with
his martial achievements, presumably many, was a certain organization known as the "Gentle Riders." He
had apparently led these men into history and a few

[7] From *Misrepresentative Men* by Col. D. Streamer (Harry
Graham).

ambuscades on the battlefield in some war; and—so
the historian would deduce from "The Badge of Policeman O'Roon"—the "Gentle Riders" were recruited
from the aristocracy of the wild men of the West, and
the wild men of the aristocracy of the East.

In addition to high mental qualities, this superman
was a kind of glorified Paul Bunyan, given to feats of
prodigious strength. That was clearly shown in the
story "Modern Rural Sports." The tale told of Andy
Tucker and Jeff Peters, two knights of the road of
obviously unscrupulous habits, who planned to augment their common bank account by separating a
modern agriculturist from some of his money. The
suggestion that they both share in the venture was
dismissed as unfair and quite lacking in decency. Jeff
Peters, flouting the idea, explains: "Two of us against
one farmer would look as one-sided as Roosevelt using
both hands to kill a grizzly."

Yet curiously, this superman, despite his exalted
station, his power, and his achievement, would seem
to have been in one section of the New Arabia over
which he ruled a stranger or at best only vaguely
known. "The Rose of Dixie" tells the story of an old
southern scholar, Colonel Aquila Telfair, who edits a
magazine, "Of, for, and by the South." No contribution from north of the Mason-Dixon line has ever been
allowed to appear in its pages. But a dwindling circulation moves the Colonel to depart from this established principle. He tells a persuasive Northern promoter of a mysterious article that he is considering.

The article [explains the Colonel] covers a wide
area of knowledge. It takes up theories and questions

that have puzzled the world for centuries, and disposes of them logically and concisely. One by one it holds up to view the evils of the world, points out the way of eradicating them, and then conscientiously and in detail commends the good. There is hardly a phase of human life that it does not discuss wisely, calmly, and equitably. The great policies of governments, the duties of private citizens, the obligations of home life, law, ethics, morality—all these important subjects are handled with a calm wisdom and confidence that I must confess has captured my imagination.

But [continues the Colonel] the only doubt remaining in my mind as to the tremendous advantage that it would be to us to give its publication in *The Rose of Dixie* is that I have not yet sufficient information about the author to give his work publicity in our magazine. He is a distinguished man both in literary and in other more diversified and extraneous fields. But I am extremely careful about the matter that I accept for publication. My contributors are people of unquestioned repute and connections, which can be verified at any time. As I said, I am holding this article until I can acquire more information about its author.

Colonel Telfair's investigations proved satisfactory, for the northern promoter, on a second visit, found the vacant space in the magazine filled by an article headed thus:

Second Message to Congress

Written for

The Rose of Dixie

By

A Member of the Well Known

Bulloch Family of Georgia

T. Roosevelt

At this ending of the tale in the year 1908, a hundred thousand American readers chuckled with merriment. They understood. To-day it would probably be entirely lost on one-half of the new generation. The imaginary historian of the future would understand it not at all. It illustrates how much the work of O. Henry was linked with the passing mood and the fugitive jest of his time.

A Sun King implies an heir apparent or an heir presumptive. In 1902 the second luminary of New Arabia, and of Bagdad in particular, was William Travers Jerome. Here again was a valiant battler against the evil jinns, the powers of Eblis. In the heart of Bagdad there flourished a fortress, believed to be impregnable and impenetrable; where a great lord said to be in secret league with various *cadis* of influence held high carnival, and through his manipulation of games of chance added the wealth of the owners of rich caravans to his already swollen coffers. There was talk of "a drunken kid," who had been despoiled of a vast treasure of gold and precious stones. Arrogant in his supposed power, maintaining that he was within the law, the great lord laughed at threats and was deaf to murmurs.

In the marts of the city there was the saying: "They can't close Canfield's." But one winter's night the fortress was stormed, and its instruments of operation demolished or carried away. All Bagdad, all New Arabia, rang with the feat. Jerome, the arch invader, was acclaimed as a mighty son of the Prophet. In "The Enchanted Profile," Mrs. Maggie Brown, said to be the third richest woman in the world, plans to give

a dinner in honor of the young girl she has temporarily
adopted as a protégée. She explains: "I don't send
out invitations. I issue orders. I'll have fifty guests
here that couldn't be brought together again at any
reception unless it were given by King Edward or
William Travers Jerome."

It was not as a caliph, surrounded by attendants,
and camels, and steeds of Arabian strain that William
Sidney Porter entered Bagdad. He came as a humble
rawi, figuratively on foot and alone. Bagdad was the
Mecca of the *rawis* of the land. They gathered from
the hills of San Francisco, the shores of Lake Michigan,
above all, from the banks of the Wabash. To be a
Hoosier in Bagdad almost inevitably meant to have the
manuscript of an historical novel concealed somewhere
upon the person.

There were *rawis* of high degree, and *rawis* of low
degree; *rawis* who lived in houses comparable to the
one in which Sinbad the Porter found Sinbad the
Sailor, and *rawis* ever engaged in fighting off the wolf
at the door. But their methods were much the same.
Unlike their predecessors of old Arabia and Persia and
Egypt, they did not sit cross-legged in the market
place, spinning their yarns in sing-song tones. In
solitude they scribbled them on odd bits of paper, or
produced them by means of complicated machines, and
then carried their wares to the editor man; or, when the
wares had proved to be particularly entertaining and
to be bartered for gold, the editor man went to them.

Porter was preëminently the *rawi*, and like every
other *rawi* in his invasion of the "big city" he brought
with him the dream of seeing himself as a best-seller.

Wandering about Bagdad he probably studied the bookshops and kiosks piled high with the literary successes of the hour. The day might come perhaps when some book of his would be displayed as conspicuously as, in the spring of 1902, were displayed such works as Conan Doyle's *The Hound of the Baskervilles*, Gilbert Parker's *The Right of Way*, Mary Johnston's *Audrey*, Thomas Dixon's *The Leopard's Spots*, Charles Major's *Dorothy Vernon of Haddon Hall*, Gertrude Atherton's *The Conqueror*, Henry Harland's *The Lady Paramount*, and Ellen Glasgow's *The Battle-ground*.

In Porter's stories are bound up his dreams and ambitions. Thinking "shop," he often wrote "shop." The magazine office and the newspaper office figure in such tales as "The Rose of Dixie," "A Sacrifice Hit," "No Story," "Best-Seller," "The Higher Pragmatism," "A Newspaper Story," and "Calloway's Code." Editors being much his companions he wrote of them and their ways, moods, and prejudices. Satirically, in "A Sacrifice Hit," he told of one editor who in selecting his stories for publication enlisted the services of readers in all stations in life. To the janitor he turned over the manuscript of Maurice Hewlett's *The Queen's Quair*. "So is the book," was the janitorial verdict.

In the tales of the *rawis* of those early years of the century, there were no Wonderful Lamps, Enchanted Horses, Cities of Brass, or Kings of the Black Isles; but many of them involved adventures and situations that exacted just as much of the reader's credulity. It was an age that ran riot with stories of Americans, usually from the Midwest, who in imaginary kingdoms or principalities of the Balkans, flashed sword play, defended castle staircases against astonishing odds, eventually marrying reigning princesses and thereafter administering affairs of state with wisdom and discretion. This kind of tale made a profound impression on Porter. He never wrote one himself, but in "Best-Seller" he championed it, paralleling its improbabilities by the story of a drummer at home.

It was in the highways and byways that reflected the political intrigue of the time that Porter learned the heart of Bagdad. The city and the land were in the throes of reform. There was much talk of venal *cadis* who bartered justice for gold. Against these thundered the District Attorney, Jerome, the Mayor, Seth Low, and the Recorder, Gough. The picturesque Devery, represented in an ephemeral campaign song as threatening "to smash in de chops of de citizens and cops," was no longer in office as the city's Chief of Police, but the Tammany Tiger was soon again to purr as he purrs in the O. Henry story, "The Social Triangle."

Iniquity flared in that old Bagdad. The Bowery was enjoying its last days as a street of colorful sin, before subsiding into the drabness of later years. There McGurk's, known to readers of O. Henry as "Mc-Turk's," was still Suicide Hall. At the corner of Sixth Avenue and Thirtieth Street, the Haymarket was carrying on the evil traditions of forty years. Almost across the way was the notorious Sweeney's, called "Rooney's" in the O. Henry story "Past One at Rooney's." Close by was the short block of Twenty-ninth Street between Broadway and Sixth Avenue, lined with the so-called dance halls, the Cairo, the Tivoli, Rennert's, and Bohemia.

Sitting silent and observant in such resorts Porter learned much of the seamy side of life in Bagdad. Until after midnight the places were usually orderly enough, the only disturbances being occasional fights between patrons. But in the small hours of the morning, after the hue and cry of factitious revelry had died down, obstreperous visitors who unwisely objected to the time-honored process of "short-changing" were dealt with by strong-arm methods. Occasionally these repressive measures were carried to extremes. Finally in one of the resorts a particularly atrocious murder was followed by the complete severance of the victim's head from his body. Commemorating the event a wag with a peculiar sense of humor prepared and exhibited at the entrance of the scene of the "little accident" a poster holding out the invitation: "Heads cut off while you wait." From that day, the glory of West Twenty-ninth Street began to wane.

Gangdom and gangsters have their share in the O. Henry stories. The gangs of Bagdad were then, as ever, in a state of transition. The Stovepipe Gang, which numbered among its membership the illustrious Kid Brady of "Vanity and Some Sables," was typical. It enlivened that particular section of the district known as "Hell's Kitchen" that runs along Eleventh and Twelfth Avenues on the river, and bends a hard and sooty elbow around little, lost, homeless De Witt Clinton Park. Appearing to pass their time on street corners arrayed like the lilies of the conservatory and busy with nail files and pen knives, the members of the gang had only one serious occupation—the separating of citizens from their coin and valuables. "Preferably," O. Henry explains, "this was done by weird and singular tricks without noise or bloodshed; but whenever the citizen refused to impoverish himself gracefully his objections came to be spread finally upon some police station blotter or hospital register."

But the Stovepipers, though typical, were merely a small band of border warriors, akin, on the battlefield of Hell's Kitchen, to the Gorillas, the Rhodes Gang, and the Parlor Mob. That section of Bagdad was ruled by the Gophers under the formidable leadership of One Lung Curran. The female of the species, according to Mr. Kipling, is more deadly than the male. That seems to have applied to Hell's Kitchen as well as to the women of Afghanistan and the squaws of the Iroquois. The Gophers had the support of the Battle Row Ladies' Social and Athletic Club, better known as the Lady Gophers, which was composed entirely of women whose mettle as fighters had been tested in frequent battles with the police. According to Herbert Asbury's *The Gangs of New York*, this organization was led by Battle Annie, the sweetheart of practically the entire Gopher gang. Like such of her illustrious predecessors in the history of New York gangdom as Gallus Mag, Sadie the Goat, and Hell Cat Maggie, Battle Annie was partial to mayhem, and is said to have held classes in the art, giving her followers the benefit of her experiences and researches.

To the east and south there were even greater gangs contributing to the turmoil of Bagdad. The Hudson

Dusters reigned in Greenwich Village. The Eastmans and the Five Pointers contended bloodily for supremacy on the lower East Side. There were great and sinister names among the *condottieri*: Paul Kelly, Humpty Jackson, Biff Ellison, Kid Twist, Johnny Spanish. Towering above all others was the redoubtable Monk Eastman. "As brave a thug as ever shot an enemy in the back or blackjacked a voter at the polls" is Mr. Asbury's tribute. No warrior of feudal days ever showed more wounds of battle or took greater pride in them. His boast was that when he climbed on the scales he had to make allowance for the bullets imbedded in his body. In 1917, with the entrance of the United States into the World War, Monk enlisted in the New York National Guard. The physicians who examined him thought they had to do with a veteran of every battle since Gettysburg. They asked him what wars he had been in. "Oh," said Eastman, "a lot of little wars around New York."

It is a curious commentary on the old underworld of Bagdad that, according to his own lights, Monk Eastman was a *preux chevalier*, a parfait, gentil knight. For men only did he carry his huge club, his blackjack, his sets of brass knuckles. He was frankly predatory. "I like to beat up a guy once in a while," he used to say. "It keeps me hand in." Once, after bludgeoning an inoffensive old man, he explained: "Well, I had forty-nine nicks in me stick an' I wanted to make it an even fifty." But in his relations with the fair sex he ever held himself to be the soul of chivalry. It was his boast that he never struck a woman with his club, no matter how much she annoyed him. When it became

necessary to discipline a lady for a lapse in manners
he simply blackened her eyes with his fist: "I only
give her a little poke. Just enough to put a shanty on
her glimmer. But I always takes off me knucks."

Above the gangsters were the aristocrats of the
underworld, the men with whom the western heroes of
The Gentle Grafter matched wits on their occasional
visits to the big city—"Big Jim" Dougherty of
"Dougherty's Eye-Opener"; the clean shaven men with
wise eyes who, in "The Poet and the Peasant," dismissed Caleb Bulltongue in his too obviously bucolic
attire as probably an agent of the Powers that Rule
("one of Jerome's men"), later to fall upon and despoil
him when he donned the habiliments of the higher civili-
zation. In their more amiable moments these men were
sports, and their talk outside of professional hours
was mostly of the race track and the prize ring—of
Irish Lad, the Picket, Africander, McChesney, of Ar-
senal, winner of the Metropolitan Handicap of 1902,
and of Reina, winner of the Brooklyn Handicap; of
Jeffries, and Fitzsimmons, and Sharkey, known respec-
tively as the "Boilermaker," the "Cornishman," and
the "Sailor."

As the result of the rapacity of too many caliphs
the giants of the ring were rarely seen in action in the
Bagdad of O. Henry's day. Pugilistica was temporarily under a cloud. With the ending two years earlier
of what was known as the Horton Law, the masters
were forced to migrate to more liberal climes of New
Arabia in order to practice their professional activities.
Yet the "manly art" continued to flourish, and more

than one humble hero of an O. Henry tale augmented his earnings by occasional appearance within the squared circle.

There was, for example, the aforementioned Kid Brady, of "Vanity and Some Sables," who before being sent to the ropes by the bright eyes of Molly McKeever, and devoting himself to the more legitimate occupation of plumber, had upheld the prestige of the Stovepipe Gang in many a professional bout. He did not, as did later, more formidable and more financially astute ringmen, erect from his earnings huge apartment houses, nor in his leisure hours lecture on Shakespeare. His battles were waged, not in open-air amphitheaters, or spacious inclosed gardens, but in stuffy, smoke-sooted halls in side streets. Known as "clubs," these halls were the speakeasies of the ring. They were for "club members" only.

Occasionally Porter was a club member, though not often, for he did not particularly enjoy the spectacle of two men battering each other. But two or three times he was persuaded to visit the old Longacre Club on West Twenty-ninth Street. The setting and the quaint ceremony appealed to his sense of the humorous. To become a club member no sponsorship was necessary. It was a mere matter of presenting oneself at the nearest corner saloon where, upon the payment of a dollar or two, a "membership card" in the name of "John Smith" and expiring the same night, was issued. The national sense of humor decreed that the fiction of club membership be ceremoniously maintained. Then, as now, the truth of the Kipling lines held. Ours is a land, indeed,

That bids him flout the law he makes,
That bids him make the law he flouts. . . .

Laughter and ironic cheers greeted the announcer's invariable preliminary admonition: "Some of youse gents have been remiss in your attendance at club meetings lately." Kid Brady, called to the center of the ring for action, was introduced as "the pride of the Stovepipe Gang" and his opponent, "in this corner, the South Brooklyn Cyclone," the master of ceremonies concluding in a ringing voice: "Both members of the club." Across the color line, beyond the barrier of race, the fiction stretched. Two negro boxers step forward for introduction. "Gents, the next entertainment on the program will be an exhibition of boxing between Joe Wolcott and Dave Taylor. Both members of the colored branch of this organization."

But the reigning kings of the ring, though professionally engaged elsewhere, were still present in the imagination of Bagdad. The ponderous Jim Jeffries held the heights, defying all challengers. Three years earlier he had dethroned Fitzsimmons, alias the "Cornishman," alias "Freckled Fitz," alias "Ruby Robert," alias the "Kangaroo." A few months after Porter's arrival in Bagdad he was to beat him again after a terrific battle. Behold Jeffries in Charles Dana Gibson's famous picture of the time, "The Champion," showing him surrounded and followed by a throng of wide-eyed admirers. Read the line in O. Henry's "The Lost Blend" describing the drink so potent that "with two fingers of it inside you, you would bury your face in your hands and cry because there wasn't anything more worth while around for you to lick than little Jim

Jeffries." There are the echoes of sports of the time other than the ring and the racetrack in the tales in which O. Henry reflected the moods and sounds of Bagdad. In "The Cop and the Anthem" the policeman excuses Soapy's welkin-shattering shouts with the comment: " 'Tis one of them Yale lads celebrating the goose egg they give to the Hartford College. Noisy; but no harm. We've instructions to lave them be."

Tempora mutantur! In the Smithsonian Institution, or in old pictures, or in advertisements of the time will be seen gasoline and electrically driven conveyances to excite the risibility of 1931. Built on the lines of the old horse-drawn carriage, humpbacked, with a door at the rear by which timorous passengers climbed into a curious compartment, and with the sides lined by long wicker baskets, these vehicles, rejoicing in such forgotten names as Pope-Hartford, Pope-Toledo, and Thomas Flyer, seem almost as remote as the contrivances of the Stone Age. Yet in the year 1902, when Porter as Haroun Alraschid first prowled the streets of Bagdad, they were regarded as lordly monsters, Juggernauts of amazing speed and devastating potentialities.

The flavor of the Arabian Nights was in these cars which were often the real protagonists of some of the earlier O. Henry stories. Shining with resplendent brass and flaming with color, they suggested magic power and mysterious adventure. In "The Fifth Wheel" the chariot is a car "splendidly red, smoothly running, craftily demolishing the speed regulations." In "While the Auto Waits" it has a white body and a red running gear, and the ownership of the car serves the purposes of fiction by establishing the hero's position in worldly affluence. In "The Third Ingredient," it is the green automobile waiting before the Vallambrosa Apartment House that stamps the supposedly poor young man with the onion as a Prince Charming, born to the purple. Usually suggesting vast wealth, in its humbler aspects the car could be made to convey the mere pretense of wealth. Make and horse power were eloquently indicative of sharp lines of social cleavages. Listen to Nancy, the wise virgin of "The Trimmed Lamp," speaking of the fascinating gentleman who has been seen by her fellow shop-girls wooing her across the department store counter with a King Cophetua air: "Him," says Nancy, "him? Not for me. I saw him drive up outside. A 12 H. P. machine and an Irish chauffeur."

XII

DISCOVERERS OF O. HENRY—RICHARD DUFFY'S NARRATIVE

"A trust is its weakest point," said Jeff Peters. "Yes, sir, every trust bears in its own bosom the seeds of its destruction like the rooster that crows near a Georgia colored Methodist camp meeting, or a Republican announcing himself a candidate for governor of Texas."   *The Octopus Marooned*

THE discoverers of O. Henry are legion. Many men have claimed the distinction of discovery, and done so honestly. There is no call to disparage any legitimate belief. Diversity of opinion is natural. Porter sent his earlier work to various publications, and every editor with the discernment to recognize the quality in the manuscript of the unknown author was entitled to a share in the honor of bringing the modern Scheherezade to the knowledge of the world. Of course the situation has led to a certain conflict of evidence.

Among O. Henry's belongings after his death there was found a notebook that was used by him when he was at Columbus. In it he jotted down the names of the stories and of the magazines to which he sent them. It is not complete, the first date being October 1, 1900; and, therefore, contains no mention of "Whistling Dick's Christmas Stocking," which appeared in *McClure's* for December, 1899; nor of "Georgia's Ruling," published in the *Outlook* for June 30, 1900. These were the first two of his stories that are now grouped in books. Later tales listed in the prison

notebook and republished in book form are, in chrono-
logical order, "An Afternoon Miracle," "Money
Maze," "No Story," "A Fog in Santone," "A Blackjack Bargainer," "The Enchanted Kiss," "Hygeia at
the Solito," 'Rouge et Noir," "The Duplicity of Hargraves," and "The Marionettes."

One day early in the year 1901 the mail brought to
the offices of *Ainslee's Magazine* in New York an envelope bearing a New Orleans postmark and containing
the manuscript of a story entitled "Money Maze." The
story was signed O. Henry, and the accompanying note
asked that either a check or the rejected manuscript
be sent to W. S. Porter at a certain New Orleans
address. The unknown first reader who saw enough
in the tale to pass it on to the man higher up has also
a claim in the honors of discovery. Eventually
"Money Maze" reached the editors, Gilman Hall and
Richard Duffy. They pronounced it good, wrote a
letter of acceptance, and asked the author to let them
see more of his work. The story was published in the
May issue of *Ainslee's*, and Porter first read it in
printed form in the Ohio Penitentiary where he was
serving the last months of his sentence.

Evidently he thought that he had found out just the
kind of material that the editors wanted, for the earlier
stories sent to *Ainslee's* were all in the vein of "Money
Maze," dealing with the atmosphere and characters of
the Central American republic of *Cabbages and Kings*.
The second tale to reach *Ainslee's* was "Rouge et
Noir." This carried the signature Olivier Henry;
which also marked the next story, "The Flag Paramount." "Rouge et Noir" appeared in *Ainslee's* for

December, 1901, and "The Flag Paramount" in the following issue. In the meantime, with stories in other fields, Porter was trying out other magazines. "A Blackjack Bargainer" and "The Duplicity of Hargraves" found their way from Columbus, via New Orleans, to *Munsey's Magazine* where they were published in the issues for August, 1901 and February, 1902; "Bulger's Friend" was sent to the *Youth's Companion;* and "The Lotus and the Bottle," another Central American story, which perhaps had been regretfully declined by *Ainslee's,* to the *Smart Set.*

But *Ainslee's* seemed to be the best market, and towards the end of the year 1901, from his room in the Iron Front Hotel in Pittsburgh, he sent three stories, "The Passing of Black Eagle," "Friends in San Rosario," both signed Olivier Henry, and "Cherchez la Femme." With these tales the editors, Messrs. Hall and Duffy, were convinced that their new contributor was no mere flash-in-the-pan, but a man to be encouraged and cultivated. After a conference with the publishers, they wrote Porter a letter urging him to come to New York and promising to accept enough of his stories to insure him reasonable support. Let Richard Duffy tell the story of his arrival and of the impression he made.

It was getting late on a fine spring afternoon down at Duane and Spring Streets when he came to meet us. From the outer gate the boy presented a card bearing the name William Sidney Porter. I don't remember just when we found out that O. Henry was merely a pen name; but think it was during the correspondence arranging that he come to New York. I do remember, however, that when we were preparing our yearly prospectus, we had written to him, asking that he tell us what the initial O stood for, as we wished to use his photograph and preferred to have his name in full. It was the custom and would make his name stick faster in the minds of readers. With a courteous flourish of appreciation at the honor we were offering him in making him known to the world, he sent us "Olivier," and so he appeared as Olivier Henry in the first publishers' announcement in which his stories were heralded. Later he confided to us, smiling, what a lot of fun he had had in picking out a first name of sufficient advertising effectiveness that began with O.

As it happens in these matters, whatever mind picture Gilman Hall or I had formed of him from his letters, vanished before the impression of the actual man. He wore a dark suit of clothes, I recall, and a four-in-hand tie of bright color. He carried a black derby, high-crowned, and walked with a springy, noiseless step. To meet him for the first time you felt his most notable quality to be reticence, not a reticence of social timidity, but a reticence of deliberateness. If you also were observing, you would soon understand that his reticence proceeded from the fact that civilly yet masterfully he was taking in every item of the "you" being presented to him to the accompaniment of convention's phrases and ideas, together with the "you" behind this presentation. It was because he was able thus to assemble and sift all the multifarious elements of a personality with sleight-of-hand swiftness that you find him characterizing a person or a neighborhood in a sentence or two; and once I heard him characterize a list of editors he knew each in a phrase.

On his first afternoon in New York we took him on our usual walk uptown from Duane Street to about Madison Square. That was a long walk for O. Henry, as anyone who knew him may witness. Another long

one was when he walked about a mile over a fairly high
hill with me on a zigzag path through autumn woods.
I showed him plains below us and hills stretching away
so far and blue that they looked like the illimitable
sea from the deck of an ocean liner. But it was not
until we approached the station from which we were
to take the train back to New York that he showed
the least sign of animation. "What's the matter, Bill?"
I asked. "I thought you'd like to see some real country." His answer was: "Kunn'l, how kin you expeck
me to appreciate the glories of nature when you walk
me over a mountain like that an' I got new shoes on?"
Then he stood on one foot and on the other, caressing
each aching member for a second or two, and smiled
with bashful knowingness so like him.

It was one of his whimsical amusements, I must say
here, to speak in a kind of country style of English,
as though the English language were an instrument
he handled with hesitant unfamiliarity. Thus it happened that a woman who had written to him about
his stories and asked if her "lady friend" and she might
meet him, informed him afterward: "You mortified me
nearly to death, you talked so ungrammatical."

To return to his first day in New York, on which
for the only time he evinced a shade of astonishment
or bewilderment, although he always humorously pro-
fessed his sense of insecurity as an outlander in the
big town, Gilman Hall and I tried to interest him in
noticing Morgan Robertson, who was passing near the
corner of Sixth Avenue and Twenty-third Street,
princely dressed in a frock coat and top hat. It was
our intention to have him meet fellow-craftsmen from
the beginning. In his own way he came to know Morgan Robertson later, but that day he had eyes only
for the elevated railroad, and gazing at it, inquired of
us, so that we doubted his seriousness, why people were
not afraid to ride on such trains, as they might so

SOME "DISCOVERERS" OF O. HENRY

William Johnston   *Gilman Hall*

Peyton Steger   *Richard Duffy*

easily fall into the street. Years later a train did
partly fall off the track, it will be recalled, through a
confusion of signals at Fifty-third Street and Ninth
Avenue. He was not surprised, he told me, which
made me remember that in our many roamings about
town he would always ride in a surface car or the subway, no matter what distance we had to go.

We never knew just where he stopped the first night
in New York, beyond his statement that it was at a
hotel not far from the ferry in a neighborhood of so
much noise that he had not been able to sleep. I suppose we were voluminous with suggestions as to where
he might care to live, because we felt we had some
knowledge of the subject of board and lodging, and
because he was the kind of man you'd give your best
hat to on short acquaintance, if he needed a hat,—but
also he was the kind of man who would get a hat for
himself. [On this point Mr. Duffy's evidence differs
from the evidence presented by Roy Norton. See page
302.] Within about twenty-four hours he called at
the office again to say that he had taken a large room
in a French table d'hôte hotel in Twenty-fourth Street,
between Broadway and Sixth Avenue. Moreover,
he brought us a story. In those days he was very pro-
lific. He wrote not only stories, but occasional skits
and light verse. In a single number of *Ainslee's*, as I
remember, we had three short stories of his, one of
which was signed O. Henry, and the other two with
other pseudonyms. Of the latter, "While the Auto
Waits" (signed James L. Bliss), was picked out by
several newspapers as an unusually clever short story.
But as O. Henry he naturally appeared most frequently, as frequently as monthly publication allows,
for to my best recollection, of the many stories we saw
of his, there were only three about which we said to him
we would rather have another instead. One of these is
a variation on the legend of the Wandering Jew, the

main personage of which is called Mike O'Bader. The
second is laid in New Orleans and is the phantasy of
a man under the influence of absinthe, abounding in
rhetorical coloring as gorgeous, almost, as de Quincey,
but wholly obscured or outblazoned as to story by
its color. The third pictured a scion of Louisiana's
seigneur days, living "remote, unfriended and alone"
in a country mansion of faded splendor; and this story
was published in a magazine that I believe is no longer
in print. The Wandering Jew story may be read in
his collected works, but I don't know what has become
of the weird New Orleans phantasy, in which there
was something of Edgar Allan Poe and Lafcadio
Hearn. . . .

He continued to live in West Twenty-fourth Street,
although the place had no particular fascination for
him. We used to see him every other day or so, at
luncheon, at dinner, or in the evening. Various magazine editors began to look up O. Henry, which was a
job somewhat akin to tracing a lost person. While
his work was coming under general notice rapidly, he
made no effort to push himself into general acquaintance. He was not unsociable, but a man that liked
a few friends round him and dreaded and avoided a
so-called party as he did a crowd in the subway.

Thus it happened that while his name had become
talked about in magazine circles, there were not many
who knew him; and he had been living here for perhaps
half a year when an editor came to me, saying with
some satisfaction that he had discovered who this elusive
newcoming story-writer was and where he could be
found. O. Henry was an undergraduate at a certain
university, he said, naming it. The man was amazed
when I told him that O. Henry had left my office only
half an hour before, that he could be found at his room
in West Twenty-fourth Street, and that to the best
of our knowledge he had never laid eyes on the particu-

lar college mentioned. Later it transpired that when
O. Henry's stories made their first stir at the college,
a young man foolishly took the credit of their authorship in gossip among his acquaintances, and, before
he could judge whither his prank or weakness would
lead, he received a letter from a magazine of the first
rank asking him to contribute. The hoax, so to describe it, was promptly shattered. O. Henry was un-
concerned, except to caution us with a smile, to be sure
and send all O. Henry cheques to him.

When Porter undertook his contract with the *World*
he moved to have more room and more comfortable surroundings for the new job. But he did not move far,
no farther than across Madison Square, in East
Twenty-fourth Street, to a house near Fourth Avenue.
Across the street stood the Metropolitan Building, although it was not so vast then. He had a bedroom and
sitting room at the rear of the parlor floor with a
window that looked out on a typical New York yard,
boasting one ailanthus tree frowned upon by time-
stained walls of other houses. More and more men began to seek him out, and he was glad to see them, for
a good deal of loneliness enters into the life of a man
who writes fiction during the better part of the day.
Here it was that he received a visit one day from a
stranger, who announced that he was a business man,
but had decided to change his line. He meant to write
stories, and having read several of O. Henry's, he was
convinced that kind of story would be the best paying
proposition. O. Henry liked the man offhand, but he
could not help being amused at his attitude toward a
"literary career." I asked what advice he gave the
visitor and he answered: "I told him to go ahead!"
The sequel no doubt O. Henry thoroughly enjoyed, for
within a few years the stranger had become a best-
seller.

O. Henry remained only for a few weeks in these

lodgings, having a dozen reasons for moving besides the fact that he had more money. Besides, the man of the house did most of the housework, he told me, and there were so many such men in New York, it was not necessary to live under the same roof to have the pleasure of their acquaintance. (Read "Ulysses and the Dog-man" if you wish to see him in hot earnest on this subject.) I asked what business the lady of the house was in, and he explained that she dealt with the incoming and outgoing guests, and she seemed to have enough to do, because he himself was apparently the only lodger that had ever made even a pretense at permanency. While here he often went to breakfast at a restaurant on Fourth Avenue and Twenty-third Street, where he had a favorite waiter. The waiter had seen better restaurants inside and out, and I have no doubt that O. Henry's inclination to tip extravagantly recalled better days. The result was that the waiter took him in charge, so no matter what O. Henry selected from the bill of fare, he would lean over and murmur: "Don't take that to-day, sir. The only thing they've got this morning that's fit to eat is ———," and he would mention the one hope O. Henry had for breakfast.

His next abiding place was at 55 Irving Place. Here he had almost the entire parlor floor with a window large as a store front, opening only at the sides in long panels. At either side of these panels he would sit for hours watching the world go by along the street, not gazing idly, but noting men and women with penetrating eyes, making guesses at what they did for a living, and what fun they got out of it when they had earned it.

He was a man you could sit with a long while and feel no necessity for talking; but every so often a passerby would evoke a remark from him that converted an iota of humanity into the embryo of a story. Although

he spoke hardly ever to any one in the house except
the people who managed it, he had the lodgers all
ticketed in his mind. He was friendly but distant with
persons of the neighborhood he was bound to meet
regularly, because he lived so long there, and I have
often thought he must have persisted as a mysterious
man to them simply because he was so far from being
communicative. It amused him to observe how curious
people are, especially the supposed hustling New
Yorker who has no room for any thought beyond his
own affairs, and he hits the type off, it will be remembered, in the story called "A Comedy in Rubber."
Any one who endeavored to question him about himself would learn very little, especially if he felt he
was being examined as a "literary" exhibit; although,
when he was in the humor, he would give you glimpses
of his life in Greensboro and on the ranch to which
he had gone as a young man, because he had friends
there and because he was said to be delicate in the
chest. He would never, however, tell you "the story
of his life," but merely let you see some one or some
happening in those days gone by that might fit in well
with the present moment, for always he lived emphatically in the present, not looking back to yesterday,
nor very far ahead toward to-morrow. For instance,
I first heard of a doctor in Greensboro, who was his
uncle, I believe, and something of a character to
O. Henry at least, when I inquired about a story he
was writing. Then he told me of the doctor, who when
asked about any of his patients, how they, Mr. Soandso or Mrs. Soandso, was getting along, would invariably reply with omniscience, "Oh, Mrs. Soandso
is progressing." But as O. Henry said, "He never
explained which way the patient was progressing,
toward better or worse." It was in Greensboro naturally that he began to have an interest in books, and
I recall among those he used to mention as having read

at the time, that one night he spoke to me of a copy-book of poems written by his mother. He spoke with shy reverence about the poems, which he no doubt remembered, but he did not speak of them particularly. They were merely poems, written by her in her own hand, and as a young man they had come to him.

It was seldom, as I have said, that you found him harking back. He was much more likely to tell you of something that had happened at the last restaurant he dined in or in the house where he lived. There was a maid-servant there, Lena, who could provide him a laugh two or three times a week. When he wrote late at night, as he did often, he slept late in the morning. Lena, who had not got past Ellis Island so very long before, would have a half a day's work done by half past nine or ten o'clock. She would knock at the door and hearing no response would open it with her pass key. Entering, Lena would goose-step to the farthest corner of the room, being so far in it that she could get no farther except by going out through the window into the street. O. Henry's head would be lifted from the pillow in his bed at the rear of the suite. When she heard him stirring, she would call out in a shrill voice attempting to purr: "May I come in, Mister Pawduh?"

He would tell her that she couldn't come in unless she went out first; and out she'd go. While Lena lasted she repeated her performance often, so that it got to be a catch phrase with us when taking something without asking permission, to say, "May I come in, Mister Pawduh?"

Richard Duffy's memories carry on through the later years. Something more of his reminiscences will be told in pages to come. But for the moment he must step aside to make way for the stories of other friends and discoverers.

XIII

BOB DAVIS RECALLS: BEING PERSONAL
FLASHLIGHTS

All the honey of life was waiting in the comb in the hive of the
world for Prince Michael, of the Electorate of Valleluna.
The Caliph, Cupid, and the Clock

MY first meeting with Sydney Porter, following his
arrival in New York whither he had been lured
by Gilman Hall and Richard Duffy, occurred on the
date of July 3, 1903, on the fourth floor of the Hotel
Marty.

Very much in the same manner that Henry M. Stan-
ley was shipped over to Africa by James Gordon
Bennett, the elder, to locate Dr. Livingstone, I was
sent uptown by F. L. H. Noble, Managing Editor of
the *Sunday World*, to find O. Henry, whose exact whereabouts were unknown. Neither Mr. Duffy nor Mr.
Hall, or any one else for that matter, seemed to be
familiar with Porter's hide-out, beyond the somewhat
indefinite rumor that he lived "somewhere over a restaurant" in the neighborhood of Madison Square,
hence, Twenty-fourth Street, which was the center of
the table d'hôte district—with lodgings.

"Wherever he may be," said Noble, "your assignment is to dig the gentleman out and make arrangements for him to write introductions to *Sunday World*
specials. We will supply him with a full set of proofs
of the various features. His job is to prepare for each

one, whatever sort of a preface, whimsical, philosophical or serious, as he deems proper. Offer him forty dollars a week. If he balks jump to fifty dollars. The third and last call is sixty dollars."

Accordingly I began a complete survey of every structure that seemed to open to the transient populace in the specified neighborhood. Through the courtesy of landlords and the discourtesy of waiters, I combed four buildings, without results. The fifth happened to be the Marty. The proprietor was French. I asked him if O. Henry or Sydney Porter occupied a room in his hospitable inn. Neither name seemed to mean anything to him. He did, however, suggest that I might go through the house and investigate.

I began on the top floor. None of the tenants was in. On the next floor, that is to say, the fourth, from hall bedroom No. 7, in response to my bombardment, I received a cheerful invitation to enter. It was a very small room opening on the usual air shaft. In spite of the dim light I was able to make out a rather corpulent figure in his shirt sleeves and with his suspenders down, seated beside a washstand upon which reposed a huge bowl containing perhaps five pounds of cracked ice in which nestled a half dozen fine Bartlett pears. The fat man arose with considerable dignity and bowed.

"Come in, mister," said he.

I entered and closed the door.

"I am looking for Sydney Porter," said I, "otherwise, O. Henry."

"I am both," he replied. "Here's a chair. Have some fruit. It is nice and cool. I suffer like hell from the heat. What can I do for you?"

"I have a proposition to make."

He fixed his blue eyes upon me, wiped the perspiration from his brow, and cupped his left ear with his hand. There was something about his demeanor that suggested the utter absurdity of bargaining.

"In fact, I have three propositions," I continued. "I will make the last one first."

I took two bites out of a Bartlett for purposes of concentration and then fired the shot:

"The New York *World* authorizes me to offer you sixty dollars a week for introductions varying from three hundred to seven hundred words in length, as leads to special features appearing in the Sunday issue."

"If this last proposition is the best," said he, gazing out of the air shaft much in the manner of the Prisoner of Chillon catching a glimpse of daylight, "you needn't make the other two; I accept your proposition. Moreover, mister, you can have the balance of the pears."

The whole transaction was completed in less than five minutes. To commemorate the operation, Porter hastily got into his coat and we withdrew to the basement of the Marty where, in spite of the humidity, we had a full course French dinner including a quart of imported wine. The banquet lasted until 3 P.M.

Within the next few days I turned over to him proofs of six or eight *Sunday World* stories, to which he wrote brilliant introductions. The following week he left the Marty and took an apartment at 55 Irving Place. Thereafter the proofs were sent to him once a week and returned to the office within twenty-four hours. Some of the material failed to inspire. He said that he would

rather not prepare an introduction to anything that
did not interest him. This temperamental display,
however, was not frequent. The arrangement lasted
several months.

Noble subsequently retired from the editorship of
the *Sunday World* and was succeeded by the late
Colonel Caleb Van Hamm.

"Who is this man Porter?" asked the new editor.
I explained that he was one of Noble's selections, and
that his rate was sixty dollars a week for such introductions as were required for Sunday features.

Van Hamm uttered one brilliant, laconic sentence:
"Can him."

As gently as possible I conveyed to O. Henry the information that his introductions were unsatisfactory.
He seemed to be very much pleased, although he later
made another connection with the *Evening World*, in
the columns of which appeared some of his best short
fiction.

The following year I came to the fiction editorship
of the Frank A. Munsey publications and made a five-
year contract for first reading of his entire output.

In the course of this relationship we carried on a
voluminous correspondence and saw each other frequently.

Elsewhere will be found many letters now printed
for the first time and a few of his adroit *billets-doux*
dealing with the gentle art of securing funds to tide
him over temporary embarrassments. He was the
nimblest-witted borrower I ever met, but in justice I
must say that at the time of his death he had cleaned

F. L. H. NOBLE

*The Sunday editor of "The World" who sent Bob Davis out,
in July, 1903, to find O. Henry*

the slate of all obligations, and went to Olympus, so far as I was concerned, absolutely solvent.

Porter was a procrastinator in more ways than one. A certain "big story" that he once promised to deliver on a specified date, did not turn up.

I called upon him at his Waverly Place address and in a casual way inquired as to the progress of the manuscript.

"Going fine! Got a great start. I could sit down any time and finish it."

"Can I read the first page?"

"Certainly, Colonel, here's the manuscript."

He tossed over a sheaf of yellow manila paper, the first page of which contained the numeral 1, and the title. Before I had time to expostulate, he gently took the sheaf from my hand and continued:

"And what's more, I can go right on with this story, without the least effort. You have already seen page one. Now here's the second page."

With marvelous deliberation he wrote "page 2" on the next sheet.

"And so on. Page 3, 4, 5. I think I shall stop here, if you don't mind; and rest."

He was a childlike individual, absolutely without guile, and at times utterly helpless. I always had the feeling that had he possessed the slightest power of resistance, he would be alive to-day, and that the illness to which he surrendered would have been defeated.

During seven succeeding years, the most productive of his lifetime, I was privileged to see him emerge from obscurity and take his place as the foremost interpreter of the short story in the English-speaking world. I take this opportunity to scotch the suggestion, frequently made by well-intentioned persons, that I was in any way, even remotely, responsible for his progress in letters. Accident threw us together in the relationship of author and editor, out of which grew an agreeable alliance based upon mutual likes and dislikes.

Had I known in the beginning that I was in after years to play a Boswellian rôle to this man, I should in all probability have made elaborate notes to be stored away against the time that is now. Had I even suspected that all he thought and said, his manner, his methods, his whole personality, was to become manna for posterity, these fugitive observations would have been completed, more intimate in detail and perforce better reading. However, I take consolation in the fact that details which I am able to summon from recollection are in some particulars equally interesting with elaborate biography more deliberately planned.

During his lifetime Porter fled from publicity like mist before the gale. He shrank from the extended hands of strangers; blushed at spoken approval and avoided conversations about himself. If alive to-day, and called upon to view a bookshelf containing the works of O. Henry, he would burst into Homeric laughter and leave the room.

The wealth of material already collected and published concerning the Caliph of Bagdad is almost beyond classification, but there will always remain an insatiable demand for new matter bearing upon his life, letters and tribulations. If the Caliph were alive I would not put pen to paper concerning him, lest in that rich southern voice he revile me for my impudence.

He desired only to be let alone; to compile his whimsical philosophies for the entertainment of those whom he hoped ever to keep at a distance.

What I here offer is but one man's contribution to those remote days before the glamour crossed his threshold and the editors like gold brokers on the stock exchange held up a finger to indicate that they would trade at any terms. I knew him in the days when over the top of the half-drawn window shade, which worked upward from the bottom, he peered out to determine whether the man on the stairs was a customer or a collector; when the question of his survival in the market of letters was under consideration; when he needed money, extra money—more money than there was—advance money; nothing but money. I saw him when his spirits were high, when the medium that he groped for seemed to be in his grasp, when his technique was beginning to take shape. He was like a man in hiding, with the door locked against interruption. Professionally we were thrown constantly together, but that did not deter us from country sports and city pastimes. There was a pub over on East Fifty-third Street that held out an amber lure, a German restaurant in Hoboken that the Eighteenth Amendment subsequently destroyed; a stube on East Seventeenth Street, where pigs' knuckles reached a state of perfection rarely attained by pork products. The Bowery had its magnetic attraction, while Union Square and the old Ashland House frequently beckoned.

It was on these excursions and across the deal table where he wrote his fiction that we came close to each other. Even so, no living man had his whole confidence.

Whosoever knew the inside story of Bill Porter's life
was present when it was unfolding—on the spot, so to
speak, an eye-witness. From the Caliph's own lips
little fell. He had a genius for taciturnity and a profound admiration for silence. Not concerning himself,
or any other, was he inclined to hold forth. When I
look back upon those seven years, which were not without certain confidences, I now come to the realization
that Sydney Porter was an uncommunicative man, and
that I was not an especially observant one. Either
that or the stupendous importance of the rôle he was
to play in letters did not impress itself upon my consciousness. Moreover I am of the conviction, from the
meager records handed down, that his other contemporaries were equally in the dark.

In truth the Caliph slipped through his "Little Old
Bagdad on the Subway," leaving but few tangible
souvenirs of his reign. How many of the tales that
were born of O. Henry exist in the original? Not a
dozen I should say. We have various letters, a sheaf
of penciled pages, some sketches, numberless endorsed
checks and some touching appeals to "hurry up with
the cash." But in comparison with the great mass he
turned out in typewritten and long-hand manuscripts
—nothing. Evidently we did not know that the Caliph
of Bagdad had arrived until after his departure. Pos-
sessing none of the manners of royalty ourselves, how
could we recognize the proximity of a king?

In addressing me, both by word of mouth and in
correspondence, he chose the terms "Mr. Man," "Bill,"
"Colonel," "Major" and, when making an appeal for
the sinews, "General," varying the form by injecting

the salutation common to his southern training of "You All." He had the habit of bestowing military titles upon his intimates, seldom addressing any one by his name. He was of soft voice and laughing eyes, with a note of confidence thrown in for effect. If asked for the time he would respond in the manner of one who was disclosing the name of the man who struck Billy Patterson. All of his conversations were prefaced with the intimation that he had decided to reveal something not heretofore communicated to living man. Throughout his speech ran a thread of earnestness, a suggestion that he had put some thought on the subject, even though the information imparted were trivial. It was his habit to take life lightly, to laugh at grandeur and scoff at pride. Ill fortune, of which he had much, left no rancor in his heart. Retiring by nature, he made the most of any situation in which he found himself a part. When thrown among his fellows he gave little but absorbed much. Without appearing to be the least bit concerned about what was going on, he heard and saw everything. Among strangers, where he was unidentified he was quite garrulous, leading the conversation, shaping the babble to his own ends.

In him the down-and-outer with whom he made speech found a kindred soul; the great and near-great wondered how a man could be so dumb and write so entertainingly. Yet it was difficult to find a subject upon which he had not some worth-while information. There were no books commonly regarded as essential to a course of good reading that he had not swallowed whole. The hidden gems of the classics were not concealed from him and the mysteries of chemistry and mathematics were at his tongue's tip. Beneath that mask of indifference was a wisdom that is revealed only in his works. What he did not actually experience, he felt, when called upon to feel it. Turn the pages of his books, pause in the meshes of his dialogue, observe his understanding of life.

One balmy summer day Porter came into my office and inquired as to what I knew about deep-sea angling.

"Everything there is to know," I announced in a firm, ringing voice and without hesitation, indecision being fatal when a fishing trip is under consideration.

"Got plenty of rods, reels and lines?" he asked.

"Nothing but."

He began to count upon his fingers.

"And kin you get some bait?"

"Clams, shedders and blood worms," I enumerated while he kept tally.

"Boat and guide, mister?" His blue eyes were filled with anxiety.

"The best. And also a lunch basket packed with all the—"

"That will do, kind sir. You have said enough; and more than I had the right to expect," he announced. "As for me, I will furnish something that up to now has been overlooked. I refer to the broad, bounding Atlantic Ocean. That is my contribution. When do we push off in the lugger?"

"Make it Friday next," said I. "We start from Port Washington, Long Island, drift down the bay on the outgoing tide, round Sand's Point, anchor off

Howard Gould's estate and begin to fish on the flow."

"With real hooks?" was the childlike query.

At a water-front restaurant in Port Washington we found a competent boatman and an incompetent boat. While waiting for the bait we were driven out into the open by the flies. They swarmed over the Caliph, driving him frantic.

"Which one of these do you suppose it is that recognized me?" he asked petulantly.

We got away finally and drifted out on an oily tide through a procession of seaweed strewn with flotsam and jetsam. The boatman, unaware of the precious cargo he had on board, began to string the author, but quit when O. Henry asked him if a soft-shelled clam put up a good fight when taken on an artificial fly.

We followed the ebb until it flattened, and threw out the anchor. A pitiless sun took up the work of parboiling us, but Porter, who was of a florid complexion and thin-skinned, cooked first and became as pink as a boiled lobster.

The fishing was atrocious and the small fry swiped bait as fast as we could put it on the hooks. Three weary hours resulted in two flounders and four sea robins.

"Let's put the lugger on Mr. Gould's beach," suggested Porter, "and bask in the predatory atmosphere of inherited wealth. He can't do any more than ask us in to lunch. Do you reckon he would like to have both flounders, or do you want to keep yours?"

The landing was made near three boathouses connected by the boardwalk to the broad lawn. In the welcome shade of these structures we sprawled on the yellow sand and made overtures to the lunch basket. A gentle breeze blowing seaward from the Gould garden brought the perfume of flowers and wet grass. Under its influence O. Henry turned to philosophizing until finally his thoughts led to the salability of the printed word.

"For example, here is a notebook," said he, taking the sheaf from his coat pocket. "It contains a dozen pages of blank paper. With a lead pencil I write on these several sheets a tale three or four thousand words in length. You buy the story and print it in one of the magazines you edit. If it is a good tale it gets into a book, or perhaps is dramatized and put on the stage. Very well; that's the beginning that has to do with its earning power. I get royalties on the volume, the serial rights, the drama and maybe some day sell it for a motion picture. It goes on and on reaping profit and yet it is never anything but the figment of my imagination converted into words. Is that clear?"

He paused and ran a stream of sand through his hands one above the other like an hour glass, his eyes searching the distant horizons. "It emanates from my mind and but for the presence of the printed name of the writer would lose its identity. But it exists; survives the years."

Another stream of sand flowed from hand to hand and trickled away.

"Now I have a daughter," he continued after a long pause, "a child of my own flesh and blood, bone of my bone. She looks and acts like me. She is my most precious possession. She is a material, breathing entity; another me. In three score years and ten, according to the Biblical injunction, she will return to the earth, and that will be the absolute last of Margaret Porter, daughter of O. Henry. But my written words set down methodically, laboriously on these sheets of white paper, fugitive reflections at best, live on. Queer, isn't it? Flesh: Mortal. Thought: Immortal."

Comment on my part seemed out of place. He fussed about in the yellow sand and uncovered a tortoise shell hairpin from which the luster had faded.

"Here's another story," was his comment. "Who owns it? Lady in waiting or lady in wading? Maid or mistress? White or black? May be celluloid. . . . Touch a match to it. . . . It if blows up——"

I took the object from his plump fingers and placed it in my pocket. That hairpin is still in my possession. In a moment his volatile imagination took him out to sea again. Rising and dusting his hands, he walked down to the boat.

"Your friend seems to be a kind of a nut," remarked the boatman, clamping his teeth on a slab of chewing tobacco. "What's his name?"

"O. Henry," I replied with emphasis.

Something seemed to struggle for exit from the fisherman's mind. "O—O—O—! Henry. I heard my daughter speakin' about him. One of them writin' men. Mebby all right at that. He's a-callin' us."

The author of "The Trimmed Lamp"—and others —wanted to go home. Clumsily but with a certain genuine consideration the bayman folded up his coat, fashioned in the stern a soft seat for his odd passenger, and placed an old tarpaulin over the sunburned hands. That was for his daughter's sake, perhaps. Nevertheless. . . .

"The thing I like most about this place," said the parboiled Porter at the depot, "is the railroad that runs out of it toward Manhattan. Do you suppose there is room in the ice cooler for both of my hands at once?"

One morning as I was coming out of the Broadway exit of the Flatiron Building I caught sight of O. Henry emerging from Madison Square. Almost at the same moment, out of the corner of my eye, I saw coming up Broadway the erect but slightly limping form of Captain Jack Crawford, "The Poet Scout." His hair was free in the breeze and rippled away from under his broad sombrero. O. Henry, concealed under a hard derby, moved among the people with engaging modesty. Everybody saw Jack Crawford. Nobody save myself saw Bill Porter.

Both men came within range of my hail at the same time. Knowing Crawford since my sixth year, having met him on the plains in the sitting-room of my father's Nebraska home at Brownville on the Missouri, and being mixed up with Porter in the so-called writing game, I brought them together with an introduction.

"Captain Jack Crawford," said O. Henry, with that glow of pride that all Southerners put into their speech when looking a soldier in the eye, "to take your deadly right hand in my trembling grasp means something in this life."

"O. Henry," retorted the gallant scout, "you have brought enough sunshine into the cañons of this accursed metropolis to justify the installation of your statue in yonder square. You have made laughter ring through the world and with your magic touched the heart of mankind. I have met during the sixty years of my life the bravest men in whom God has planted the breath of life, but you, O. Henry, are the kindliest. There is nothing that I would not gladly do for you."

"Captain Crawford," said Porter, with a wistful look in his blue eyes, "could you teach me to twirl a six-shooter, that is, to spin it on my trigger finger so that at the right moment, while apparently surrendering the weapon to an enemy, I could blow his entire digestive apparatus through his backbone?"

"It takes a lifetime to do that," said the scout, "but I'll be happy to instruct you any time or any place."

I steered the potential assassins down the street to the old Continental Hotel and into those leather cushions that were part of the barroom. "Give Jack Crawford a list of the editors you want killed," I said to Porter, "and let the waiter have the order."

"I don't want 'em killed," spoke up the Caliph, "—just crippled and left to suffer. Besides, there is only one vital spot in an editor, though nobody knows where that is."

"Not even the editor himself," added the Poet Scout, whose wares had been moving in and out of magazine offices for many years. "Authorship is my meat, but I couldn't read or write until I was fifteen.

A Sister of Charity taught me the alphabet and gave
me some simple books, which I took to war with me.
After the Rebellion I went West and served as a Government scout under General Crook in the Indian campaigns. It was in Nebraska that I met Bob's father,
a missionary. He helped me finish my education.
During the Apache campaign I carried telegrams by
pony for the New York *Herald*. Operated for Miles,
Howard and others in the Sitting Bull campaign—"

"When did you take up poetry?" asked Porter,
pushing back the remains of a steak.

"I was always a poet," replied the old Indian fighter.
"I have always been perfectly at home with poetry, as
far back as I can remember. For example, just listen
to this: 'Where the Hand of God Is Seen.'"

Crawford began rather quietly, but on the third
verse left his seat and shook out his locks. Jack had
elocutionary gifts and a belief in his own poetry.

"I have memorized every poem I ever wrote, something over a hundred and fifty. Listen to this: 'The
Sunshine Trail.' I cover the whole of life in these
lines and no man can hear them without applying their
lesson to himself." He rolled it out with all the de-
clamatory tricks at his command. "And I want you
to keep in mind that not a drop of alcohol ever crossed
my lips. I'm a teetotaler. The Lord never made a
tongue that needed fire-water."

"What could old Captain Jack do with poetry if
he got a slug of redeye under his belt?" asked O. Henry
aside while the Injun fighter was reciting a thunderous
epic to the wild and free life of the border. At this

O. HENRY CARICATURES ONE OF HIS BIOGRAPHERS

*An artistic assault on Robert H. Davis made by Sydney Porter
at a baseball game in Brooklyn in 1903*

juncture on the program the Poet Scout had all the waiters stacked up against the wall and O. Henry backed into the corner. He piled up poetry with no intimation of fatigue. Poem after poem gushed from his lips, his fine voice vibrating under the spell of his elocution. Once he sat down and somebody began to applaud. Jack took the call and, throwing his napkin on the floor, went back again.

To cap the climax, Crawford introduced O. Henry to the audience and dragged the blushing genius to his feet. It was perhaps the most embarrassing moment in the career of Sydney Porter and made him mob-shy the rest of his life. The thing that astonished both of us was Crawford's familiarity with Porter's entire list of short stories. Jack named twenty of them and was on the point of retelling each separate plot when the proprietor of the Continental Hotel passed me the high sign and we took the air.

It was perhaps just as well, for by that time the Prince of Story Tellers was about all in, while the Poet Scout had hardly begun.

Out in the street, after he had shaken hands for at least twenty minutes, I separated the teetotaler from his new-found friend and opened up the traffic of the town. Pointing O. Henry in the direction of his Waverly Place hangout, I gave him a gentle shove and led Crawford away.

"That's a fine young man," remarked Jack, "and I'll make it my business to see more of him. What's his address?"

After a week of silence I received from the exhausted Mr. Porter this note:

55 Irving Place, New York, Nov. 11, 1904.
DEAR BILL:
No. But I have bought a bottle of Hunyadi.
                              Yours as truly,
                         CAPTAIN CRACK JAWFORD
                         THE GO IT SPOUT

P.S.—D— the lunch. Noon grub puts me on the
blink. Don't you ever wander in the mead after sun-
down? Dodge the curfew some evening, and I will
prove my devotion.
                              PITTSFIELD SIS

XIV

FLASHLIGHTS IN CORRESPONDENCE

If we can earn a run (in life we call it success) we get back to
the home plate and sit upon a bench. If we are thrown out, we
walk back to the home plate—and sit upon a bench.
Society in Serge and Straw

O. HENRY, reflected in his own letters, is also
reflected in the letters that were written to
him; the letters of supplication, admonition, and reproach from suffering and anxious editors. The picture is often complete from one side of the correspondence. Between the lines one can read the suave,
evasive reply, and the probable suggestion that a little
further advance on the projected and promised story
would be highly gratifying.

O. Henry's connection with *Munsey's Magazine* extended over a period of nearly ten years, beginning
with the appearance of "A Blackjack Bargainer" in
1901, and ending with "A Technical Error," in the
issue for February, 1910, the last O. Henry story to
be published before his death. The close association
with the magazine, as has been told, began in 1904.
The story of that association is revealed in some of the
correspondence from the files. The omitted signatures
are of course those of Davis.

Friday, Sept. 30, 1904.

DEAR MAN:
It's just 4 o'clock P.M. I've had your letter about
ten minutes. Exhibit A, enclosed, shows its foreign

labels and wanderings. I'd admire to eat noon grub with you any day. Your habit of getting your invitations in three hours after the appointed time is extremely disconcordant to deglutition. The only mottoes I can give you to hang on the wall are these:

Munsey is the route of all eatables.

Bill can never dine with the waiter that has passed.

As you are the man with many engagements, you set some other day, and I'll joyfully be with you, if you'll address me in North America, proper street and No.

To show you that I ain't forgot you, how's this for a memory portrait of our dear Captain of the Sunday World ball team? [1]

Yourn constantly,
SYDNEY PORTER

October 15, 1904.

Sydney Porter Esq.
55 Irving Place, N.Y.C.
DEAR BILL:

I thought perhaps—well, never mind—you know what I mean.

Yours as before,

New York, Oct. 17, 1904.

Dʳ Mʳ Dˢ.

You know damwell that—but what's the use!

Yours unscathed,
WILHELMJ

P. S.—Still, I would say that I telephoned on Friday, but you were—

P. P. S.—Editor man been standing over me with Big Stick for copy. Same to-morrow. After that, why—

[1] Portrait facing page 216.

November 12, 1904.

Sydney Porter Esq.
55 Irving Place, N.Y.C.

DEAR BILL:

I had an idea that your appetite was better after sunset. But beef has been high, and all luxuries are up since Roosevelt was elected.

Your noonday appetite always delighted me.

Sometime this coming week we will gather by the river in the gloaming, and you can take your choice of rivers—either the East or the North.

The same as ever,

Thursday.

DEAR MR. BOBDAVIS:

Funny you wouldn't care if a fellow handed in his checks, whether they were good or not. I am taking two kind of dope out of the two boxes from old Doc Wildman a distinguished specialist on 94th St. And I rid up there in a Ridgway-Thayer automobile.

I am getting some good sleep of nights now, and feel like hitting out a story to-day. Much better. My trip never done me no good. But the dope is all right. I will send you in the story in days a very few.

Got $50 more up there you want to advance to a hypochondriac? Let it be in cash if so. I must sell a little part of my soul to buy some bread and sharlot rust.

I strike my forehead three times on the floor before Colonel Titherington, than whom the Flatiron holds none more worthy of being Second Cousin to the Moon and Brother-in-law to the Sidereal System. As for you, the fairest could not win me from your smiles.

If you ain't got the money let me know, and I will tackle the Philistines.

Continuously,

SYDNEY PORTER

P. S. Except the Christmas story I ain't done any work for the World nor nobody else.

December 9, 1904.

Mr. Sydney Porter,
55 Irving Place, N.Y.C.
DEAR BILL:

What is the prospect for receiving that story you began for us years and years ago?

You know I told the man who pays the bills that you had agreed to deliver the goods, whereat he became greatly concerned and showed much satisfaction. I told him the price and he kept his color. There is nothing left for you to do but produce the document.

Why are you so cold?

Yours,

DR. BILL:

Here she are. I reckon you or some intelligent person in the office can tell where the patches fit. If you don't like the new title say so. There are others.

Fulsomely,
WILLIE

February 24, 1905.

Sydney Porter Esq.
55 Irving Place, N.Y.C.
DEAR BILL:

It is important, desirable and necessary that you begin sending a wad of copy into this office.

Having left off secondary heads, all bars are down and there is no reason why you should not produce a tale fit to read ere the week is gone.

You will get this letter probably at 9 o'clock Saturday morning—that will give you until 4 o'clock to write 4000 words. How can they stop you.

Very sincerely yours,

March 1, 1905.

Sydney Porter Esq.
55 Irving Place, N.Y.C.
DEAR MR. PORTER:

COPY?

Yours respectfully,

Monday.

DEAR MISTER:
Would you put a tail on this kite for me again? She
will fly on the date advertised. Please send the cash
if you've got it on hand.
Say—the story will be brought to you by me on
WEDNESDAY. It will be an all right one. Maybe
on Tuesday if I get it copied.

Hoping &c. & yours truly,
SYDNEY PORTER

April 10, 1905.

Sydney Porter Esq.
55 Irving Place, N.Y.C.
MY DEAR BILL:
If the sun sets on Monday without—well, you know
the rest!

As ever,

DEAR PERSONAL BILL:
She will set without - - - - - - - come on with the
rest.

The Same,
S. P.

Excuse same paper—just up.

May 4, 1905.

Mr. Sydney Porter,
55 Irving Place, N.Y.C.
DEAR BILL:
We are still desirous.

Yours willingly,

N' York – Friday

Say – Bill!

Lend me
$15 'till Monday.
My banker is out
of town. Have
a couple of checks
coming in Monday.
Need that much

today. What?
Return on Monday
sure. In haste
Yours as ever
Sydney Porter
47 W. 24th
P.S. If it isn't convenient
I'll love you just the same

"OWING TO THE ABSENCE—"

*A sample of the importunate correspondence,
always in good humor, of which he was a
master*

Saturday.

DEAREST BILL:

Enclosed P. O. order for $25. Fact is,- er- that-that is to say-er-er-you know-I-er-er-well, I was-er-er-I mean-the-er-er-you know.

Hoping the explanation is entirely satisfactory, I remain

As ever thine
S. P.

May 19, 1905.

Sydney Porter Esq.
55 Irving Place, N.Y.C.

DEAR BILL:

This is for you if something in the nature of short fiction is not turned in to this magazine poco pronto.

Yours,

May 31, 1905.

Sydney Porter Esq.
55 Irving Place, N.Y.C.

MY DEAR PORTER:

If you don't come up to see me purty soon, I'll come down and drink up everything in your house, including the ink and the mucilage.

Are you sick?

Do you need help?

Are you in love?

Respectfully,

Saturday.

MON CHER BILL:

Can you raise the immediate goods for this, and once more rescue little Ruby from certain death?

The big story will be handed in Monday for you to try on the piano.

From next week I'll show you a story every week. I'm going to make some of the best special samples of 2,000 and 25,000 word stuff that's possible. That's the length that counts.

I am a story ahead at the World now.

I'm feeling fine, and hope these few lines will—say—don't forget to send the $25.

Don't do it if you refuse to do it.

Yours 's ever,
S. P.

June 13, 1905.

Sydney Porter Esq.
119 Fourth Ave., Pittsburgh, Pa.
MR. AND SIR:

Please convert the scrambled eggs into an omelet burned on one side, and ship it East by the first mail. Also, upon your return, come in and discuss the proposition of giving us a peek at some of the World stories you have been writing, as we would be mighty glad to have something along that line for the short story department—at the established rates that we have fixed between us.

I think you are losing a few honest dollars by not hauling a little closer to the wind which we are prepared to blow in your direction.

Let me know as soon as convenient when I can see you in the flesh.

Salaam twice, and yet again.

Thine,

DEAR UNCLE WM.:

Thanks
"<br>"<br>"

I will bring you the $50 in the morning.

Thanks

"

"

I am just typewriting the closing words of the other story. I will hand it to you in the morning *en personne* between 10 & 11.

Again thanks,

Your old

BILL

July 6, 1905.

Sydney Porter Esq.
55 Irving Place, N.Y.C.
MY DEAR PORTER:

We are all wondering up here what happens to have happened to you. Your letter from Pittsburgh over a month ago, stating that the goods were being unpacked and would be shipped shortly, looks like a joke.

Is there any chance of getting a manuscript out of you this week? Do you think I had better come down and cuss you a little to your face?

Please let me know what to expect, and whither we are drifting.

If you don't happen to be in when this message reaches your menage will you call me up on the 'phone later, and greatly oblige,

Yours as ever,

July 8, 1905.

Sydney Porter Esq.
55 Irving Place, N.Y.C.
MY DEAR BILL:

If you are not otherwise occupied, and feel in the mood, I will be pleased to take sufficient time off to-morrow to go with you down to Port Washington, and mingle with the Yeomanry. It will be a pleasant trip for both of us, particularly to you, as I am light and gay in the country.

Let me know by this boy whether or not you are next, and I'll get busy looking at the time tables, etc. If the idea appeals to you, why not 'phone me?

Ever and anon,

July 21, 1905.

Sydney Porter Esq.
55 Irving Place, N.Y.C.
HONORABLE O. HENRY:

I leave today for Maine. You will get a letter from me at the end of the week, stating that everything has been arranged for your recipe. And if you don't come, I will see that when you die you are buried at Port Washington overlooking the sea, as I am of the impression that you can observe as much under ground as you can on top of that section.

Sincerely,

August 15, 1905.

Sydney Porter Esq.
55 Irving Place, N.Y.C.
DEAR BILL:

Back from Maine. When can we converge at your shack? Are you busy turning out a story every ten days, as previously threatened?

Ever yours,

Monday.

DEAR BILL:

Herewith submitted one ms. Have another one ready to typewrite, which you can read to-morrow.

Give the full speed ahead signal and whoop 'em through, pro or con. Great business. The mill is grinding at the old gait.

Yours,
BILL 2ND

August 19, 1905.

Sydney Porter Esq.
55 Irving Place, N.Y.C.
MY DEAR MAJOR:

After reading "In Care of the Pilot," it is clear just why the same is still in your possession.

I hope to see you some day next week, but any reference to the subject will be met with violent physical resistance.

Why don't we go to the theater some evening, to some vaudeville performance, and hiss the actors?

Yours,

October 28, 1905.

Sydney Porter Esq.
55 Irving Place, N.Y.C.
DEAR BILL:

??????

Yours,

October 31, 1905.

Sydney Porter Esq.
55 Irving Place, N.Y.C.

Lie perfectly still and don't shake the bottle. Will call shortly—at the regular rates of $2.50 per visit.

November 13, 1905.

Sydney Porter Esq.
55 Irving Place, N.Y.C.
DEAR BILL:

If this here doc'ment, clipped from the World, ain't entirely rong, you must be pretty good. I lave it to you. Is there anything into it?

P. S. How's your pulse?

Sunday.

DEAR BILL:

I'm coming up to see you with the goods right away. I can't make no sociable calls until I am fixed. Send you some money to-morrow.

Adoo till then.

Yes, slow but still,

BILL

November 20, 1905.

DEAR O. HENRY:

Your selection was a winner, except that we have not $100. in cash in the office. I should think, however, that you can easily cash this check with your grocer, manicurist, barber or florist. We could easily have fixed it for you at the bank had it not been after three o'clock. Or, if you do not raise the money by ten o'clock to-morrow, let us know, and we will arrange it for you.

Yours very truly,

November 20, 1905.

Sydney Porter Esq.
55 Irving Place, N.Y.C.

DEAR BILL:

Go to the New Paltz with the firm determination to do the best you can, and remember the old adage "Lips that touch liquor shall never touch mine." Them Paltz girls is pretty particular you know.

I see Ainslee's makes the announcement that they are going to hurl you at the American public in 1906, that your stories are "marvels of literary excellence" and that you stand "without a rival." All right. Let us see some of them.

You never come to the wrong man when you come to me, no matter what you want.

The Same,

Here is one of those enigmatical letters typical of the man and his whimsical humor:

Friday.

MY OWN LUCILLE:

I should say about Monday or Tuesday next week or any other day thereabouts that conforms to your convenience.

Indeed the Child Slaves appeal to me immensely, though they don't get anything. I should admire exceedingly for to help strike off their shackles. Count me in and on and up against it with you.

Paralyzed be the hand that refuses to bestow a kindly wink upon these little ones.

Yours to the last exit,
S. P. (C. C.)

December 12, 1905.

Mr. Sydney Porter,
New Paltz, Ulster County—N.Y.

MY DEAR BILL:

Everybody's, McClure's, New York World—Munsey next, Yes?

Yours,

January 10, 1906.

Sydney Porter Esq.
55 Irving Place, N.Y.C.

DEAR BILL:—O'HENRY:—SIDNEY PORTER, ET AL.:

Is there anything doing in your career of unchecked crime that I can select out and use in a high class magazine?

Delicacy forbids my appealing in a loud voice—so this is merely a hint.

More anon.

January 22, 1906.

Sydney Porter Esq.
55 Irving Place, N.Y.C.
DEAR BILL:

"It's a long time"—said the Governor of North Carolina to the Governor of South Carolina.

Yours,

Feby. 2d, 1906.

MY DEAR MR. DAVIS: (ain't that formal?)

It was my intention not to approach you again without the goods; but it is calorified atmosphere once more for yours.

Whereas Justus Files Mormon or any other of the white lights could take a barge for Europe for a month's rest on being proven paretic, I, having no v.m.o.s. (visible means of support) have had to continue treading the winepress, though the exudation of the real juices has been so that you could scarcely notice it at all. If I were the Waterworks Commissioner of the Pierian Spring I could guarantee a flow of the negotiable Croton; but I ain't.

I have sat or sot at my desk day after night, and, as Colonel J. W. Riley says, haven't been able to think of a damn word. Perhaps you may have noticed that the columns of the WORLD have been Ohenryless. You would also discover, should you make inquiries, that no magazine, magazines or imitations thereof have received a line of ms. from me that puts the slightest crimp in our arrangement. I have explained so many times the cause of my protracted drought, that it would weary you for me to repeat them.

I've got a scheme in sight whereby I can at least clear up all financial obligations the first of next week, anyhow; and that will help some.

Yours as ever,
SYDNEY PORTER

P. S. Why in the h——l pussonally don't you ask me
out to eat? Sometimes I don't have enough. Bobda-
visically you shall forever bloom, an amaranth in my
heart. Also I kotow three times to Datto Titherington, whom I cherish fondly. I don't care how much
you abuse me professionally. I am going to put everything under one roof next week.

Semper yours,
S. P.

April 16, 1906.

Sydney Porter Esq.
55 Irving Place, N.Y.C.
MY DEAR BILL:

That fling at the ten-cent magazines in yesterday's
World will cost you dear.

It looks like bloodshed to me.

May 21, 1906.

Sydney Porter Esq.
55 Irving Place, N.Y.C.
MY DEAR BILL:

We are going to run your story, "A Man for a
Man" in the August number, with a very fine, five-color
picture for a frontispiece.

In the same issue we have another story entitled "A
Man from Hong Kong," which is very near to your
title,—that is to say, half of it is.

Do you think you could change "A Man for a Man"?
You need not change him into a lady, but alter it so
the "Man from Hong Kong" and your story don't
seem to sound alike. Of course they don't read alike.

"The Ethics of Pig" has just arrived. It is a beaut
and gets the money tomorrow. It is the best graft
story you ever wrote.

Ever yours,

May 22, 1906.

Sydney Porter Esq.
55 Irving Place, N.Y.C.
DEAR BILL:

Knowing the proximity of poverty in all its phases, I send your check by this messenger, who is dressed especially for the occasion. Please take his number, you might like to see him again.

When am I to get a look at that other story?

Titherington has gone to England for six weeks. Therefore you can sit around here and talk to me in bad English without hurting anyone's feelings.

Always sincerely yours,

Friday.

Listen to the voice of business, with personal regards undiminished, relegated to one side.

I've been writing nothing for a month on account of having no abiding place in which I could work.

And I've got to move from here in 3 or 4 days because Gilman Hall is coming back to town.

I've got to have some money—some to send home and some for expenses. I'm not asking "Munsey's" for it (still less you personally) but I'm going to raise $250 to-day sure. If your magazine doesn't care to advance it I'll have to get it somewhere else, which I won't have the slightest trouble in doing.

Of course I'll have to abandon short story work to do it; but it's a case of "must." I'll have to go up town and make arrangement for a serial right away.

Dropping the short stories will be a big set-back for me, but I've got to have the money; and if your people object to investing it with me I've got to get it where I can.

Please give me a definite final answer at once.

As ever, Yours,
SYDNEY PORTER

May 25, 1906.

Sydney Porter Esq.
55 Irving Place, N.Y.C.
DEAR BILL:

After fighting with my conscience all night, and
clinging to this classic as a mother embraces a child
that she fears will look like somebody else, I am at
last resigned to let it go. It is the best thing of the
kind I ever saw, and if you would make one change in
it we could use it, but that change would mean the
assassination of a master-piece, and with tears stream-
ing down my face I herewith surrender it.

It is not known that we have seen it here, so it may
be offered elsewhere as the first strawberries of the
season.

Pray for me.

June 12, 1906.

Sydney Porter Esq.
55 Irving Place, N.Y.C.
DEAR BILL:

Can you drop in this afternoon to discuss a trivial
matter of a trivial change in our seats among the
haughty? We want to get a better view of the stage,
as there is a lady with a large bonnet sitting right in
our path. We like the show, and it is our intention
to sit through the entire performance, but at the price
I think we ought to get a little bit nearer the orchestra.

Ever yours,

June 18, 1906.

Sydney Porter Esq.
55 Irving Place, N.Y.C.
To the MAHARAJAH OF PHUNK. PRINCIPALITY
OF BLINK:
Enclosed find the Turkish delight.
Salaam.
KING OF ROPEK

Thursday Morn

Dear Old Mr. Bob:

Your story is
being typewritten. I had to
knock off for a day or so
to do the <u>World</u> stunt. It
is a fine large Texas story
full of fresh air and mescal.

Ong passong — that wa'nt
no dig at 10¢ magazines. — It's
only the 25¢ & 35¢ ones that have
those bum illustrations. Why,
man, the 10¢ magazine's, not only
being the best, raised me from
a pup. Peace unto thee

Bill, the Highbinder

BUSINESS CORRESPONDENCE

June 21, 1906.

Sydney Porter Esq.
55 Irving Place, N.Y.C.
DEAR BILL:

"Calloway's Code" is understood and appreciated in this office, and we have about decided that the 80,000,-000 readers of this magazine shall have a chance to decipher it on its own account.

If you have any more loose words lying around, gather them up and send them to us.

Always sincerely yours,

Thursday.

DEAR OLD BILL:

At last I have a home at 126 Waverly Place, and have an address to give you. I am in Gilman Hall's apartment, and can now continue to turn out the old blown-in-the-bottle brand of fiction.

I am a man of dam few words. I want $125 (don't read that a dollar and a quarter). That, in addition to the $150 that I screwed out of the high-browed and esteemed B. Merwin during your absence will make a total of $275 which will be more than covered by the moral and entertaining tale that I agree to have finished and delivered to you all by 10.30 A.M., Monday, Aug. 27 or perhaps earlier.

Pursue the liberal policy and get the best stuff.

Personally and officially I greet you and make obeisance.

Consistently,
BILL, THE BEDOUIN

P. S. Bet you never caught a damfish.

P. P. S. I want the dough not a check (but a check will do) by the bearer, or else a few well-chosen words of refusal. Come down and see my 7 room apartment with well stocked refrigerator. Tell old B. Merwin to call too.

March 12, 1908.

O. Henry Esq.
The Caledonia Apartments, 28 W. 26th St., N.Y.C.
MY DEAR O. HENRY:

Some time ago we sent you proofs of "A Moment of Victory." I believe you said you wanted to make some changes in it, but if you are going to do so will you please do it at once and let us have the proofs back, as we want to use the story. It reads very well to me as it stands, and we should be perfectly well satisfied without any changes.

Very sincerely yours,

The stories covered by this correspondence represented what should have been O. Henry's years of relative affluence. For the earlier stories appearing in *Munsey's* he was paid at the rate of one cent a word or even less. The first check sent for "A Blackjack Bargainer" was for thirty-five dollars, though the records show an additional payment of fifteen dollars in December, 1902. It was printed in the issue for August, 1901. Thirty-six dollars was also the price paid for "One Dollar's Worth," bought by the magazine. For "Jimmy Hayes and Muriel," bought April 10, 1903, the price was thirty-six dollars. A little better rate was given for "The Duplicity of Hargraves," bought November 27, 1901, and published in *Munsey's* for February, 1902. It was sixty dollars for a story of approximately five thousand words.

But soon growing recognition with the attendant

Friday

Kind Sir:

Thanks, thanks,
thanks for the papers
to Mrs R. E. Jane.
Je vous remercie
beaucoup de oolong.

Had it not was
for the fact that I
was having me
bawth when your
message arrived
I should have ans-
wered yestereve.

But hark! the
chateau is surrounded —

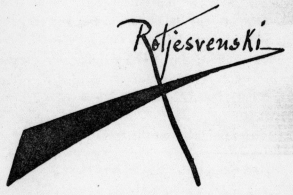

Once aboard the lugger, and the girl is ours.
Again — thanks
Yours Au revoir.

Rotjesvenski

O. HENRY BECAME A LINGUIST
OF PARTS, AS THIS LETTER TO
DAVIS SHOWS

competition moved these prices along a decimal. In
January, 1905, O. Henry entered into an arrangement
with the Munsey Company by the terms of which he
was to give them the first reading of all his short
stories, in return to be paid ten cents a word for such
stories as were accepted. Thus for "Hostages to
Momus" (July, 1905) he received five hundred dollars; for "Telemachus Friend" (December, 1905),
$280; for "The Handbook of Hymen" (July, 1906),
$300; for "The Higher Abdication" (August, 1906),
a total of $500, $200 of which represented three advance payments; for "Calloway's Code" (September,
1906), $250; for "The Ethics of Pig" (October,
1906), $340; for "Seats of the Haughty" (Decem-
ber, 1906), $500; for "The Moment of Victory" (May,
1908), $436.50; for "Schools and Schools" (October,
1908), $300; for "Helping the Other Fellow" (Decem-
ber, 1908), $280; for "The Higher Pragmatism"
(March, 1909), $230; for "Best-Seller" (April,
1909), $350; for "A Technical Error" (February,
1910), $240.

The stories published in the early part of 1902 were
also sent on from other cities. The O. Henry bibli-
ography for 1902 lists nineteen tales appearing in that
year. The mediums, in addition to *Munsey's*, *Ainslee's*, and *Everybody's*, includes the *Smart Set*, the
Black Cat, the *Era*, *Town Topics*, and *Brandur's*
"Rouge et Noir," appearing in December, 1901, was
the first to bear the signature Olivier Henry, which
was again used in 1902 for "The Passing of Black
Eagle" and "Friends in San Rosario."

By 1903, O. Henry had found himself and was in

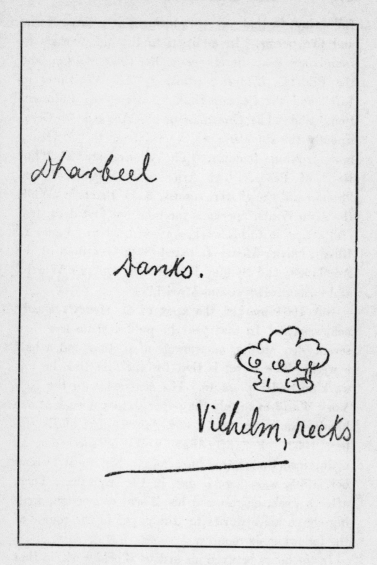

A NOTE OF THANKS FROM THE CALIPH
TO DAVIS

full swing, in that year producing thirty-three stories and five poems. In addition to the old markets he found new fields in *Harper's*, the *Cosmopolitan*, and the *Pilgrim*, *Harper's* printing "The Whirligig of Life" and the *Cosmopolitan* "A Retrieved Reformation," and "The Guardian of the Accolade." Occasionally the signature was varied from the O. Henry now growing familiar. The *Ainslee* stories, "The Robe of Peace," "At Arms with Morpheus" and "Sound and Fury" were signed "S. H. Peters"; "While the Auto Waits," perhaps the tale that first drew general attention to his work, was credited to "James L. Bliss"; Olivier Henry fathered "The Guardian of the Accolade"; and Sydney Porter "One Dollar's Worth" and "Jimmy Hayes and Muriel."

But 1904 marked the apex of O. Henry's steady achievement. In that year he published no less than seventy-five stories, an average of a story and a half a week. The secret is that for the first time he was working under pressure. His contract with the New York *World* to supply the paper a story a week at one hundred dollars a week had begun the first of December, 1903. For fifty-three weeks in succession he maintained that astonishing pace. Not until December, 1905, was there a gap in the sequence. Then, after a week, he resumed his *World* connection, writing eleven more stories for the paper in the course of the following six months.

In the hours between his ardous *World* work, in that rich year of 1904, he found time to write for *Ainslee's* "The Hypothesis of Failure"; for *Everybody's*, "Hearts and Crosses," "On Behalf of the Manage-

ment," "Two Renegades," and "The Emancipation of
Billy"; for *McClure's*, "A Tempered Wind," "Holding up a Train," "The Ransom of Mack"; for the
Metropolitan, "The Enchanted Kiss"; for the *Cosmopolitan*, "The Door of Unrest"; for the Associated
Sunday Magazines, "The Reformation of Calliope";
for the *Century*, "The Missing Chord"; for the *Critic*,
"A Dinner at ————"; and for the *Northwestern
Miller*, "The Church with the Overshot Wheel." Of
the *World* stories "The Furnished Room," "The Defeat of the City," "A Lickpenny Lover," and "From
the Cabby's Seat" are O. Henry at his very best.

XV

PROMISES AND EVASIONS

Catching suckers in New York is like dynamiting a Texas lake for bass. All you have to do anywhere between the North and East rivers is to stand in the street with an open bag marked "Drop packages of money here. No checks or loose bills taken."
Innocents of Broadway

SCHEHEREZADE, spinning the tales of *A Thousand Nights and a Night* for the diversion of an exacting lord and for the preservation of the lives of the virgins of his kingdom, contrived so to time her narrative that it reached its most exciting point the moment the cock crew in the morning; thereby, through the royal curiosity as to what "continued in our next" might have in store for him, ensuring herself another twenty-four hours of mundane existence.

O. Henry had not one exacting overlord, but several of them. Like Scheherezade, he found it expedient to serve them piecemeal. Readers of the O. Henry stories have often been puzzled by a certain dislocation in many of the tales; a break between the opening paragraph and the main body; then perhaps another break before the twist at the end. That is primarily due to the fact that his working life in the period of his greatest activity was one of promises and evasions.

"Propitiatory fragments" is what Alexander Black has called the bits of manuscript that O. Henry was in the habit of advancing "on account" of the promised

246

tale. One of the several editors of the *World* who
came in contact with the O. Henryian vagaries, Mr.
Black in *American Husbands and Other Alternatives*,
wrote:

The coming of the first fragment of an O. Henry
story acknowledged the reasonableness of my official
anxiety, for the weekly stories in the *World* had to be
illustrated, and the illustrations needed a little more
information about scene and characters. Often this
preliminary part (on the last day of grace) held no
adequate hint for the draughtsman, but an accompanying line would wig-wag: "The picture might be of a
traffic cop holding open a pathway for a pretty girl."
The offender [according to Mr. Black] could awake
to sparkling excuses. Sometimes they were not more
original than those offered by an office boy with his
eye on a ball game. Again, they would be ingenious.
Always they would be joyously colloquial. Promises
had a like flavor. "You can bet your variegated socks
that I will send you an Easter story" was typical. Or
the reassurance might run (as it did in 1907), "May
the ink in my bottle turn to Old Crow on the day that
I hesitate to use it at the desire of you and the still
dear World!"

Editors were not the only ones to have to learn to
accept with philosophical resignation these O. Henryian vagaries. Miss F. M. Holly, the authors' representative, recalls an experience at the beginning of
her professional career, when one particularly cheering
morning had brought her news of sales, among others,
of a story by Gertrude Atherton, and an article on
"How to Buy a Piano," by Rupert Hughes. Fortune
seemed to be coming on bright wings when, capping

these pleasant successes, the telephone rang and a voice announced: "This is William Sidney Porter, O. Henry speaking."

He wanted, he explained, to enlist her good help for an old sweetheart of his, a Miss Sara Lindsay Coleman, who was from the South and had some stories that she wanted to sell. Miss Coleman would call at Miss Holly's offices with the stories. Would Miss Holly, as a personal favor to him, try her best to sell the stories at some good place? "Certainly," said Miss Holly, "I'll do my best for that old sweetheart of yours. But how about giving me a chance sometime at an O. Henry story?" "I'll do that, too," said O. Henry. "I haven't anything on hand just now. But I won't forget. It's a promise."

Miss Holly sold the stories of the "old sweetheart" who was to become the second Mrs. William Sidney Porter. Incidentally one of them, "The Man in the Valley," appearing in *Tom Watson's Magazine*, attracted considerable attention at the time. Some years passed and Miss Coleman had become Mrs. Porter, before again over the telephone came the sound of O. Henry's drawling voice. "I have not forgotten that promise I made you. I've got a fine story that I want you to sell. But there is a plumber's bill to pay down at the Long Island home, and I'll have to have five hundred dollars for the story." "Leave it to me," said Miss Holly, closing her desk for the day.

In the course of the next few hours the bright dreams dissolved. Bob Davis was the first editor to be approached. Eloquently he tossed his hands to high

heaven. "He owes me four stories already. Not
another cent until he delivers the copy for which he has
been paid." In turn other editors were visited; the
entire round of the New York magazine offices made.
Everywhere the experience was the same; everywhere
the suggestion was met by outraged expostulation and
reference to debts already incurred. It was late in the
afternoon, after having tried every possible market,
that Miss Holly returned to her office. There, according to the agreement of the morning, O. Henry called
her up. "I couldn't do it, Mr. Porter," she explained
unhappily, "I've tried everywhere and it's no use."
Reassuring, comforting, came back the gentle suave
voice: "Don't let that worry you in the least. You
see I made it into a Christmas story, and I've just sold
it myself to the New York *Herald*."

Approximately corresponding in time to Miss
Holly's experience was an experience of George Barr
Baker. To that Long Island home where there was a
plumber's bill to be met, O. Henry had gone, not of his
own volition, but at the suggestion of friends, particularly of Gilman Hall, who was ever solicitous of Porter's health and work. Friends saw to it that a
comfortable house was found in an attractive locality,
close to the water, and superintended the transportation there of Porter and his family, consisting then of
Mrs. Porter and Margaret. Porter himself was relieved of all the arduous details of furnishing, and
hiring servants. The friends felt that away from the
distractions of the city the story-teller would be in a
better position to produce and deliver the tales for
which he had contracted. They saw him settled there

'12. 45'

Just phoned to you. to go
to lunch. Dont lose faith in
inhuman nature. I'll have
some work ready for you
just as soon. I can pay
my bill at Munsey's at 2
hours notice any day. I
can pay my bill with you
next week.   Now, be quiet.
The American Magazine hasn't
got a line of ms. from me on
hand. Be good, + give me a
chance. When I get out of the

hole I'll heap coals of fire
on your head.

Come around to c me
any time. I'm always at
home.

Yours as fair as
possible.

Bill

P.S. If I ~~fire~~ cant work &
you people wont feed me shall
I starve or hunt grub elsewhere?

THE CALIPH DISCUSSES
QUESTIONS OF FINANCE
WITH DAVIS

and then they left him. But the result was not quite
the one for which they had hoped.

On one of the summer's hottest afternoons Mr.
Baker, then on the staff of *Everybody's*, was confronted with the familiar situation of waiting for an
O. Henry story that had been promised for an early
issue and had not been delivered. He took it for
granted that Porter was in his Long Island home. But
as anxiety grew, on a chance he decided to make a visit
to the town apartment in the Caledonia. Usually it
was difficult to effect an entrance there. The Cerberus
on guard in the lobby had general instructions to ex-
clude all visitors. A tip would move him to pretend to
telephone and then announce that "Mr. Porter was
not in." On this occasion, however, knowing Mr.
Baker, he accepted the explanation that "Mr. Porter
expected him," and directed the visitor to the elevator.

Treading softly Mr. Baker turned the door knob of
the Porter apartment and entered. Porter was seated
at his table, his pencil poised over the familiar yellow
writing pad. The three windows of the room were
open, and an electric fan, revolving at its highest possible speed, was blowing directly upon the writer. Entirely unconscious of the presence of the new arrival,
he continued his mental search for the exact word that
was needed in the story.

Little Old Noisyville on the Subway was at its noisi-
est. From nearby Broadway came the clang of the
surface cars. The Sixth Avenue L rumbled and clat-
tered. Fifth Avenue contributed to the din. It was
the hour of the outpouring from the shops, and the air
was shrill and raucous with the shouts of thousands of

girls escaping from their daily toil. But seemingly unconscious of the riot O. Henry sat there waiting for the word to come.

"Ah, I have it!" There was a sigh of relief and the pencil moved for a moment. Then for the first time Porter realized the presence of his guest, and waved his greetings to the accompaniment of the appellation of "Doctor" or "Colonel." "Here's your story, not quite done, but you will have it on Monday morning."

"That's good," said Mr. Baker. "But I certainly did not expect to find you here. Thought you were down in the country."

"The country." Porter shook his head emphatically "Couldn't stand it! It drove me to distraction!"

"What did?"

"Why, the noise, the terrible noise. Do you know there is a bird, a malignant little bird, that comes to my window and calls to me most annoyingly. Calls to me? That bird howls at me from morning to night. Does so deliberately just to disturb me. Then those cows, those two cows! They are forever mooing. And then the water, continually plashing, plashing. Couldn't stand it any longer. The noise was driving me mad. Prevented me from even thinking of work. Had to come up here for peace and quiet."

"Quite true," assented his visitor, "and now that the story's done—"

"Not quite done," corrected Porter, "but nearly done. And while we are on that subject let me suggest that if I were a different kind of a man, which of course I am not, I would hint that with a starving wife and daughter, and one or two servants who are also starving, as well as a hungry dog, an advance of say one hundred and fifty dollars would be exceedingly welcome. But, as you understand, I am not that kind of a man."

"Up to the time he last touched pencil to paper O. Henry was never known to get a piece of work into the hands of an editor except at the last possible moment," recalls Isaac F. Marcosson[1] in *Adventures in Interviewing*. "Upon some occasions he completely failed to meet the schedule." Mr. Marcosson illustrates the point with a story. O. Henry had received a large advance, as usual, for a story ordered by a prominent magazine. The head and tail pieces had been drawn and the space allotted in the number. Ten days before the date when the copy was due the editor began to telegraph the author for the manuscript. From long experience he knew what an ordeal was in store for him. He received no answer from the author. On the night before the last day that the manuscript could be used, he wired the following couplet to O. Henry:

[1] Mr. Marcosson was responsible for making Sir James Barrie an O. Henry "fan." In 1917, he told Sir James about the American story-teller, and two months later on his return from a trip to Russia, was informed: "While you were gone I read all of O. Henry's books that I could find. I thank you for telling me about them." "Then," says Mr. Marcosson, "he proceeded to tell me his version, of at least a dozen of the best O. Henry yarns, ranging from 'The Trimmed Lamp,' which was one of his favorites, to 'The Rose of Dixie.' As an expression of his appreciation he wrote a letter to O. Henry's daughter Margaret, who was then living in New York. Barrie became such an O. Henry enthusiast that he presented a complete set of the American author's works to Mr. Asquith."
A letter from Colonel E. M. House to the authors of this book reads: "When Lord Balfour was at the Washington Conference he told me that he found a long row of books in the apartment he occupied by an author called O. Henry. He had never heard of him but he took up one of the volumes at random and before he left Washington he had read every line that Sidney Porter had written. I have never heard any of O. Henry's admirers speak with more enthusiasm than did Lord Balfour."

> O. Henry, in your hour of ease
> Send us that story, please.

O. Henry was taking a rest in the mountains of North Carolina. The final poetic appeal stirred him to action for he wired back the reply:

> When care and sorrow rend the brow
> I cannot send that story now.

Yet despite the constant need for money there were times when the mood moved him to decline offers of rich promise. In the New York *Sun* for January 10, 1915, Mr. Clarence L. Cullen related the following story:

I was with him at the Twenty-sixth Street place one afternoon when a batch of mail was brought to him. One of the envelopes caught his eye. On the envelope was printed the name of one of the leading fiction publications in all the world, if not indeed the most important of them all. Many times during the years when he had been struggling for a foothold as a writer of short stories he had submitted his tales, including the best of them, to the editor of this publication. Always they had come back to him with the conventional printed slip. When he reached the topmost rung of the ladder he meticulously refrained from submitting anything to that particular publication, the writers for which comprised the leading "names" in the world of fiction.

He ripped open this envelope which attracted his eye. There was a note and a check for one thousand dollars. The note asked him briefly for something from his pen—anything—with that word underscored— check for which was therewith enclosed. If the thousand dollars were not deemed sufficient, the note went on, he had only to name what sum he considered fair and the additional amount would be remitted to him.

Porter, who was probably the least vainglorious writer of equal fame that ever lived, smiled a sort of cherubic smile as he passed the note over to me. When I had finished reading it, without comment, he, saying never a word, addressed the envelope to the editor of the publication, slipped the check into the envelope, stamped the envelope and went out into the hall and deposited it in the drop. Not a word passed between us about the offer.

The writing of stories was O. Henry's vocation; his avocation was the invention of excuses when the stories were not written in time. To that there is rich and diverse testimony. As William Johnston, the editor with whom he was directly in touch during the thirty months when he was supposed to supply the New York *World* with a story a week, has expressed it, his letters explaining why the stories were late in being delivered, show almost as much his powers of invention as do the tales themselves.

Evasive is the word that best sums up the personal O. Henry. It is the one word that explains all; covers all. Those who were nearest to him, those with whom he reveled and played in his quiet way, were always conscious of this quality of evasiveness. Much of it was due to native shyness; much to his Old Man of the Sea. That was the mental side of the quality. The fact that in all directions of the compass there were anxious or irate editors clamoring for promised copy contributed to the practical side. That explains his various movings, and his mysterious absences. He was always the "Elusive Pimpernel."

Form No. 2.

THE WESTERN UNION TELEGRAPH COMPANY.

INCORPORATED

23,000 OFFICES IN AMERICA. CABLE SERVICE TO ALL THE WORLD.

ROBERT C. CLOWRY, President and General Manager.

Receiver's No.   Time Filed   Check   190

SEND the following message subject to the terms on back hereof, which are hereby agreed to.

To

Dear Bill:

I am moving today from Mawdy St. to #29 West 25 St. ff. Am feeling pretty fine for to charge. Have a good story about 500 words done which I'm sure you will like. Can I come in and read it to you on your way home. Can you send me $50? I need it. He will be all ready for you tomorrow night.

Your Sydney Porter

☞ READ THE NOTICE AND AGREEMENT ON BACK.

THE POLICY OF DELAY

A specimen epistle rushed hurriedly from the Westminster Hotel to the editor of "Munsey's" for the obvious purpose of gathering the sinews

The evasiveness grew with the years, as the burden of his moral debts became heavier. Mr. Johnston's experiences were rather happier than those of later editors. The task of providing an original story every week for the *World* left O. Henry little time for outside work and involved a close association of editor and author. The two men lunched and dined together frequently, and spent occasional evenings over the pool table or in the bowling alley. In addition, an almost daily correspondence was carried on for many months. Of this Mr. Johnston has left a record.

On O. Henry's part the correspondence was largely of specious excuse. Sometimes it placed the blame on a visitor who had outstayed his welcome and would not be dismissed. The next time for the sake of variety it would be something about "dizziness on rising," or a description of "Colonel Bright and his justly celebrated disease," candor compelling him to say in conclusion: "Good old doc says it ain't the genuine thing but it took six prescriptions and wasn't any slouch of an imitation."

At another time, Mr. Johnston records, a stern editorial demand, "Where's this week's story?" would elicit a note whimsical and utterly irrelevant, as follows:

What you say? Let's take an evening off and strike the Café Francis for a slight refection. I like to be waked up suddenly there by the music and look across at the red-haired woman eating smelts under an original by Glackens.

Peace for Yours.

S.P.

Another excuse for a dilatory story:

Being entirely out of tune with the muse, I went out and ameliorated the condition of a shop girl as far as a planked steak could do so.

These letters were written in his round, regular hand, sometimes in pencil, sometimes in ink, and usually signed "S. P." or "Sidney Porter." There was one typed, and signed with the initials "O. H." that Mr. Johnston considered the brightest gem of all. It was written probably late in September, 1905. At all events it concerned the story "The Guilty Party," a sermon on parental responsibility. It had been delivered late, as usual, and on receiving it and reading it, Mr. Johnston wrote:

There was once a celebrated author who appeared before the judgment bar. A host of people were there saying nice things about him, when up spoke a weary editor and said, "He never kept a promise in his life."

In reply to this came from O. Henry by special messenger a note which read:

Guilty, m'lud.
And yet—
Some time ago a magazine editor to whom I had promised a story at a certain minute (and strangely enough didn't get there with it) wrote to me: "I am coming down to-morrow to kick you thoroughly with a pair of heavy-soled shoes. *I* never go back on *my* promises." And I lifted up my voice and said unto him: "It's easy to keep promises that can be pulled off with your feet."

XVI

HAROUN IN HIS GOLDEN PRIME

Alraschid administered justice, rewarded the deserving, and punished whomsoever he disliked on the spot. He was the originator of the short story contest. Whenever he succored any chance pick-up in the bazaars he always made the succoree tell the sad story of his life. If the narrative lacked construction, style, and esprit he commanded his vizier to dole him out a couple of thousand ten-dollar notes on the First National Bank of the Bosphorus, or else gave him a soft job as Keeper of the Bird Seed for the Bulbuls in the Imperial Gardens. If the story was a crackerjack, he had Mesrour, the executioner, whack off his head. The report that Haroun Alraschid is still alive and is editing the magazine that your grandmother used to subscribe for lacks confirmation.

The Discounters of Money

THE sixty dollars a week that Bob Davis, in that first interview in the room over Marty's, held out as an inducement to O. Henry to write for the New York *World*, could be made to go far in the Bagdad of a quarter of a century ago. The later arrangement by which he received one hundred dollars a week for a story a week enabled him to establish himself in what he called "the business of caliphing," and to indulge in the vagaries and extravagances appropriate to the generous-handed rôle. Figuratively, he was in a position to toss about his "purses of gold." In the years from 1904 to 1907, O. Henry was Haroun in his golden prime.

The road to those years had been hard to travel. "Well, Man," asks Ida Bates, the stenographer and typist of the Acropolis Hotel in "The Enchanted Profile," "how are the stories coming?" "Pretty regularly," is the scribe's reply, "about equal to their going." That was O. Henry's case. The rejections had outnumbered the acceptances. In 1902 and 1903, when he found a market for his tales and occasional verses, it was necessary to work it hard. His relations with *Ainslee's Magazine* illustrate that point.

For example, in its issue for April, 1903, *Ainslee's* printed one of his great stories, "Roads of Destiny." In the same number appeared the short sketch, "The Robe of Peace," credited to S. H. Peters, and the poem "April," signed John Arbuthnot. *Ainslee's* for June of that year carried his first story with a New York background, and the first story fully flashing the color of the Arabian Nights. That was "While the Auto Waits." It was signed James L. Bliss. No one outside the office knew who James L. Bliss was, and few then knew who O. Henry was; yet the sheer quality of the tale moved a critic on the New York *Times* to write: "We do not know who James L. Bliss is. The name is new to us. But we defy anyone to produce a French short story writer who is capable of producing anything finer than 'While the Auto Waits.'" Evidently as yet Porter attached little importance to the signature O. Henry; for he was calling himself, in addition to James L. Bliss, S. H. Peters, Sydney Porter, Olivier Henry, T. B. Dowd and Howard Clark.

Meanwhile he had been writing for other editors besides the editors of *Ainslee's*. In *Everybody's* for October, 1902, were published "The Cactus" and "Round the Circle." "Hearts and Hands" appeared in *Everybody's* for December of the same year. Other occasional markets were *Munsey's*, *Smart Set*, the

Black Cat, Brandur's, the *Era,* and *Town Topics.*
The prices paid for the tales thus contributed belong
to literary history, and serve to illustrate Porter's
struggle when on the road to his "caliphry."

Ainslee's bought the stories for sums ranging from
fifty to seventy-five dollars apiece. The old records of
Munsey's Magazine contain such entries as: "Sidney
Porter, 47 W. 24th St., N. Y. City. Bought Dec. 23,
1902: 'One Dollar's Worth.'" "Sydney Porter.
$36.00. Bought April 10, 1903: 'Muriel.'" "Sydney
Porter, c/o W. W. Harris, 289 Spring Street, Columbus, Ohio. $25. Bought May 21, 1901: 'A Blackjack
Bargainer,' 5,000 words." A note under this entry
records an additional payment of fifteen dollars made
June 25, 1901. The original rate had been half a
cent a word. Later the magazine was to make amends
for the early hard bargains when it established by
agreement a rate of ten cents a word for any story by
O. Henry that it found suitable for its needs. But in
the meantime there is the record: "$60. Bought Nov.
27, 1901. O. Henry, 119 Fourth Avenue, N. Y. C.
'The Duplicity of Hargraves'—4,000 words."

Even smaller were some of the figures in the checks
that filtered in to O. Henry. Charles Hanson Towne,
who at that early stage of his career was associated
with the late Arthur Grissom in the editorship of the
Smart Set, has a story to tell. One day in 1902, Mr.
Towne, engaged in the tiresome daily task of going
through submitted manuscripts in the dim hope of finding a new note, came across a handwritten story, a
story so neatly prepared that it was a relief to read it
after so many typed scripts.

I never saw so bold and legible a hand [Mr. Towne recalls]. It was like copperplate. I wish I had it now, but so much that is valuable is lost in printers' offices; and how was I to realize then what a great writer I had come across, how he would one day be considered one of the world's finest story-writers? I whooped as I read. Then, after an even louder whoop, I took the manuscript to Mr. Grissom. "If you don't take this, I resign," I remember I cried; and I literally forced him to read it—it was only seventeen hundred words in length—as I stood beside his desk.

"Again you're right," he said, looking up as he finished the last page. "Make out a voucher, please, at our usual rate." Our usual rate was one cent a word; there I wrote on one of the blue slips that we had for the cashier: "Pay Sydney Porter (O. Henry) for a story entitled 'By Courier,' Seventeen dollars ($17) ['By Courier' was published in the *Smart Set* for May, 1902]. And when another story came in from this author, for he sent another (he was then in Pittsburgh), he wished to know if we could send the check immediately, as he wanted to come to New York and settle down to write. He further stated that if we could pay him at once, we might deduct ten dollars for cash, so anxious was he to be on his way to the metropolis. The story ["Madame Bo-Peep of the Ranches"] was six thousand words in length, but we did not deduct anything. We sent him the full amount and asked him to call on us when he arrived in town. But he didn't; and it was some months later that I first met him.

In outline somewhat similar to Mr. Towne's story is the story told by Witter Bynner. In the autumn of 1902, Mr. Bynner, a young man fresh from Harvard, sought and obtained employment with the McClure

Company as a first step in a literary career. His position was that of a super office boy, with a variety of duties, including that of a subordinate literary adviser. In the distribution of the flood of unsolicited manuscripts that found their way into the office, those that seemed the least promising were intrusted to him for a first reading, with instructions to sift out a few to be passed on to the man next higher up, or, in the event of a real find, to call the manuscript to the immediate attention of the head reader of the house, Miss Viola Roseboro.

For months it proved dreary work, a hopeless search that called for all the patience and enthusiasm of youth. The winter passed without any sign of the desired "find." Then one day in the spring of 1903 young Mr. Bynner came upon a manuscript called "Tobin's Palm." It bore the signature Olivier Henry. The name meant nothing. He read it, reread it, and then went straight to Miss Roseboro. "Here is the long-sought story," he said. "It's a crackerjack, a new note in fiction. We simply must take it."

Following up the matter a few days later he learned to his dismay that the story had been returned to the author with a letter of encouragement and a request that further stories be submitted in the future. The situation did not satisfy the eager discoverer. He went to S. S. McClure and told his tale. In glowing colors he painted the qualities of "Tobin's Palm," and insisted that it be recovered if possible. At length Mr. McClure caught fire from his young employe's enthusiasm. "Have you the man's address?" he asked. "Yes," said Bynner. "Then write him and ask him to

let us see it again." "That won't do," said Bynner.
"We can't wait. We've got to get it at once and
accept it on the spot." "Will you back that with your
judgment?" asked S. S. "I will," said Bynner.
"Then go after it. We take it."

Clapping on his hat Witter Bynner hurried to the
address in West Twenty-fourth Street. There, in that
room over the restaurant, he found his man sitting in
his shirt sleeves. The first impression, never to be forgotten, was of a stoutly built man, seemingly plunged
in the depths of despondency. The room was bare of
furniture and destitute of the appurtenances of physical comfort. A bed, a chair, and a trunk—that was all.
On top of the trunk was lying a long stamped and
addressed envelope. There was no word of self-intro-
duction; of explanation. The visitor pointed to the
envelope and asked: " 'Tobin's Palm'?" "Yes," was
the reply. "It's sold," said Bynner. "Good," said
O. Henry, "I'm flat broke."

That was the beginning of an association and friendship that lasted until Witter Bynner's departure from
New York to the West in 1906. "Tobin's Palm," appealing to S. S. McClure as much as it had to its discoverer, was bought for one hundred dollars, an
advance on the usual prices of fifty or seventy-five
dollars then paid by the magazine for stories by writers
without any particular reputation. It was followed
by many other stories with Bynner always as the intermediary. In *McClure's* appeared "The Pimienta Pan-
cakes" (December, 1903); "Holding Up a Train"
(April, 1904); "A Tempered Wind" (August, 1904);
"The Ransom of Mack" (December, 1904); "An Un-

finished Story" (August, 1905); and "The Trimmed Lamp" (August, 1906).

Of course, Bynner's experience was the usual experience. The magazine presses would be waiting and not a line of the promised tale at hand. Then Bynner would hurry off in quest of the author. "It's all written," Porter would explain when finally cornered. "Then let me have the copy." "Oh, I don't mean that it is down on paper; but it's all here." The culprit would point to his head. Then, to the last word as it eventually appeared in print, O. Henry would tell the story while Bynner listened. He had memorized it in its entirety before putting down the first word. "Now write it," Bynner would say. So O. Henry would sadly turn to the irksome task with Bynner at his elbow gathering up the tale as it came sheet by sheet.

It was soon after the beginning of the acquaintance that Porter moved from his room over Marty's to the more commodious quarters at 55 Irving Place. On occasion he played host. In the apartment there was a sofa at the disposal of the welcome guest. Bynner was then living in Brooklyn, and once or twice a month it was his habit to spend the night with Porter, sleeping on the sofa. Usually at such times the two men dined together. There was a restaurant on Eighth Avenue that they often frequented where for the sum of twenty-five cents a dinner of a kind was served. It included wine, or what went by that name.

Contrary to the general experience, Bynner's impression of Porter was of a man who kept his drinking of hard liquor within the bounds of reason. The wine with dinner and then two or three carefully measured

night-caps before retiring. He does not recall ever
having seen Porter obviously "under the influence,"
and the only suggestion he ever had of secret indul-
gence was the fact that Porter was addicted to the use
of a perfume or sen-sen which might have been for the
purpose of hiding a tell-tale breath.

A dominating quality of the Porter of Witter Bynner's memories was his gift of silence. In their walks
together and their meals together there were long
periods when not a word was spoken. The companionship had reached a degree of intimacy where any
attempt at forced conversation was unnecessary. In
silence the two men would eat, and in silence make their
way back from the restaurant to Irving Place.

A bond that drew Porter and Bynner very close
together for a time was the preparation for publication of the book *Cabbages and Kings*. It was O.
Henry's first book, published late in 1904. In the
rough it was merely a collection of the various short
stories, based upon his experiences in his Sinbad days
as an exile in Central America. These tales, some of
them written while Porter was still in the Ohio Penitentiary, had been scattered about in various publications.

Porter had the notes for as many more tales, and
wrote "The Admiral," "Dicky," and "Cupid's Exile
No. II." But volumes of short stories were then regarded by publishers with unfavorable eyes, so it was
Bynner who conceived the idea of running through the
collected tales a plot thread that would weld them into
a continuous narrative. With that suggestion in mind,
Porter proceeded to the writing of the Proem and "Fox
in the Morning," with which *Cabbages and Kings*

begins; "The Vitagraphoscope," with which it ends;
and between, carrying on the mystery, "Caught,"
"The Remnants of the Code," "Smith," and "Two
Recalls." Bynner's share in the collaboration deserves
lasting recognition. Porter did the work of writing
the additional tales at a time when work was comparatively easy to him. But it was Bynner's interest, his
spur, his suggestion of the thread linking the first story
with the last, and his adroit sequence, that made *Cabbages and Kings* the narrative of suspense and surprise
that it is.

For the stories in what has come to be accepted as
the typical O. Henry manner, Porter, according to
Witter Bynner's impression, cared but little. He often
disparaged them, or spoke of them flippantly in intimate talk; and was always genuinely fearful that the
reading public would "find him out" and grow tired
of his vein. But there was one story that was ever
dear to his heart. It was one of his earliest. Again
and again he urged Bynner to read it. "That is the
kind of story I want to write. But the editors won't
let me." The story was "Roads of Destiny."

In the Bagdad that knew Haroun O. Henry in
his golden prime, that Eighth Avenue restaurant where
Porter and Bynner dined and wined at a cost of twenty-
five cents each was by no means exceptional. Throughout the city there were hundreds of establishments
catering to the appetite at corresponding prices.
Twenty-five cents was the charge for a luncheon or a
dinner at Marty's over which Porter was living when
Bynner found him, and when Bob Davis found him.
The Café Francis in West Thirty-fifth Street, which

was one of Porter's favorite haunts, and where, as will
be told, he saw the girl whose face led directly to the
writing of "The Enchanted Profile," served a luncheon
for thirty-five cents. At either of the old Mouquin
restaurants, the downtown place on Fulton Street, and
the uptown place at Sixth Avenue and Twenty-eighth
Street, the latter particularly dear to Porter's gastronomical heart, fifty cents was the price of an order of
half a cold roast chicken with a bowl of salad, while
an addition of fifteen cents provided a *carafon* of pass-
able red or white wine.

When O. Henry felt in the mood to caliph on the
grand scale he could turn to the greater hotels and
more magnificent restaurants without inviting financial
disaster. There the prices were in proportion. The
dollar dinner of the men's grill of the old Manhattan
was elaborate and famous. At the Waldorf-Astoria,
then at the height of its glory, at the Holland House,
at the Knickerbocker, one could sit down to a meal at
a cost that to-day would hardly stay hunger at an
automat. But suppose the Caliph, as often happened,
was for the moment hard pressed for funds. Bagdad
was open-handed in its hospitality. The respectably
dressed man, which meant Porter with his natty gray
suit, his rich blue tie, his everlasting glove and cane
in his right hand, and the usual little Cecil Brunner
rose in his buttonhole, might have only a few coins
jingling in his pocket. For him there was always the
free lunch at the old Fifth Avenue Hotel where he
could regale himself substantially and satisfactorily at
an expenditure of ten cents for a glass of beer.

Within the compass of Bagdad, especially in its

hostelries and refectories, the Caliph could find the flavor of other lands. I. F. Marcosson has told of the atmosphere and food of the Levant when dining with Porter in a restaurant known as Little Syria in New York's Syrian quarter far down on the lower West Side. Robert Rudd Whiteing has related the adventure of the quest of viands designed to recall Porter's experiences in Honduras in the Latin-American hotel in Fifteenth Street. France was always at hand with Mouquin's, or Martin's, or the Lafayette, or the Brevoort; and at Old Tom's, in the shadow of Trinity's spire, at Browne's chop house, at Sam Martin's, or the Clifton, the vicarious traveler, by a little play of the imagination, might make himself believe that he was within the sound of Bow Bells. At the tables of Shanley's or Rector's were to be heard western voices reminiscent of Porter's early days. That Bagdad of the four million was a great transient city. Hourly the caravans with their pilgrims of pleasure arrived from all parts of New Arabia, and the ships from countries across the sea.

As became Haroun Alraschid, Porter knew the garish emporiums of upper Broadway and the grime and dirt and squalor of the low haunts that lined the Bowery. They held out to him the promise of adventure and material, but in neither of the extremes did he find the comfort and quiet for which he yearned. But in those days, in the first decade of the century, there was another kind of establishment that offered hospitality. It was known as the family saloon. There was one such saloon in particular, that played a highly important part in his life. It was his club, his only

NUMBER 55 IRVING PLACE

It was here, through the triple window, that O. Henry studied the heart of his City of Razzle Dazzle, his Little Old Bagdad on the Subway. Porter's rooms were immediately to the left of the entrance

club. There he spent hours that amounted to months
if not to years. It was reflected again and again in
his stories; it was described in detail in "The Lost
Blend."

That saloon was at the northeast corner of Eighteenth Street and Irving Place, diagonally opposite
Porter's quarters at Number 55. Perhaps proximity contributed to the choice of a man always reluctant to stray far from home. But it was a kind
of saloon that was occasionally to be found and that
has been entirely forgotten in the denunciation of the
institution as a whole. It was a neighborhood establishment in an orderly neighborhood. Just round the
corner was the conservative aristocracy of Gramercy
Park. The patronage was respectable while ranging
up and down the social scale. There were tradesmen
from the Third Avenue shops who preferred the
saloon's quiet and orderliness to the noise that prevailed
in similar establishments on their own avenue. English
writers from the Gramercy Park clubs dropped in
when homeward bound for a glass of ale that reminded
them of their own native land. The occasional touch
of aristocracy was provided by the presence of some
old-time New Yorker of Irving Place whose boyhood
memories of the street carried back to the days of
Washington Irving. At "Con's" he sipped his night-
cap toddy before proceeding homeward.

Behind the bar was Con, white-aproned and seriously sober. "Clean, temperate, clear-headed, polite,
white-jacketed, punctual, trustworthy, young, responsible," O. Henry described him. For the purposes of
fiction, in "The Lost Blend," O. Henry called the place

"Kenealy's," and demoted Con from his proprietorship to make him the bartender timorously in love with his employer's daughter. Con in the tale, he was also Con in real life. Handy with the bung-starter, which was rarely needed but always at hand for a possible emergency, he was fiercely proud of what he called the respectability of his place. No prohibitionist was ever more hostile to the noisy, offensive drunkard than Con. No plea from the man who obviously had already had too much moved him. His eye cold with dislike, his face a mask, he would produce and push across the bar a seltzer and lemon instead of the beverage ordered. " 'Tis that you need; no more whisky."

The worst adjunct of the old saloon was what was known as the "back room." Most of the back rooms were the resorts of the painted women of the night. There were plenty of these women in the Bagdad of Porter's day. They swarmed in particular in the region between Third and Fourth Avenues and the neighborhoods of Gramercy Park and Irving Place. But experience had taught them to avoid Con's. No woman ever had access to his back room. That was kept sacred for himself and his intimate friends, or on occasion placed at the disposal of two men planning a business deal, like Riley and McQuirk of "The Lost Blend," figuring and mixing in the hope of rediscovering the long sought drink. The object of their quest was a concoction that was the elixir of distilled battle, money, and high life, and had once moved a little Central American republic to the point of repudiating the national debt, removing the duty on cigarettes, and declaring war on Great Britain and the United States.

At Con's Porter found ease and solitude from the world. There he could indulge in the kind of argument that appealed to him with the proprietor or the casual stranger. He could be alone in his corner or he could have company which was never prying or intrusive. There he was beyond the reach of most of his editors and other creditors.

The world's outstanding short story-tellers, Poe, De Maupassant, Stevenson, and O. Henry, all dying young, are all reputed to have been addicted to excesses in some form or other. O. Henry drank, and drank hard. He was a two-bottle man; that is, his average daily consumption in the years of his caliphing in New York was two quarts of whisky. Later, in Asheville, in the mood in which he wrote "The Rubaiyat of a Scotch Highball," he "cut it out" entirely. Perhaps that abstinence, after years of steady drinking, contributed to hasten his end. Certainly the abnormal amount of liquor that he consumed between 1903 and 1907 seriously affected his health. But Porter "carried" his liquor. Unlike Poe, who despite the legend, drank comparatively little, being lashed to irritable excitement by a single glass of wine, Porter could consume a vast amount of strong spirits and not show it. His bibulous habits rarely affected his deportment, swayed his gait, or altered the tenor of his low, even voice. That power of control explains a certain conflict in the testimony.

Another side of William Sidney Porter must be discussed if a clear understanding of the personality of the man and his work is to be reached. Kipling has said that single men in barracks don't grow into

plaster saints. Neither do full-blooded men living
bachelor lives without restraint in a great city. Like
Stevenson in his early Edinburgh days, like Maupassant almost to the hour when it was necessary to confine
him in the asylum of Dr. Blanche at Passy, O. Henry
turned to women. In the quest for adventure that was
his most natural pursuit. He had his light affairs,
many of them, and his conquests were more or less easy.
Many of his heroines were drawn direct from the life,
being polished up and whitewashed for the purposes
of fiction. Lindsey Denison will tell of a remark of
Porter's throwing a curious light upon himself and the
Dulcie of "An Unfinished Story." Yet some of the
affairs were presumably entirely innocent.

There was no avenue leading to possible adventure
that Haroun neglected. He even sought adventure
through the medium of the "personal columns" of the
newspapers. According to the story told by Ethel
Patterson in *Everybody's Magazine* for February,
1914, the New York *Herald* for September 10, 1905,
carried the following "Personal":

Two neighborly "literary fellows," 35 and 30, seek
social acquaintance of two intelligent, attractive and
unconventional young ladies interested in artistic
ideas, with a view to mutual improvement and entertainment. Omar. 116 Herald.

Miss Patterson, living in a skylight room in Harlem
because the hall-room, being heated, would have cost
fifty cents more a week, was moved to answer the "Personal" in the "Rubaiyat" verse that was prevalent at
the time.

Oh Thou, who didst with pitfall and with gin
Beset the Road I was to wander in,
Thou wilt not with Predestined Evil round
Enmesh, and then impute my Fall to Sin!

The Bird of Time has but a little way
To flutter—and the Bird is on the Wing.

Then followed:

Indeed I am awfully lonesome. You can't understand, for there's two of you. There's only one of me.
Take my word for it that it is not nice to be a girl
working all alone in a city where you scarcely know
a human soul. I am at a point where I talk to elevator boys and car conductors. That is why—and
because I am also a bit of a gambler—I thought I
would write to you. I have been brought up to believe
"gentlemen do not do that sort of thing" *you* are
doing. But I have been brought up to believe "ladies
do not" either. And as I am unwilling to admit I am
not "a lady," that gives *you* just the one chance on
which I propose to gamble.

Who *are* you? Out of space you have spoken a
name I love. Out of space I am answering you. Will
you come within signalling distance, you ships that,
perhaps, shall not pass in the night?

Pardon me that I do not give you my own name and
address. You might, you know, be—well—almost anything. An entire matrimonial agency, for example. I
wonder. I am just—

A WOMAN

In reply came this letter:

Sept. 17, 1905.

MYSTERIOUS "A WOMAN":

I never particularly noticed that—"Oh Thou who
didst with pitfall and gin" until you quoted it. Then

I reached for my dictionary. It told me that "gin"
was a trap, a snare. Then I drew upon my memory
and saw another "gin" and heard a fizzing sound in
connection with it.

My Dear Madam "A Woman," believe me, there is
no trap or snare. Not by our "Personal" shall you
fall; we hope it will be a dirigible balloon in which you
may soar into the more pleasant strata of clouds and
ether.

My brother "Omar" and I are not connected by any
more binding tie than that of similar tastes and well-
established mutual friendship. Weary of the counterfeit Bohemia into which people who "write" are
dragged, we sent forth the "Personal" into space with
the hope of winging some wild, free creature of the
aerial regions above who might prove congenial company in our quiet excursions in search of the (genuinely) romantic and the (reasonably) adventurous.

I came from the saddle of a Texas bronco four
years ago to New York. The conventionalities and
the routine of the little circle I have been revolving in
have about caused me to stampede. The more "people" I meet the "lonesomer" I get. I can well sympathize with a woman who is lonely in the Big City.

Please, ma'am, will you try a chat with us instead
of the car conductors and the elevator boys?

You—"a bit of a gambler at heart"? Let's see if
you are. You made a very careful lead with your
"A Woman" signature. Well, I must admit you were
right to do that. But I'm playing a trump—here's my
picture (which you won't recognize) and here's my
card and address. You won't recognize the name, for
I write over a *nom de guerre*.

I trust you thus because you say you are "a literary
fellow" and I have confidence in "the gang." If you
would care to come within speaking distance and give

us a hope that we may gather "underneath the bough" with you we would be glad to hear from you again.

Yours to the bottom of the jug,

THE TWO OMARS

The correspondence continued. Under date of Sept. 22 the lady replied:

DEAR MR. OMAR No. 2:

Shake hands. Six years ago *I* "came from the saddle of a Texas bronco." "Stampede!!!" Sometimes I feel as though I just naturally can't stick it out. You know the feel. You *must!* How—

I want *free* life!
And I want *fresh* air!
And I *long* for the canter after the cattle
The crack of the whip like shot in battle.

And—and—*you* know!

And I have two more years than you have of pent-up loneliness. I said in my letter I was "lonesome." You said you were "lonesomer." I know I am "lonesomest." How could you be as "lonesomest" as I, you two who are bound by the tie of "similar tastes and a well established mutual friendship"?

Well, anyway, I feel better now. I know that somewhere else in this jungle of houses there is another human whose eyes and heart turn backward toward "Home."

It was decent of you, Mr. Porter, to send me your card and address. Your confidence in this infinitesimal portion of "the gang" will not be misplaced. I don't know whether or not I should show my appreciation by being equally frank. I'm afraid I can't. I shall have to remain "a paper sport." Will you let me be unknown to you a little longer? You can't lose much, you see—you literary fellows. But for me—it's so unfairly different.

And now—I am at a standstill. I *want* to accept your invitation to "come within speaking distance," but I do not know how. Of course the simplest method is to tell you where I will meet you. But how in the name of Heaven am I to know you when I get there? Shall I wear a red rose? Isn't that the proper thing under such circumstances?

I suppose I ought to tell you what I look like. I do not know. Let's see. I'm dark—*frightfully* dark. I do not imagine my best friends could call me "pretty." But if by chance you care to remember that beauty is, after all, only skin deep, you may address a letter to me as you did before, while I remain to you just a little longer just—

A WOMAN

To this Haroun made reply:

Saturday—

Goodness me! Did you really come from the bronco country, or was that only a figure of speech? If you did, I can talk your language. Don't you know that you are always safe in approaching the campfire of a Texan?

I would have been disappointed, O mysterious "A Woman," if you had revealed yourself and given me permission to "call." I'm glad you didn't do that. These are but wireless signals through space. Why should they be spoiled by a "call"? Why should I add to the awful tedium of your life by sitting on a slippery couch in your "parlor," hitching up my trousers an inch at the knees to preserve the crease (when you weren't looking) and drinking a cup of English breakfast tea (which is no good—always get uncolored Japan), and asking you whether you like "Man and Superman" or the Hippodrome the better.

Not for Old Bill Omar, the Texas Scout.

My dear "A Woman," I can do these things sometimes. I can be a perfect gent when I want to. They
used to round me up a year or two ago and drive me
to "functions." Once I was corralled with a bunch of
poets and poetesses up-town. The poets sat in semi-
circles on the floor and read "things of their own."
And the poetesses didn't do a thing to a couple of
old portfolios with eighty pounds of unpublished
"pomes" in them.

Truth is, I'm tired of the New York bluff. I want
a pal who hates this sort of conventionality, who will
be a "good fellow"—in the best sense of the term—
and would like to go about and enjoy the Arabian
Nights that can be found here by the true followers
of the Commander of the Faithful. *Unconspicuous
unconventionality*—these two large words seem to hit
off the idea. Let's see if I can tell you?

One evening I'd like to dine at the Café Francis or
Mouquin's—rather in style, and shaking hands with
well-known artists and hungry writers. The next day
I'd go down on the lower East Side and watch the
police break into joints and get the "local color." The
next evening I'd go home and lock my doors and read
one of Clark Russell's sea stories and swear at anybody that dared disturb me. On the next I'd go to a
theatre and after it was over go to a dance-hall and
entice somebody into a corner and inveigle them into
telling me THINGS!—the things that make literature
if only the editors should let us write 'em. Then the
next evening I'd be a direct descendant of my Puritan
ancestors—I'd write letters to my relatives and read
Macaulay's Essays.

Twenty-four hours later would find me bored, dis-
gusted, angry, dissatisfied—why?—because I haven't
got a "pal" to help me enjoy these things.

Say, A. W., you're all right. Will you excuse camp-fire talk? I slept on the ground three years in the cattle and sheep camps, and I don't care for society phrases. Still I can do 'em if necessary. I don't make no breaks in conversation when there's fine-haired folks around, you bet.

Really, isn't it awful, this way of getting acquainted? I never put an ad in a paper before since my last reincarnation. I am glad you work—it is good, very good for you. I am glad your best friends don't call you pretty—it's a proof that you are. I am glad you are dark—I have admired blondes all my life, and my judgment and taste have been proven faulty. And I like very much your hesitancy at revealing your identity.

Perhaps you'd rather know something more about the tent-makers. My accomplice, Omar No. 1, is the editor of a magazine. He is no mystery, and you would run no risk if you should see him standing on a corner with a red rose in one hand and a corkscrew in the other for purposes of identification.

I will give you a brief but revolting description of myself. First comes a newspaper clipping:

"———, who has brought out his first novel in '——— ———', a rollicking tale of humorous doings in a small Central American republic, is a true soldier of fortune. He is still a very young man, but has lived a varied life. He has been a cowboy, a sheep-herder, merchant, salesman, miner, and a great many other nameless things in the course of very full years spent doing our West, Southwest, Mexico, South and Central America. Mr. ——— (which of course is not his name) went about with a keen eye, and supplemented it by a ready note-book, into which he jotted down his impressions and things noteworthy that happened on the way. He carried an abundant good fellowship, and saw the bright and amusing side of things, as his stories bear sufficient witness."

This is an accurate description except that I am not a very young man, I have never been a cowboy, a sheepherder, merchant, salesman, or miner—I can't deny the "nameless things" so readily. I never carried a note-book in my life. I am reasonably "good humored" except when irritated. Now let's get down to personalities.

In appearance I resemble, more than anything else, a retail butcher who is worried about his bills. I acknowledge to being rather inconstant, and reserve the right to change my opinion every thirty minutes.

Enough of me! Now the important thing is how are we "ships who pass in the night" to exchange signals?

Of course I could walk up Broadway at 7:45 with one shoe off and a fur boa around my neck screaming "Murder!" every thirty seconds. You could come down the street singing "Hiawatha" in a pink kimono and your hair cut short—and so we would know each other. But that is unconventional; isn't it?

Lemme see! I'll tell you.

(This is all new to me. I'm accustomed to lasso ladies to whom I take a fancy, throw them across my saddle, and gallop away, firing my trusty revolver as the horse's hoofs strike fire from the asphalt pavement on the prairie.)

An' it please you, let's say that you come to the 125th St. and Lenox Ave. subway station at a certain time, one evening this week. I will be there with my friend Omar (or alone if you prefer it). I thought perhaps the three of us could meet with less constraint. Upon our singling you out from the common herd (don't mention it) we will respectfully approach you and talk about the weather. Then, if we are so fortunate as to enlist your confidence, we can run out somewhere for a quiet little dinner, and discuss Shakespeare and the musical glasses. Of course we would humbly acquiesce in your declination of the invitation to dine, if you should see proper, but I lay my hand on the cigars in my upper left hand pocket and assure you that your lightest wish shall rule all the procedure after we meet.

If this strikes you all right, please answer, naming the day and time and something by which we can recognize you—say a handkerchief in your left hand or anything that will give us the clue.

Hoping that this will meet with your approval and that you will name an early day,

I remain,
Sincerely yours,
SYDNEY PORTER

That letter, for some reason that she cannot explain, Miss Patterson never answered. There was no meeting at the subway entrance. Two years later chance brought about a more conventional meeting in the home of a friend. In time she told O. Henry that she was the "Personal Girl." After that he used to call her "The Miss Terry," and delighted in teasing her with the reminiscence.

XVII

BAGDAD DAYS AND BAGDAD NIGHTS

Haroun took around with him his vizier, Giafar (a vizier is a composite of a chauffeur, a secretary of state, a night-and-day bank); and old Mesrour, his executioner, who toted a snickersnee. With this entourage a caliphing tour could hardly fail to be successful. *The Discounters of Money*

NIGHT was the revealing hour for the magician of Bagdad [said Al Jennings]. When the million lights flashed and throngs of men and women crowded the thoroughfares in long, undulating lines like moving black snakes, Bill Porter came into his own. . . . At every corner adventure waited on his coming. A young girl would skim stealthily around a corner, or an old "win" would crouch in a doorway. Here were mysteries for Porter to solve. He did not stand afar and speculate. He always made friends with his subjects. He learned their secrets, their hopes, their disappointments. He clasped the hand of Soapy the bum, and Dulcie herself told him why she went totally bankrupt on six dollars a week. New York was an enchanted labyrinth, yielding at every twist the thrill of the unexpected—the wonderful.

Jennings, after being freed from the Columbus Penitentiary, had courageously set himself to the task of winning his way back as a respectable member of society. Wiser than Porter, he made no attempt to hide or obscure his prison record. On the contrary, he shouted it from the house-tops until it lost any possible value it might have had as a weapon in the

284

hands of his political enemies. Consequently in his life there was no Old Man of the Sea.

In the years that followed their association in Columbus there had been occasional correspondence between the two men, and when Jennings reached Bagdad, Porter, arrived at his full glory as O. Henry, undertook to show his friend the sights of the city. The first afternoon was devoted to the grand tour in a "rubberneck" wagon. Late that night they started out again. "Where are we going?" asked Jennings. "Everywhere and nowhere," was the reply. "We may land in Hell's Kitchen or we may find ourselves in Heaven's Vestibule."

It was not long after their reunion that Jennings became acutely conscious of Porter's sufferings from the burden of his Old Man of the Sea. In view of their relations in the past Porter was likely to be outspoken to Jennings when he was reticent to other friends who might have grown closer to him in his new environment. Jennings quotes one utterance, which, laying bare the particular Calvary that was in his heart, was the summing up of his later life. "Colonel, every time I step into a public café, I have the horrible fear that some ex-con will come up and say to me: 'Hello, Bill, when did you get out of the O. P.'"

Rare were the moments when O. Henry was able to put entirely aside those searing memories and that brooding fear. The imagination that ran riot in his writing was the great enemy to his happiness when applied to his own life. The pity of it is that it was all so unnecessary. Will Irwin recently summed up a

regret that has probably been shared by every genuine
friend of Bill Porter.

Why didn't some one speak out? Why did we all
keep up the polite pretence of ignorance? How different it might have been. Why didn't some one of us
go to him and say, "Bill, we know all about it and it
doesn't make the slightest difference. If you ever
owed a debt to society you've paid it in full. At that,
maybe it was an unjust debt. But that's all past.
What counts is that every man in the crowd, every
man with whom you go to dinner, or with whom you
take a drink at the bar, knows all about the years
at Columbus, and no one cares a damn. You're the
only person who thinks about it; nobody else does.
We like you and we respect you. You're O. Henry.
You're doing great work. That's the only thing that
counts. Snap out of your mood. Stop trying to hide
yourself from strangers for fear of running across
some one with a knowledge of a secret that is no secret
at all. Stiffen your shoulders and once for all throw
off your Old Man of the Sea."

Had such a course been followed by an accepted
friend early in the New York days the entire tenor of
O. Henry's life would certainly have been changed;
possibly his existence might have been prolonged for
many years. Unfortunately, no one had the courage
to speak. It would not have been an easy task. With
all his capacity for friendship there was always a warning reserve; a dignity that was maintained even in the
most ludicrous situations. Like others, Will Irwin
recalls the immaculate attire, the low voice, the almost
impenetrable reticence. Manner and dress were bar-
riers. The very gloves that he wore, and the gold-

headed cane that was always in his hand were in themselves a kind of armor against instrusion.

So no one spoke and the Old Man of the Sea maintained his iron grip. The full extent of the yoke is still shrouded in mystery. How far did it explain certain of O. Henry's goings and comings; his constant need of money even in the years when his earnings from his pen should have been more than ample for his needs and his occasional extravagances? At the time of his death and before it there were ugly rumors in the air—talk of blackmail that he paid under threat of exposure of his *secret de Polichinelle*. The rumors have persisted to this day. In connection with them there was whispered the name of a man who twenty years ago was well known in the New York magazine and newspaper offices. Another story circulated just after O. Henry's death had it that he was paying blackmail to three persons, two men and a woman. Al Jennings quotes Porter as saying one night in his rooms in the Caledonia: "I can't stand it much longer. She comes after me regularly, and she's the wife of a big broker here at that. To-night I told her to go hang. She'll get no more from me." To this confidence Jennings adds the comment: "Not a former convict at the penitentiary—none of these, so far as I know, ever bothered him—but a woman of high social class, a woman who had lived in Austin and flirted with Bill Porter in his troubadour days."

But to turn to a pleasanter topic: some of Will Irwin's reminiscences. It was two years after O. Henry settled in New York that Will Irwin came on from the West. Before leaving California he and Gelett Burgess

Saturday

Hello, Mr. Bill

Say — a fool and his money &c.

Is there anything doing for about $49.98 today for the purpose of purchasing things offered for sale in the marts? I had to send most all of that stuff abroad that you

A LETTER TO DAVIS WHICH
ILLUSTRATES THE PECULIAR
AND MYSTERIOUS ECONOMICS
OF O. HENRY

gimme the other
day.
      Dont press
the matter if
it seems out
of order. I'll
be even & ahead
of the game
pretty soon.
      There we'll
come to you
on Monday the
new story — I
want it type-
written first.
      Greetings and
Undying veneration
in either case.
Yrs   Sydney Porter

had been collaborating on two books made up of stories
of old San Francisco told with an Arabian Nights
twist. One day in New York Burgess called Will
Irwin's attention to a story in *Brandur's Magazine*
called "A Guthrie Wooing," a highly humorous tale
of a waitress in a Western restaurant whose daily contact with gobbling men temporarily dispelled all dreams
of love and romance. The story, renamed "Cupid à la
Carte," appears in the volume *Hearts of the West*.
"Here is a man," said Gelett Burgess gloomily, "who
is beating us on our own ground."

It was that chance reading of "A Guthrie Wooing"
that led to the friendship between Will Irwin and
Bill Porter. In time Mr. Irwin became the editor of
McClure's Magazine in which many of the O. Henry
stories were published. Before long he was meeting
with the same promises, the same evasions, the same
whimsical requests for advance payments; and like
other editors was often driven to distraction when the
tale for which space was being held open was not
forthcoming on time. More than once Will Irwin was
forced to sit relentlessly by O. Henry's side, refusing
to leave until the last line was written and the manuscript reluctantly yielded.

A Will Irwin memory involving his highly gifted
collaborator and brother Californian, Gelett Burgess:
All the world knows how the Englishman best remembered as Lewis Carroll wrote *Alice in Wonderland*, the
tale that has been the delight of millions, and lived
to repent it. At least he made the pretense of repent-
ing it. In a somewhat similar unfortunate moment
Gelett Burgess wrote "The Purple Cow." It won him

THE SALOON OF "THE LOST BLEND"

This establishment for the dispensing of liquid refreshments stood at the northeast corner of Irving Place and 18th Street, New York, and was a favorite haunt of O. Henry when he lived across the street.

an unexpected and undesired fame. The lines of the skit, nonsensically intended as a satire on certain of the art eccentricities of the hour, were chanted from one end of the land to the other.

> I never saw a Purple Cow,
> I never hope to see one.
> But this I tell you here and now,
> I'd rather see than be one.

In dashing off the nonsense Burgess had builded not wisely but too well. Try as he would he could not live down "The Purple Cow." It obscured his more serious work; it actually proved an obstacle in his career. Strangers meeting him for the first time invariably brazenly quoted it to him. In time it became a nightmare. The slightest reference to it brought sulking, brooding misery. In the midst of a burst of gayety the remotest allusion to the hated lines plunged him into the depths of silence and gloom.

One evening O. Henry, Will Irwin, and Gelett Burgess were of a party in a merry mood. In the group was the exceedingly vital young woman who in the early years of the century enjoyed some celebrity as the "Queen of Bohemia," a title inherited from an earlier "queen" who had reigned in Pfaff's Cellar. A diversion said to have been popular among earlier Americans but now since the passage of a certain amendment relegated to the limbo of forgotten things, had its share in stirring the spirit of adventure. Finally some one suggested that they all adjourn to the apartment of the Queen of Bohemia for dinner. In the general applause of the idea, the Queen's voice was the only one raised in dissent. She had, she protested, nothing in the apartment of which a dinner could be made, and no money with which to repair the deficiency. But that made no difference, the others urged. They would provide the materials. "And I," announced O. Henry, "will cook the dinner."

The "Queen" overruled, the party proceeded on a round of purchases, and laden with provisions enough to feed a small army, stormed the apartment of the reluctant hostess. There O. Henry installed himself as cook, placing a great steak on the fire and dexterously preparing the ingredients of certain mysterious sauces. One of them involved the beating of eggs. A particular egg roused his suspicions. He paused, spoon in air. He scanned the waiting, hungry circle until his glance fell upon Gelett Burgess. A malicious smile spread over his face and he solemnly began to chant:

> I never beat a rotten egg,
> I never hope to beat one;
> But this you'll understand, I beg,
> I'd rather beat than eat one.

George Jean Nathan is one of the men who recalls prowling with the Caliph in Bagdad days and Bagdad nights. Once, Mr. Nathan tells, O. Henry was in company with H. H. McClure in a Broadway restaurant. "What are you going to do to-night?" asked McClure. "I'm going to persuade a hobo to give me three hundred dollars," was the answer. "On a bet?" asked McClure. "Not at all. That's the price of a story, and I'm going to rub up against some tramps down on the Bowery until one of them suggests a plot to me."

In pursuance of the plan O. Henry moved about the
Bowery until finally he got in touch with a typical
bum. Together they strolled down the street and asked
a passer-by for the time. "Almost midnight." "I feel
like a cup of coffee," said Haroun to his ragged companion. "Come on, I've got a quarter and we'll blow
some of it in this place." They entered the dingy eat-
ing-house, sat up to the counter and each ordered a
cup of coffee and a ham sandwich. Although the two
men had been together for some time, the writer had
detected the gleam of nothing definite in the tramp
that promised to provide the copy he was seeking. But
he felt sure that he had picked his man right and that
the suggestion would eventually come.

Rarely leading the conversation, preferring to let it
come naturally, he said nothing to his companion of
the night, who was busily engaged with the food before
him. When they had finished and had reached the
street, Porter suggested that they walk leisurely up
the Bowery and see if there was anything to be seen.
They wandered aimlessly for fully an hour and a half
and then Porter said that he felt like another cup of
coffee. In another eating place, two more cups of
coffee at two cents a cup. Then more walking, but still
no idea from the tramp. Finally tired out, Porter told
his companion that he was going to leave him. He
reached out to "shake," and as their hands met, Porter
surprised the hobo by laughing. "What's up, cull?"
asked the other. "Oh, nothin'," replied Porter, "I just
thought of something."

The "something" in point was an odd twist for a
new story. But the oddest twist of all—and a typically

O. Henry twist—was that the idea that he had suddenly found for his story had absolutely nothing to do
with the Bowery, with tramps, with two-cent coffee, or
anything even remotely related thereto. "Well, then,"
remarked a friend to whom he had related the adventures of the night, "what good did the Bowery sojourn
do you? You didn't get your three-hundred-dollar
idea from the tramp after all, did you?"

"Indeed I did," was the answer. "That is, in a way.
The tramp did not give me the idea, to be sure, but
he did not drive it out of my head—which is just as
important. If I had not gone down on the Bowery
and had chosen an uptown friend for a companion instead of that tramp, my more cultured companion
would not have allowed me a moment's conversational
respite in which my mind could have worked, and, as a
consequence, the idea would never have come to me. So
you see, the Bowery hobo served a lot of good, after
all."

Mr. Nathan has told how, strolling one night
through Madison Square after the theater, O. Henry
came upon a young girl crying bitterly. The man
with O. Henry approached the girl and inquired the
cause of her grief. She told her story. She had come
to the city from a town in central New Jersey, had
lost her way, and was without money, friends, or a
place to sleep. Deeply touched, the man with Porter
gave the girl a couple of dollars, put her in charge of
a policeman, whose latent sympathy he managed to
arouse with a one dollar bill, and, satisfied with his act
of charity, locked arms with Porter and continued
through the Square to Twenty-third Street. "Why

didn't you speak to her?" he asked. "I'll bet that there was a corking story in that girl that you could have dragged out." Porter smiled. "Old man," he said, "there never is a story where there seems to be one. That's one rule I always work on. It saves time and, let me see—two plus one—yes, three dollars."

Across every counter of the New York department stores is the shadow of O. Henry. "Shop girls"—he wrote of Nancy in "The Trimmed Lamp"—"no such persons exist. There are girls who work in shops. They make their living that way. But why turn their occupation into an adjective?" At Sixth Avenue and Eighteenth Street is Sieber-Mason's, the scene of "The Ferry of Unfulfilment," whence "a thousand girls flowed along the sidewalk, making navigation danger-ous to men." Discharged from the "Biggest Store" Hetty Pepper made her way to her home high up in the Vallambrosa Apartments, there to assist in finding romance as related in "The Third Ingredient." Ma-dame Beaumont, who in every-day life answered to the name of Mamie Siviter ("Transients in Arcadia"), having lived her annual glorious week in the Hotel Lotus, went back to her place behind the hosiery coun-ter at Casey's Mammoth Store. The heroine of "The Buyer from Cactus City" was of the sisterhood. A saleslady in the "gents" gloves, Maisie of "A Lick-penny Lover," was one of three thousand girls in the "Biggest Store." "Do you ever go into the depart-ment stores to study them?" some one once asked Porter. "Indeed not," was the reply. "It's not the sales-girl in the department store who is worth studying, it is the sales-girl out of it. You can't get romance over a counter."

One evening in December, Mr. Nathan relates, O. Henry was walking down Broadway in company with two friends. Near Herald Square the men were approached by a rather well-dressed young man who in a calm, gentle voice told his hard luck story, and begged for the loan of a quarter. One of the men handed over the twenty-five cents to the stranger and the latter disappeared round the corner. "Seemed like an honest, worthy chap," said the dispenser of charity. "Yes," said Porter quietly, "he seemed like an honest, worthy chap to me, too—last night."

While walking down Broadway on another occasion O. Henry accidentally bumped against a man who was not looking in the direction in which he was walking. "I beg your pardon," said the writer, "but really you ought to look where you are going." "If I did in this town, I probably wouldn't go far," replied the man with a sarcastic smile. "Ah," said O. Henry quickly, "and how are all the folks in Chicago?"

O. Henry never missed a favorable opportunity to have a chat with an amiable policeman. "Policemen know so many odd things and so few necessary ones," was one of his sayings. One night he was talking with one of the bluecoats in Hell's Kitchen, a region described in "Vanity and Some Sables." There was the sound of two loud revolver shots. "Some one's been killed," said O. Henry. "Don't worry, only injured. It takes at least three bullets to kill any one in this part of town," was the cop's reassurance.

To most of his friends and acquaintances O. Henry

was "Bill." To Roy Norton he was "Sid." "I could cover twenty pages with personal stories of Sid," Mr. Norton writes. "I was inclined to add another, showing his carelessness in money matters, but don't know whether it's just to dwell too much on his drinking habits." Roy Norton was a near neighbor of the Caliph when the latter was living in the Caledonia, Mr. Norton having an apartment up four flights of stairs at 13 West Twenty-eighth. That proximity had its conveniences. When either of the two was short of funds, by no means an unusual condition, the other was near at hand for a "quick touch." One hundred dollars was the limit of these "touches." Fifty dollars was the usual amount and once the Caliph suggested that they should write a joint ode to a rebounding fifty dollar bill.

One night [writes Mr. Norton] I went over to his rooms in the Caledonia to pay back fifty I had borrowed about a week before. He was bothered about a story that he said he owed Archie Sessions for advanced money, but after a few minutes chucked his pencil down and said: "Hey, Kunnell! Seems to me it's time to observe our immemorial custom"—which was that whenever either of us got that fifty from the other, the recipient bought something. "Let's go up to the Knickerbocker," he said. "I owe that fellow Tom a dollar he lent me the other night when I was short." So we ambled off up there; Sid ordered one round, which we drank; then insisted on another, and when he came to pay, looked blank. He didn't have the price of those four drinks in his pocket. He had gone off leaving the fifty dollars on top of his desk. What is more I have an idea that when he went out he left the door open.

Illustrating another side of O. Henry, Roy Norton goes on to tell of his prowess as a marksman. He writes:

A man of constant surprises, was Sid Porter! And the surprises ran a gamut, whimsical usually, grave at rare intervals, then unexpectedly betraying some hidden knowledge, or unboasted skill. We had been friends for some years, bordering at times on intimacy to an extent when seldom a day passed without our seeing each other, before I ever knew of his proficiency in firearms.

"Didn't know you could shoot," he said one night when, as he frequently did, he climbed the stairs to a little apartment I maintained—up near the roof and but three or four minutes from his rooms. He had a newspaper in his hand which gave the results of a rifle contest in which I had blundered to a winning record. "Used to shoot some myself," he said. "Come on around to a gallery I know on Seventh Avenue. I'll see whether all that newspapers publish is lies."

He more or less dragged me out and led me to what proved to be about the best of the underground ranges with which Seventh Avenue was, more than twenty years ago, infested. I wasn't surprised when he and the proprietor greeted each other like old friends, because one never knew what kind of friends he would meet, or where, or how. I was forewarned when the man behind the counter went to the rear and returned with a beautiful regulation Colt's revolver, evidently something reserved for experts.

"Nothing doing," I remarked. "I've never got to be anything you could notice with a gun like that. Just average out where I came from, and guns were the first presents given to the newly born by proud godfathers."

The obliging proprietor brought out a special rifle

and after a few minutes O. Henry said, "Well, you've restored my faith in the probity of the press. Also you've stuck me for about one dollar. Now it's my turn with the small cannon."

And it was! I hadn't even a chance when it came to all round shooting with a revolver, and although brought up on what was then the frontier, I have seldom seen a better pistol shot than Sid Porter. Making perfect scores at a target is not rare—nothing to write about; but he did something that I doubt if there is one in five thousand comparatively good pistol shots can do well, consistently perfect "string shooting."

String shooting consists in suspending a light weight by a white twine from the ceiling against a black background, and shooting to cut the string. It can be done only with a dead center shot, owing to the delicately selected weight. The weight is just heavy enough so that anything but a dead center shot causes the string to slip to one side, leaving a black mark on the white twine, if it has been hit at all. Sid Porter not only made me open my eyes at that style of shooting, but did something that was astounding, shot at the string when it was swung like a long, slow pendulum. He would wait until it had come to a gentle, regular, short arc, and if he did not succeed cutting the twine, nearly always left a mark on it. I couldn't do it. I dropped out. The proprietor could give Sid a match, but expert though he was (I understand a retired champion) got the worst of it. He told me one time, months afterward, that he considered Sid Porter one of the best revolver shots at a moving target that he had ever known. Later I discovered another peculiarity in my friend's make-up; he always selected an hour so late for a visit to the range that we could be practically certain of being alone, and if even a few curious loafers intruded, would glance around at me and say, "We'll have to go now if we're going to keep that date with Mr. Witherance," a signal for immediate departure.

One night when the late Charles Jennings happened into my rooms while O. Henry was there, I tried to stir up a match, for Charley Jennings was himself very expert with a revolver, having passed nearly all his life in the far West; but although Charley and Sid were excellent friends, the latter could not be enticed out. After Charley had gone Sid said, almost plaintively, "Please don't tell folks I can shoot. My reputation's bad enough as it is and besides somebody might try to get me on the police force."

That room had many memories of him. There was a sideboard in it which in those days, before Mr. Volstead, offered hospitality. One night he came up and deposited three bottles on top with the explanation, "It's not fair, Kunnel, for me to be coming up three or four nights a week empty and going away full. Too much of a reversal of that Biblical story about the virgins' lamps."

I protested somewhat vigorously. He grinned and made no reply. A week or so later he came up while I was working on a story. We had a rule that when either visited the other and found work under way, there was to be no interruption, the visitor chucking himself into a chair with a book, staying as long as he pleased or departing when he chose. In the course of the evening he went to the sideboard two or three times and finally I noticed, absent-mindedly, that each time he did so he very carefully took some change from his pocket. It wasn't until I pulled the last sheet from the typewriter that he said, "Come on out. Some fresh air does one good after work." Then as we were going out he stopped abreast the sideboard and I saw several exact little piles of coins. He picked them up, one by one, counted them, put them in his pocket and as he

reached for one of *my hats* sighed and said, "A man
spends an awful lot on drink. I saved ninety cents for
booze and thirty cents in tips by coming up here to-
night. Kept count of it by paying each time. Now
I'm going to take you to a dive I just found where we
can get the biggest schooner of beer you ever saw for
a nickel."

I mentioned his taking *my hat*. He handed me occasional annoyance and frequent amusement by this
idiosyncrasy of his. He would lounge up to my place
just about the time I had bought a new hat, and sooner
or later, before he left, would spot that hat and try
it on in front of the mirror in the hat rack. Unfortunately we wore the same size and shape, and almost
invariably he would remark that he liked mine best
and—walk off with it! It made no difference if mine
cost five dollars and his two, or vice versa. That part
never entered his mind. When I packed up and left
that apartment I found no less than five hats with the
initials S. P. in them. When recently I returned to
New York after seventeen years' absence abroad and
took some trunks out of their long storage, almost the
first thing I found was a crumpled hat, now old-fashioned, with S. P. perforated in the hat band, and it was
with a sad heart that I hung it above my book case in
which there are many autographed books and one in
particular which is oddly defaced on the title page with
interlineations making it read: To Roy Norton, my
friend, a *very* "Gentle Grafter," from another one.
Sidney Porter, alias O. Henry.

Sometime during the winter of 1906-7, William
Griffith, who had then recently succeeded Theodore
Dreiser as the editor of the *Broadway Magazine*,
sought out O. Henry with the idea of enlisting him as
a contributor. The first meeting led to a close acquaint-

ance that lasted until O. Henry's death in 1910. Not many months elapsed after that meeting before O. Henry was writing as follows:

DEAR COLONEL BILL:

Please send me $25. I've invited a friend to dinner. From the looks of him, he isn't going to pay for it; and I can't.

At that time, Mr. Griffith points out, O. Henry, though much sought after by the magazines, was far from being well known to the public at large. Nor, in spite of his almost chronic need of money, was it a simple matter to secure him as a contributor; and for various reasons, valid or paradoxical. In the first place, a few publications, to which he had contributed before and after his arrival in Bagdad, had secured prior liens on his work by advancing him hundreds, if not thousands, of dollars for stories which had not yet been written, much less delivered.

Parenthetically, says Mr. Griffith, it is a matter of record that O. Henry was as scrupulous in discharging his obligations to the editors for whom he wrote as he was as an artist pursuing his art. It remains to be recorded that he never borrowed a plot, or misappropriated an idea knowingly; although in his later years it was a custom of editors to send him outlines for stories such as they hopefully fancied would appeal to him for fiction treatment.

Mr. Griffith writes:

On one occasion, being in despair of a story from him to fill a yawning gap in the magazine I was editing, I ventured to suggest to him the possibility of a story based upon the idea of a Romeo cop and a Juliet housemaid having a lovers' quarrel below stairs in a Fifth Avenue mansion, the master of which was an international financier. Distraught by the threatened loss of her blue-clad beau, the maid irritated the cook, who, in turn, succeeded in decocting an atrocious brew of coffee the next morning, a beverage of which the master of the house was particularly fond. As a result the latter took his wife to task for having such a cook, and was properly cautioned as to the limitations of his province, domestically speaking. Arriving at his office with his temper ruffled, the financier was to preside at a board meeting to consider an international transaction which might involve the country in war, and so on.[1] O. Henry listened patiently to the warmed-over Mother Goose suggestion, and remarked:

"Not so bad, in its way; but I'm afraid it would curdle the ink."

Richard Duffy has told how Porter came to New York. Mr. Griffith adds a point or two to that account:

A propos of his becoming a resident of New York at the age of forty, many accounts have been given. I am repeating his own, saying that he had been staying for some months with relatives in Pittsburgh, when he was invited by the editors of *Ainslee's Magazine,* to which he had contributed several stories, to go to New York with their guaranty to take one story a month at one hundred dollars each. He accepted the invitation with the proviso that he was to be paid for the first story in advance. To the surprise of the editors, the

[1] Innocently seizing upon the idea in the air, Mr. Griffith was borrowing a conventional plot of Richard Harding Davis, then in the full swing of his popularity. Compare the general outline with Davis's story "The Boy Scout," for example.

publisher of the magazine authorized the advance payment, and a cheque was duly forwarded.

A week passed, with no word from Porter. But presently a letter arrived, explaining that the one hundred dollars sent him had mysteriously evaporated, and asking for another hundred. Again the publisher authorized the sending of the money, and in the course of a day or two O. Henry arrived on the scene. After meeting the editors, to quote himself: "They escorted me, with fear and trembling, to the office of the publisher, Mr. S———, who abruptly closed his office door, and motioned me to a chair. Fearing the worst was yet to come, I hastened to thank Mr. S——— for his generosity, and assured him that his confidence was not misplaced. 'Don't mention it, my dear sir,' he rejoined, 'I was born and brought up in Pittsburgh, and was only too glad to assist in your escape.' "

Of the personal O. Henry, Mr. Griffith writes:

He was more interesting as a talker than in his stories—that is when with a congenial companion. First, however, there was his barrier of natural reserve. Till this was penetrated—and he had to penetrate it himself by sensing a potential friend in the casual acquaintance—there was no geniality. I am not of the opinion that this was due to innate modesty, so much as to his natural disposition to be a looker-on in his Bagdad. To have been a cynosure or a personage would have meant distraction from taking notes for future reference and use in his tales.

Mr. Griffith quotes a woman novelist:

Unquestionably he was a great *raconteur*. Had his table-talk been taken down in short-hand, it would have sounded very much like his written dialogue, only it

was not circumscribed and curbed by the limits of the
story and the necessity of keeping the narrative upper-
most. . . . His wit was urban, sophisticated, individual, quite free from tricks and the desire to obtain
effects. It was never mordant or corrosive, but struck
clean and swift as lightning. It was packed with
worldly knowledge, designed to delight the woman of
thirty or forty, not of twenty.

One of the earliest letters that Porter wrote William
Griffith was in the summer of 1907. After the usual
manner it bore simply the date of Friday. It was
written from the Caledonia. In addition to revealing
the writer's chronic need of money, the letter contains
some interesting information about the story "Thimble,
Thimble," which, apparently, was destined to appear
in the *Broadway Magazine* sometime in 1907, but was
not printed until *Hampton's* published it in the issue
for December, 1908. The *Broadway* evidently paid
two hundred dollars for the tale, a bargain price, as
Porter facetiously says, in view of the fact that he was
arriving at the period of high prices, when he was
commanding five hundred dollars, seven hundred and
fifty dollars and even more for his stories. The letter
reads:

MY DEAR COLONEL GRIFFITH:
   If you've got one hundred dollars right in your desk
drawer you can have my next story, which will be ready
for delivery next Thursday at the latest. That will
pay half; the other half on delivery. I'm always wanting money and have to have a century this morning. I
just wanted to give you a chance at the story at summer
rates, if you want it. Please give the bearer a positive

answer, as I will have to know at once so as to place
it this afternoon.

Yours very truly,
SYDNEY PORTER

P. S.   Story guaranteed or another supplied.

"I never want to be anywhere where I have more
than three faces to watch," O. Henry once told Lindsey
Denison. "I can keep track of those three faces,
study them, and guess what is going on in the minds
behind. I am willing to be one of four at a dinner
table, but there must never be more than four." In
the days when the Lotus Club was famous for its dinners given in honor of celebrities, Chester S. Lord, a
leader of the organization, sought to have O. Henry as
a guest. Mr. Lord applied to Lindsey Denison as an
intermediary, and through him sent a message to Porter saying that he would not be called upon for a speech
or in any other way made conspicuous or uncomfort-
able. Denison urged his friend to attend, pointing out
that the mention of his name in the next day's newspapers as being among those present would have a
practical value, and also that he would establish contacts that were sure to be of service. O. Henry shook
his head. "More than three faces to study," he said,
and would not be moved.

One evening O. Henry and Lindsey Denison, after
wandering together through the early hours, found
themselves at the door of the Denison apartment.
"Come in," urged Denison. "Who's there?" "Only
my wife and a couple of girls." "And who are the
girls?" "Oh, they're the right sort. Not up-stage or
anything like that. Of course, they're lion hunters,

especially when the lions happen to be authors, and they're particularly interested in you and your work."

"Nothing doing," said O. Henry, and started to walk away. Denison called him back as an idea came to him. "Listen," he said. "There's no reason why I should introduce you under your own name. I'll tell you what I'll do. I'll say that you are your own old friend Arthur Williams of Texas, of whom you've told me so much. Then I'll mention that you know O. Henry very well. In that way you may have a chance to get the real low down on yourself."

The suggestion appealed to O. Henry's whimsical sense of humor. "Arthur Williams" was formally presented, and Mrs. Denison, sensing at once the spirit of the jest, lent herself whole-heartedly to the deception. In the course of talk Mr. Denison casually mentioned that Mr. Williams was an intimate friend of Sydney Porter, as the writer was generally called in the Denison household. That was enough. The girls insisted on sitting figuratively at Mr. Williams's feet and questioning him about his friend.

Soon their hero-worship vanished. The tongue of Iago was at work. The imagination of this false friend of O. Henry ran riot, rising to heights of vilification. Sydney Porter, according to his account, was a dangerous man, one of the worst men in New York. He was not to be trusted. He never had had an original idea of his own and had stolen the plots of all his stories. He lived in dubious ways, cadging upon his friends and acquaintances, and often even extorted money from shop girls. One of the listeners, appalled by these revelations, shook her head sadly. "And to think that a man like that could write such a beautiful tale as 'An Unfinished Story!' " "I'll tell you about that too," said Iago. "Sydney Porter wrote that story for the sole purpose of revenging himself on a shop girl in Wanamaker's who had turned him down."

Later in the evening, when the girls had departed, there was general laughter over the success of deception. Suddenly O. Henry became serious. "In all that rigmarole," he said, "there was just one bit of truth. The real Dulcie *was* a shop girl in Wanamaker's and she did turn Piggy down. And Piggy—I was Piggy."

PART IV
SCHEHEREZADE

XVIII

CONCERNING THE STORIES AND THEIR STORIES

If I could have a thousand years—just one little thousand years—more of life I might, in that time, draw near enough to true Romance to touch the hem of her robe.   *He Also Serves*

OF THE O. Henry stories there are many stories to be told. The above quotation illustrates one aspect of his work. From time to time during his lifetime and after his death charges or at least hints of plagiarism were in the air. Behind some of these were envy or malice. The charge of plagiarism is one that few writing men have escaped. There is an old saying which runs: "Rivals will run up to thee and call thee plagiary; and rather than that proof should be wanting, similar words to those of thine will be thrown in thy teeth out of Leviticus and Deuteronomy." More bluntly Mr. Kipling has said the same thing in the lines:

> When 'Omer smote his bloomin' lyre,
> 'E'd 'eard men sing by land and sea;
> An' what 'e thought 'e might require,
> 'E went an' took—the same as me.

That occasionally O. Henry "went and took" is not to be denied. Very often the appropriation was probably entirely unconscious. A haunting line, long stored in the memory, suggested itself at the moment of writing. The quotation is an example of that. "He Also

Serves" was written in the autumn of 1908. Fifteen
years earlier when Porter in Austin was going through
his early receptive and imitative stage of authorship,
Kipling had published his verses "To the True
Romance":

> Thy face is far, from this our war,
> Our call and counter-cry,
> I shall not find Thee quick and kind,
> Nor know Thee till I die.
> Enough for me in dreams to see
> And touch Thy garments' hem:
> Thy feet have trod so near to God
> I may not follow them.

The inspiration of the lines with which "He Also
Serves" begins is obvious. But the fair inference is
that the memory had been a dormant one, and
that the imitation was neither conscious nor intentional.
The whole history of literature abounds in such resem-
blances. Take some of the most familiar of sayings.
Wordsworth writing: "The good die first," was preceded by Byron's "Heaven gives its favorites early
death"; by Drummond's "Who yet was good that ever
died old"; by Plautus's *Quem di diligent adolescens
moritur?*"

Shakespeare's "There is a tide in the affairs of men"
was forestalled by lines of Chaucer. Tennyson's
"Godiva" was based upon the same subject as an earlier
poem by Leigh Hunt; and when Tennyson wrote:

> I hold it true, whate'er befall,
> I feel it when I sorrow most,
> 'Tis better to have loved and lost
> Than never to have loved at all,

there was perhaps somewhere in the back of his mind
the faint memory of Houghton's:

> He who for love has undergone
> The worst that can befall,
> Is happier thousandfold than one
> That never loved at all.

But after this intrusion of a literary essay, to come
back concretely to the subject of the O. Henry stories.
Three of them that in particular have been singled out
as resembling closely in plot and outline other stories
written by other men are "The Song and the Sergeant," "A Retrieved Reformation," and "The Duplicity of Hargraves." Immediately after the publication
of "The Song and the Sergeant" in the New York
World for February 26, 1905, the *Bookman* received
several letters, which were not printed, pointing out its
similarity to a magazine story that had appeared many
years earlier.

Likewise the plot of "A Retrieved Reformation,"
appearing in the *Cosmopolitan* for April, 1903, was
traced to a story, "The Diamond Drill and Mary,"
which had been published in the *Black Cat* in 1900.
Before the writers of this book there is now a letter
from a correspondent who shall be nameless, charging
that Porter himself was conscious that he had "skated
too close," and had urged the correspondent to say,
"if it came to a show-down," that he had given Porter
the idea in conversation as an original story.

The most striking resemblance of all, however, is
that of the O. Henry story "The Duplicity of Hargraves" to the Leonard Merrick story "A Very Good

Thing for the Girl." In each the plot is practically the same. An ambitious young actor studies a projected part from the life, and scores a tremendous hit. In each story the unsuspecting model, attending a performance of the play, recognizes himself in the stage character, and is stirred to hot resentment. Leonard Merrick's hero is in love with the daughter of the little Church of England minister who is the victim of the innocent plot and loses her on account of what she considers as a betrayal of her father. In the O. Henry version there is no love element, and the model from whom Hargraves builds up the rôle that makes the success of "A Magnolia Flower" is a fiery Alabama major of the old school.

The charges of plagiarism directed at O. Henry on account of "The Duplicity of Hargraves" were charged with circumstantial detail. One version was that in the original writing of the story the following of the Leonard Merrick plot was even closer, and that O. Henry, conscious of his "borrowing," as an afterthought added the twist at the end in order to divert suspicion. The belief that O. Henry "borrowed" his story has long persisted in many quarters. Let Mr. Merrick forever clear O. Henry's memory of that charge, and inferentially of similar charges. "The Duplicity of Hargraves" was originally published in *Munsey's Magazine* for February, 1902. The present authors wrote to Mr. Merrick to check up on "A Very Good Thing for the Girl."

Mr. Merrick's reply, under date of May 3, 1930, is in part as follows:

I wrote to A. P. Watt for the information you want and they reply as follows: "According to our records, 'Very Good Thing for the Girl' was published serially in this country (England) in the *English Illustrated Magazine* in September, 1903." So if the O. Henry story was published about 1902, as you say, he got there first. I have not read that story of his to this day, and I should very much like to if you will let me hear what volume it is in.

The charge of plagiarism against O. Henry may be for all time dismissed. The deliberate plagiarism is invariably the work of the unintelligent amateur. Detection is certain. O. Henry, being neither an amateur nor unintelligent, knew that. On the other hand, he was acutely conscious of the idea in the air. The contention of his best friends that he not only never borrowed a plot but that also he resented a plot being outlined to him is hardly to be accepted as complete. Presumably the plots so offered did not appeal to him. Some Frenchman is reputed to have said that there are only seven original plots; and that all the stories of the world have been based upon these seven plots or variations of them. No one, however, seems to know who the particular Frenchman was, what the occasion of his utterance, or what the seven original plots exactly were. Presumably most of them are to be traced back through the fairy tales collected by Charles Perrault in the seventeenth century. Certainly one of the basic plots is that of Cinderella and the Glass Slipper. Like other writers of all lands and times, O. Henry told that story in various versions over and over again. It is the germ idea of "The Count and the

Wedding Guest," "The Brief Début of Tildy," "The
Enchanted Profile," "Past One at Rooney's," "The
Buyer from Cactus City," and a score more.

There is also the echo of more modern tales. But
rarely was there any attempt to disguise the source.
When himself conscious of a resemblance he was quick
to emphasize it. Take "Thimble, Thimble," the story
of the Northerner, the Southerner, the Old Nigger
Man, the Hunting-case Watch and the Open-Faced
Question. The story appeared in *Hampton's Magazine*
for December, 1908. "Mostly borrowed from the late
Mr. Frank R. Stockton, as you will conclude," says
O. Henry; and a little later: "Of course you can per-
ceive at once that this flavor has been shoplifted from
Mr. F. Hopkinson Smith, in spite of the 'et' after the
'Carter'." His "Best-Seller," which appeared in 1909,
was frankly a Zenda or a Graustark novel converted
into a short story with a United States twist. In
"Next to Reading Matter" he drew openly from Rostand's "Cyrano de Bergerac," just as Mr. Booth Tarkington drew openly from Rostand's "L'Aiglon" in his
story "Great Men's Sons."

Occasionally in an O. Henry story there is to be
found an amusing discrepancy or inconsistency. The
wonder is that there are not more; due to his habit of
writing one part of his tale to placate an insistent editor waiting at his shoulder, or as an earnest of the
promised copy to accompany a plea for a further payment in advance. There is a curious blunder, for example, in the story just mentioned, "Thimble,
Thimble." But have not authors been making these
little "breaks" since the beginning of time? Did not

Dickens in *Nicholas Nickleby* make Wackford Squeers in one breath order the pupils of Dotheboys Hall to crack in the ice in the pond and weed the garden? Did not Thackeray in *The Newcomes*, kill off Lord Farintosh's mother only to bring her back to life in a subsequent chapter; and repeatedly in *The Adventures of Philip* call Philip Firmin, Clive Newcome? And quite recently there was Mr. Sinclair Lewis, in *Dodsworth*, describing his hero's stimulated thirst when returning to the "experiment" of his native land, picturing him taking a drink in the morning, "something he had not done since after a certain football game at New Haven"; quite overlooking the fact that Yale's athletic history has never included morning football games.

But to turn to a subject pleasanter and more constructive than those of discrepancies and allegations of plagiarism. Of the geneses and development of the O. Henry stories there are tales to be told. To the gathering of these tales many who knew O. Henry have contributed. Some of the tales, as will be shown, vary from others. At times they are in direct conflict. For example there are two versions of how O. Henry came to write "A Municipal Report," generally ranked as very near the apex of his work.

The more familiar of the two versions is that O. Henry wrote the story in answer to the challenge of Frank Norris, who had said:

"Fancy a novel about Chicago or Buffalo, let us say, or Nashville, Tennessee. There are just three big cities in the United States that are 'story cities'—New York, of course, New Orleans, and, best of the lot, San Francisco."

Very well, said O. Henry, I *will* write a story about
Nashville, Tennessee; and proceeded to tell the tale
of the pathetic Azalea Adair, and her scamp of a husband, and of the faithful old Negro hack-driver who
had been a slave and a descendant of Zulu kings, and
who did not hesitate at murder in defense of his beloved mistress. Then, realizing for once that he had
builded well, he flashed back to Norris a defiance of his
own with the concluding line: "I wonder what's doing
in Buffalo."

That last line certainly supports the above version.
Yet there is another, to the effect that on one occasion
O. Henry and a caller at the Caledonia were discussing
the material out of which a story writer built his tales,
O. Henry maintaining that it was almost entirely a
matter of technique, and that the trained craftsman
should be able to construct a story on any subject,
however trivial, that was offered to him. "I've got
some of my best yarns," he explained, "from park
benches, lamp posts, and newspaper stands." The
caller happened to have in his pocket a Rand and Mc-
Nally pamphlet dealing with Nashville. It consisted
mainly of statistics. He tossed it over. "Write a
story based upon that," he challenged. "I'll do it,"
said O. Henry.

Whichever of these two versions of the ultimate
source of "A Municipal Report," is the correct one, its
subsequent development in O. Henry's mind is illustrated by a letter written to William Griffith.

My dear Colonel:
This story (you will please understand that this
scenario does not give the effect) ends as follows:

The old nigger hack-driver is a relic of the old South. He is a night-hawk and a ruffian (probably) but his piratical depredations upon travellers and transients are for the sole purpose of supporting an old lady (the poetess) who is the last of the family to which he once belonged. All his small earnings are contributed to that end.

Major Caswell, a type of the degraded Southerner, is living off the slender income of his relative (Azalea Adair). He is the rat thoroughly despicable.

Azalea Adair is a type of the tenderly nursed lady of the old régime, but she is drained of her resources (furnished by the old negro) by her impossible relative.

In the end there is a dramatic and mysterious murder, the victim being Major Caswell. The "snapper" comes in the last paragraph, revealing the slayer by a bare intimation. The whole scheme is to show that an absolutely prosaic and conventional town (such as Nashville) can equal San Francisco, Bagdad, or Paris when it comes to a human story.

The beginning of this story is not written yet— there will be 2 or 3 pages (to follow) containing references to Frank Norris's lines in which the words occur "think of anything happening in Nashville, Tennessee." I have to look this up in Putnam's Magazine.

It will work out all right.

P. S.   Your money back if you want it.

P. S. S.   Send the dough to the Caledonia.

There are the stories that O. Henry planned to write, or at least had an idea of writing, but never did. Mrs. Sara Coleman Porter has been quoted as saying: "Once at a dinner, my brother told him of a man who hated the particular locality in which he lived so bitterly that he had gone far away, but at his death his body had been brought back to the very spot he disliked for burial." O. Henry was seen to make a note of the idea on his cuff, but it does not appear in any of his stories.

Another story of a story that O. Henry did not write is recalled by George Rector of the once famous restaurant that bore his name. Occasionally in his moments of particular financial prosperity Porter dined at Rector's. Meeting the proprietor one evening he asked the curious question: "Have you a marine clock on your yacht?" Being answered in the affirmative, he further asked: "Can you explain to me the striking of the bells?" Mr. Rector told him that the even bells were on the hour and the odd on the half hour. There were further questions; as to whether ship's time ran from one o'clock to twenty-four around the clock or from one to twelve; as to whether a man in a dark room who heard a ship's clock strike eight bells would know whether it was morning, noon, or night. Finally he explained the reasons for his careful questioning. To quote Mr. Rector:

O. Henry continued: "I require some technical information. A man is found murdered in a cheap tenement house far in the heart of New York. No one in the house knows anything about him except the landlady, who remembers one solitary visitor of a Latin-American type who came around about two or three times a year. Each visit was the signal for violent quarreling, and the slamming of a door when the South American departed. After one of these visits and an unusually violent argument, the man is found dead in his room the next morning. The visitor is picked up on the landlady's testimony to the police that she heard the sounds of a blow, the falling of a body, and the slamming of a door just as the clock struck eight.

"The South American claims that at eight o'clock he was in a barroom on the water front and brings witnesses to prove it. Of course, you understand that I am jumping rapidly and we are now at the trial of the accused man. He is about to be convicted on the landlady's testimony, when his lawyer—he has a lawyer, of course, because it develops that he is the agent for a rich banana republic on the Isthmus—his lawyer brings in last-minute evidence that the landlady's testimony is worthless because the striking of the clock meant nothing. It struck eight all right, but the striking was eight bells, which not only could have been eight P.M. but also eight A.M. And in addition it could have meant four in the morning, four in the afternoon, or noon, or midnight. It was a ship's clock."

O. Henry scratched his head a trifle, and then said: "There's one thing I forgot. Even with the striking of eight bells the landlady would have been able to tell whether it was night or day, because, though the windows in tenements are dirty, they are never that dirty. I will have to make the landlady blind, and I hate to do that, because landladies are my best friends —when I have the rent. . . . Thank you very much, Mr. Rector."

Occasionally an O. Henry story was suggested by an odd bit of local color. That was the case with "The Last Leaf." Porter's shy and almost suspicious attitude toward the stranger who was not the casual stranger, the acquaintance scraped in a mood on a bench in Madison Square or Sheridan Park, or at some corner of "that thoroughfare which parallels and parodies Broadway," has already been emphasized. To his little circle of intimates he was usually accessible. But all these intimates understood perfectly the futility of attempting to arrange formally a meeting between O. Henry and some one who wanted to know him; realized that at the first hint the quarry would take fright and disappear.

So the encounter had to have every appearance of mere chance. Into Porter's rooms on Irving Place, or in the Caledonia, the friend would drop, apparently for a word or two of business. If in the business there was a possibility of an advance, so much the better. With the friend there would be a stranger, whom the friend had chanced to pick up on the way. Nine times out of ten the friend would not introduce the other two. But after a few minutes' talk, and in response to a prearranged signal, the stranger would remark that he had stumbled on a joint near the Bowery where there was a cocktail mixer who had tended bar in forty-nine cities of the United States. Before he had finished Porter had reached for his hat. The friend was forgotten, and arm in arm, stranger and story-spinner sallied forth into the night.

One man established almost immediately a common, sympathetic ground by describing what he called "the most picturesque bit of rear tenement that remains in New York." In three minutes he and Porter were in the street. "I led him down Irving Place to Fourteenth," Porter's new found companion has told, "to Sixth Avenue, past the Jefferson Market Police Court, into Greenwich Village, past Sheridan Park, and down Grove Street to the very end. There, between the front houses, Numbers 10 and 12, there is an opening. Be-

OLD GREENWICH VILLAGE

*A section of the city before its invasion by pseudo-
Bohemians, which was always particularly dear
to O. Henry's heart*

yond the opening is a triangle, in the middle of which is
a tall telegraph pole, and at the back there are three
three-story brick houses, the front windows of which
look out diagonally at a wall against which leaves are
growing.

" 'There is a story there,' said O. Henry, 'a story
that reminds me of an episode that I was reading a
little while ago in Murger's *Vie de Bohème*. Do you
know the book? It is where the *grisette*, at night,
waters the flowers to keep them alive. The lifetime of
the flowers, you remember, was to be the lifetime of
that transient love.' He wrote that story, I am sure,
in 'The Last Leaf,' and when I see that bare, dreary
yard, and the blank wall of the house twenty feet away,
and the old ivy vine, I recall the pathetic tale of Sue
and Joanna and the masterpiece that old Behrman
painted at the cost of his life."

Will Irwin has written: "His tales were conceived
in all manner of ways. . . . Mostly the plots sprang into
his mind in flashes, generated from some remark, some
picture, some slight accident of the day's work." He
left an unfinished story called "The Dream." It had
been ordered by the *Cosmopolitan Magazine*, and after
his death the unfinished manuscript was found in his
room, on his dusty desk. What had been written was
published in the *Cosmopolitan* for September, 1910.

Mr. Irwin has told how the idea for "The Dream"
came. It was about two weeks before the end. As
Porter was resting, his eyes on the clock languidly noting the time, he fell into the intermittent slumber of
the sick. And he dreamed a long dream which seemed
to hold the experience of a lifetime. He awoke with

his eyes still on the clock. He had been asleep less than two minutes. Immediately the story came. He told it to a member of the staff of the *Cosmopolitan*, but he did not begin it then.

The story of "Springtime à la Carte" is also Will Irwin's story. It grew out of a dinner at the old up-town Mouquin's, always one of Porter's favorite restaurants. The talk turned to the subject of Porter's work. "I think I'll make a story out of this table." His eye fell on the bill-of-fare. He picked it up. The *carte du jour* was typewritten. "Here it is, Colonel," he said after a moment. And straightway he told the tale substantially as it was written, of the long search in the great city by the farmer lover for his missing sweetheart, fruitless until chancing into a restaurant his eye falls upon the strange entry on the bill-of-fare that has been typed through tears, and he realizes the significance of "Dearest Walter, with hard boiled egg."

There are two versions of the origin of "The Halberdier of the Little Rheinschloss." According to both of them the tale, like so many other of the O. Henry stories, grew out of a restaurant and a dinner. In other points they differ materially. Al Jennings tells of a German restaurant somewhere on Broadway where the Pilsener was good but where the thing of chief interest to him was a ridiculous figure standing at the landing of the stairs tricked out as an ancient halberdier. One evening when Jennings and Porter were seated at a table in the restaurant in question with steins before them, the former called attention to the figure, saying, "Look at that weak-kneed sap, Bill. Picture him as an ancient man-at-arms. Porter finished his beer and then said: "It's a good story."

Instead of sitting up to talk till one or two in the morning, which was his usual custom, that night Porter insisted on going home early. The two men had an appointment for the next day at noon. When Jennings arrived at Porter's rooms he found the big table where the writing was done littered with sheets of paper, while all over the floor were scraps of discarded manuscript. "I've just finished the yarn," said Porter. "He read it to me," says Jennings, "Just the merest glint had come to him from that steel-plated armor. The Halberdier would never have recognized the gem Porter's genius had polished for him. The story just as it stands to-day was written by Porter sometime between midnight and noon."

More circumstantial is George Barr Baker's version of the origin of the tale. According to him the restaurant that furnished the background as well as supplying the seed idea from which the story grew was one of Porter's familiar haunts, known as Allaire's or Scheffel Hall, at the northwest corner of Seventeenth Street and Third Avenue. For the purposes of fiction Porter called it Old Munich, and described the big hall, with its smoky rafters, rows of imported steins, portrait of Goethe, and verses painted on the walls—translated into German from the original of the Cincinnati poets—all of which seemed atmospherically correct when viewed through the bottom of a glass. Also it was through the bottom of a glass that Porter found his story.

At Old Munich one evening O. Henry, Mr. Baker, and a third man whose name Mr. Baker has now for-

THE STORY OF A SUIT OF ARMOR

The original of the Old Munich of "The Halberdier of the Little Rheinschloss"

gotten, decided to dine. From Porter's home on Irving Place it was just a step, but the way led past the emporium for liquid refreshment presided over by his friend Con, and there he stopped for a friendly word and glass. In consequence his arrival was somewhat late, and he was well fortified. With the progress of the dinner, washed down by copious draughts of the brew for which the establishment was famous, Porter dropped out of the conversation, lapsing into musing silence.

But his story-telling mind was active. An unusually good-looking waiter, who seemed out of place in his occupation, riveted his attention. "Do you see that waiter?" he whispered to his companions. "He's not a real waiter. He's waiting on a bet, or to prove his ability to earn his own living." The waiter disappeared, or at least seemed to do so. That puzzled Porter. Finally he found the solution. Again he confided to his companions. He pointed to a suit of armor that decorated the hall, "That waiter is hiding behind the suit of armor. Yes, he's inside of it." Relapsing once more into silence, he kept studying the armor through the thickening smoke.

Through the open doors came the sound of what in those days was considered to be a high-powered motor car that had stopped before the restaurant entrance, and there was a general stir caused by the appearance of two late arrivals who seemed rather out of place in Old Munich's Bohemian atmosphere. They were an elderly man in faultless evening clothes, and a highly attractive young woman, exquisitely gowned. The management led them to the room above known as the Little Rheinschloss, but not before Porter had appraised them according to his fancy.

"Those people," he announced, "think that they are slumming. Ah, I have it! It's all on account of the handsome waiter! He is in love with the girl and she is in love with him. The old man wants to keep them apart. He has bet the young man that he cannot make his own living, to say nothing of supporting the girl. The young man is trying to prove the old man is wrong. That is why he is waiting on the table. He can't get anything else to do. Now he is hiding behind the armor in order to keep out of sight. No, he's inside the armor." Not a word more would Porter say. Sleepily he surveyed the scene through the bottom of his stein. But the following Monday morning the story was laid on George Baker's desk.

Gilman Hall's testimony tends to bear out the George Barr Baker version. In 1915, a pilgrim, engaged in gathering material for a book about the literary haunts of New York, had prowled about the city in search of the background that would best fit the O. Henry description. The quest proving fruitless, he applied to Gilman Hall for information on the subject. Mr. Hall laughed. "Do I know the real Old Munich? Very well, indeed. Often I dined there with Porter. No wonder you have not found it. You have been looking too far to the north, to the south, to the west. Don't you realize that Porter would never have walked that far if he could have helped it? The only time I ever persuaded him afoot as far as Seventy-second Street and Riverside Drive he stopped, and with an injured air, inquired if we had not yet passed Peekskill. Here we are in front of Number 55. Why not try around the corner? Old Munich is Scheffel Hall."

Al Jennings believes that the genesis of the story "The Furnished Room" came one night when he and Porter visited a dancehall at the corner of Sixth Avenue and Twenty-second Street and there found two girls whom Jennings calls Mame and Sue. Touched by their obvious hunger Porter finally made the suggestion that the party of four adjourn to his own rooms. "It was after one o'clock in the morning," says Jennings, "when we reached the hotel. Porter ordered a beefsteak, potatoes, coffee, and a crab salad. He served the supper on the table where so many of his masterpieces were written. It was in that outlandish situation, with Mame sitting on a box, Sue in an easy chair, and Porter with an apron over his arm like a waiter serving us that 'The Furnished Room' came into being."

Then there is the story of "The Gift of the Magi." The tales that O. Henry had been contributing to the *World* had been highly successful. With the planning of the magazine section for the Christmas number for 1905, it was decided to make the O. Henry story the principal feature, printing it on the first page, with illustrations in color. Dan Smith, then the paper's leading illustrator, was directed to make the drawings, which, to be made ready for the press naturally required considerably more time than the text.

There was the usual desperation when time grew short and no copy was forthcoming from O. Henry. Finally Dan Smith started out on a hunt for the delinquent. Cornering him in his rooms he extracted the confession that not a line had been written, nor had the author the faintest idea of what the story was to be about. Smith urged the seriousness of the situation. "I must get to work at once. Can't you tell me something to draw and then fit your story to it?" For a time O. Henry sat in silence. Then in his slow Southern drawl he said: "I'll tell you what you do, Colonel. Just draw a picture of a poorly furnished room, the kind you find in a boarding house or rooming house over on the West Side. In the room there is only a chair or two, a chest of drawers, a bed, and a trunk. On the bed a man and a girl are sitting side by side. They are talking about Christmas. The man has a watch fob in his hand. He is playing with it while he is thinking. The girl's principal feature is the long beautiful hair that is hanging down her back. That's all I can think of now. But the story is coming."

Paraphrasing O. Henry, the story of that story should end here. But hardly had Dan Smith descended the flight of brownstone steps from Number 55 to the sidewalk of Irving Place than Lindsey Denison received an urgent, imperative telephone call to "come right over." Complying, Denison found his host seated at his writing table, penciling sheets of the familiar yellow copy paper. But the story on which he was working was not the one that had been promised to Dan Smith.

With Lindsey Denison's arrival O. Henry pushed aside his manuscript, rose, locked the door of the apartment, produced from a cupboard material entertainment, and pointed to the sofa in the corner of the room. "Lie down there," he said, "I've got to forget this story and write another one. Have to have it done this afternoon and not a line written. I've thought of an idea for it but I need a living model. You are that model. I'm going to write a story about you and your wife. I've never met your wife, but I think that you two are the kind that would make sacrifices for each other. Now stay on the sofa and don't interrupt." Three hours later O. Henry had written the last lines of "The Gift of the Magi."

There was one story that might well have involved O. Henry and the publishers of the magazine in which it appeared in an action for libel. That was "The Enchanted Profile," which told of Mrs. Maggie Brown, an elderly lady of enormous wealth and parsimonious habits. Mrs. Brown was strangely attracted by the beauty of Ida Bates, the stenographer and typist of the Acropolis Hotel, and adopted her for a period, loaded her with lavish presents, and then, when the bill for a certain dinner came in, had to resort to drastic and irksome economies. In Mrs. Maggie Brown there was more than the daring suggestion of a very wealthy woman who was conspicuous in the news of twenty-five years ago.

The original seed idea of "The Enchanted Profile" may be traced back to the early Texas journalistic days, when Porter had written for the Houston *Post* a skit about the Philadelphia young lady whose countenance was the best beloved in the land for the reason that it had been the model from which the artist for the government had drawn the design for the head to be used in the minting of the silver dollar. Probably for many years the thought of some day turning the point to use had lurked in the back of Porter's mind. But apparently he never saw the setting for it until the night he found his Ida Bates.

The real Ida Bates was not like the girl in the story, a hotel stenographer and typist, but a Miss K. G., a chorus girl who had enjoyed a highly exciting career. One night early in the winter of 1907-8, there was a merry dinner in the old Café Francis. By chance ten persons who knew one another found themselves there, and the management, sensing the situation, put two tables together to accommodate them. Lindsey Denison was one of the party. Miss K. G. was another. There was much animated talk and the clinking of many glasses.

Mr. Denison, chancing to look across the room, saw O. Henry seated alone at a nearby table in a corner. He had been watching and listening intently. "I knew by his expression and dancing eyes that he was getting copy," recalls Mr. Denison. To have invited him over to join the merry revellers would, of course, have been out of the question. It would merely have embarrassed him and probably have moved him to hurried departure. So Mr. Denison left his own table to join his friend.

"Getting a story?" was his greeting as he sat down. "I am, and it's a crackerjack," was the reply. "It's that girl sitting there at the end. She's a beauty. And that profile. In this light it's a silvery gray." "It isn't entirely the light," suggested Denison. "The poor girl has been down on her luck for a number of weeks now, and that's largely responsible for the coloring." "At any rate," persisted Porter. "It reminds me of something. Look at it from here. Can't you see the resemblance to the lady's face on the silver dollar?" "Would you like to meet her?" "Is she dumb?" was the parrying question. "Not an idea in the world." "In that case," said O. Henry spaciously, "bring her over."

XIX

THE BAGDAD THAT THE CALIPH KNEW

"The 'argot' to which you refer was the invention of certain
of your literary 'discoverers' who invaded the unknown wilds
below Third Avenue and put strange sounds into the mouths of
the inhabitants!" *A Little Local Color*

IT is eleven centuries and a quarter century since
Haroun the Just, amid the lamentations of Bagdad on the Euphrates, shuffled off his mortal coil to be
gathered to the arms of the *houris* of the Paradise of
the Faithful. Were he to return to-day to contemplate
the city that was the scene of his wise rule and his
various adventures, his astonishment at the changes
wrought by time would be only relatively greater than
the astonishment of the Haroun of Little Old Bagdad
on the Subway at the transformation that has been
brought about by a brief twenty-one years.

In rough outline the streets and squares in which the
modern Haroun wandered and which he peopled with
his creations remain much the same, but from them
have gone the flavor and color that he knew in the days
of twenty-five years ago, when the world was young
though hardly innocent. There is a drab street known
as the Bowery. Once it blazed with light, and the
blare of strange sounds came from its open doors.
There is another drab street known as Sixth Avenue.
In Haroun's day it still retained much of the evil glory
that had won for it the appellation of Satan's Circus.

The squares that he frequented, Union and Madison, have changed almost out of recognition. Wide avenues cut through the labyrinthine Greenwich Village that he knew. Gone is the Fourth Avenue that moved him to dreams of men rusting in armor and a medieval solitude.

If the modern Haroun were to return to-day to his Little Old Bagdad on the Subway, his Big City of Razzle Dazzle, his Noisyville on the Hudson, his City of Too Many Caliphs, his City of Chameleon Changes, his first visit would almost certainly be to that structure at 55 Irving Place, on the west side of the thoroughfare between Seventeenth and Eighteenth Streets, where, in the front room on the second floor, he lived in the richest years of his adventures and his achievement. He had other homes, but that was preëminently O. Henry's New York home.

To-day the rooms occupied by O. Henry are the offices of a relief organization. The edifice is a dingy four-story brownstone house dating from the Victorian era if not before. The projecting stoop still remains. The casements of the upper stories frame vacancy; the vacancy that stares down at the passerby with a kind of hurt blindness. The structure seems to sense an early demise; a swiftly coming demolition; to be saying: "Next year, next month, next week, to-morrow, perhaps, my remains will be clattering down a chute, and in my place there will be a towering skyscraper."

Porter's constitutional aversion to anything that involved arduous physical exercise has already been emphasized. Therefore, the quintessence of O. Henry-Land lies within a circle of half a mile radius, with 55 Irving Place as the center. Within that circle were to be found the hotels of the Spanish-American New York stories, Chubb's Third Avenue restaurant, the Old Munich of "The Halberdier of the Little Rhein-schloss," and the particular saloon that served as a background for "The Lost Blend." Where that saloon was, diagonally across the street from Number 55, there is a florist's shop now, and were Haroun to re-turn, he would undoubtedly sigh at the transformation.

Also within that half-mile radius were the four sides of Gramercy Park, conspicuous in the tales of aristo-cratic flavor; the bench in Union Square, which could be confused with no other bench in the world, which Stuffy Pete, of "Two Thanksgiving Day Gentlemen," regarded in the light of personal property; and those other benches in the other square, a few blocks to the north, where prepossessing young women, inspired by Robert Louis Stevenson's *New Arabian Nights*, were moved to romantic exaggeration; where disconsolate caliphs, shorn of power and stripped of ill-gotten pelf, sat brooding over the judgments of Allah; where fifth wheels rolled along asphalted pavements, and jinns came obedient to the rubbing of the lamp.

A close associate of Porter whose name has already appeared once in the course of this book was the late Robert Rudd Whiteing. Bob Whiteing, who gave his life in the Great War, was one of the best beloved of men. He followed Gilman Hall and Richard Duffy as an editor of *Ainslee's Magazine*. Once Porter extended to Bob Whiteing an invitation to luncheon. It was to be a Spanish-American luncheon in the course of which Porter was to introduce his guest to certain flavors and dishes that he himself had learned to like or at least to endure in the days of his exile in the Lands of the Lotus-Eaters. The two men were crossing Union Square.

"Come with me," said Porter. "I will show you the real place. Over at M———'s [he mentioned a restaurant in a street to the south] you may find the Señors, the Capitans, the Majors, the Colonels. But if you would sit with the Generalissimos, the Imperators, the truly exalted who hail from Central and South American countries, accept my guiding hand." So from the square they turned in Fifteenth Street and found, on the south side, some seventy-five yards east of Fourth Avenue, the Hotel America, with its clientele of gesticulating Latins, who, if not planning revolutions, had all the appearance of arch-conspirators. It was the atmosphere that went to the making of "The Gold That Glittered," which, the reader may remember, began at the very spot at which the invitation had been extended, "where Broadway skirts the corner of the Square presided over by George the Veracious."

In his nightly wanderings through old Bagdad, Haroun the Just did not confine himself to those thoroughfares that were analogous to London's Park Lane, Paris's Avenue Bois de Boulogne, now Avenue Foch, or New York's Fifth or Park Avenues or Riverside Drive. On the contrary, he preferred to learn in the purlieus, to listen in the shops of the hunchback or the tailor. Likewise the modern Haroun. When editors became too importunate he would say good-by to the companions with whom he had been sitting in a Broadway restaurant, proceed downtown, and stroll along the Bowery or some adjacent street until he found the particular tramp who seemed most promising as copy. Sometimes he found the story and sometimes he did not.

In twenty or thirty of the tales, usually with very definitely marked backgrounds, O. Henry's wanderings about the lower East Side are reflected. He was almost surprisingly careful in his search for local color, though he sometimes took liberties with it for the sake of humor. As an illustration take the relatively unimportant story "The Sleuths" (*Sixes and Sevens*). A man from the Middle West visits New York to find his missing sister. At her last address he learns that she has moved away a month before, leaving no clew, and to help in the search he enlists the services of the famous detectives, Mullins and Shamrock Jolnes. The "science of deduction" leads to 12 Avenue C which is blandly described as an "old-fashioned brownstone house in a prosperous and respectable neighborhood."

Now if any neighborhood in O. Henry's day was *not* prosperous and respectable, it was that about Avenue C and Second Street, which in unsightliness rivaled the Mulberry Bend of earlier times. O. Henry had sensed its offensiveness through his eyes and nostrils. The selection of Number 12 was not mere chance, a meaningless jotting. He knew that there was no such number; that on the southeast corner was a saloon bearing the number 10, and on the northeast corner the pharmacy was designated as 14. Just as there is no 13 Washington Square, there was no 12 Avenue C. Also there is no 162 Chilton Street, where the missing sister was eventually found, for the reason that in the Borough of Manhattan there is no Chilton Street at all.

O. Henry knew his East Side and usually worked from a definite structural model; though most of these models, in view of the changes wrought by the years, are hard to identify to-day. Somewhere on the East Side was the famous Café Maginnis, where Ikey Snigglefritz of "The Social Triangle," in the proudest moment of his life, shook the hand of the great Billy Macmahon. An indication of the exact whereabouts of the Café Maginnis was given in the information that Ikey, leaving it, "went down Hester Street, and up Chrystie and down Delancey" to where he lived. Ikey's home was in a crazy brick structure, "foul and awry," and there Cortlandt Van Suykinck found him and shook his hand, thereby completing the triangle.

Somewhere in the lower East Side was the saloon of Dutch Mike where the Mulberry Hill gang and the Dry Dock gang met in the Homeric conflict the outcome of which sent Cork McManus to strange lands remote from the Bowery and to the adventures related in "Past One at Rooney's." Somewhere there was the Second Avenue boarding house where Miss Conway showed Andy Donovan the locket containing the portrait of her purely imaginary lover as told in "The Count and the Wedding Guest." Between the Bowery and First Avenue, "where the distance between the two streets is the shortest," was the Blue Light Drug Store, where the unhappy hero of "The Love Philtre of Ikey Schoenstein," concocted the mixture that was to work the downfall of his rival, Chunk Macgowan.

In Orchard Street were the rooms of the Give and Take Athletic Association where, as told in "The Coming Out of Maggie," Tony Spinelli played Prince

Charming at the ball of the Clover Leaf Social Club
under the pseudonym of Terry O'Sullivan. Farther
up on the East Side were the Beersheba Flats from
which the variegated tenants were driven forth by official edict to the grass of the park and the sufferings
of "The City of Dreadful Night."

The very first allusion to a New York scene in an
O. Henry story was in the chapter "Two Recalls" of
Cabbages and Kings. There two men were pictured
sitting on a stringer of a North River pier while a
steamer from the tropics unloaded bananas and
oranges. One of the men was O'Day, formerly an
employe of the Columbia Detective Agency. In a
burst of confidence stirred by the sight of the too
familiar bananas, he told his companion of the mistake
that had brought him to his unenviable condition, incidentally clearing up for the reader of the tale the
rather ugly mystery that had obscured the marriage of
Frank Goodwin and the lady known in "Coralio" as
Isabel Guilbert.

There were gateways to the Bagdad that the Caliph
knew. In the story "The Lady Higher Up," O. Henry
pictured a dialogue between Mrs. Liberty, on her
pedestal in the Bay, and Miss Diana at the top of the
tower of the vanished Madison Square Garden. Even
the thick brogue that Mrs. Liberty had acquired could
not hide her envy of the other lady. In the matron's
opinion, Miss Diana had the best job for a statue in
the whole town, with the Cat Show, and the Horse
Show, and the military tournaments where the privates
"look grand as generals, and the generals try to look
as grand as floorwalkers," and the Sportsman's Show,

and above all, the French Ball "where the original
Cohens and the Robert Emmet-Sangerbund Society
dance the Highland Fling with one another."

But even before sighting Mrs. Liberty, "made by a
Dago and presented to the American people on behalf
of the French Government for the purpose of welcom-
ing Irish immigrants into the Dutch city of New
York," the visitor from a foreign shore had a glimpse
of a far-flung outpost of Bagdad as, from the deck of
a transatlantic liner, the great wheels and towers of
Coney Island were pointed out to him. Among these
wheels and towers Alexander Blinker, owner of "Brickdust Row" (*The Trimmed Lamp*), walked with Florence, his chance acquaintance of the boat, learned a
lesson, and saw a light. No more was the jostling
crowd a mass of vulgarians seeking gross joys. Counterfeit and false though the garish pleasures of the
spangled temples were, he perceived that deep under
the gilt surface they offered saving and apposite balm
and satisfaction to the restless human heart. Here, at
least, was the husk of Romance, the empty but shining
casque of Chivalry, the breath-catching though safe-
guarded dip and flight of Adventure. He saw no
longer a rabble, but his brothers seeking the ideal.

Again here was the enchanted chicken-coop of
Madame Zozo, who read "Tobin's Palm" and from it
predicted a dark man and a light woman, trouble and
financial loss, a voyage by water, and a meeting with a
man with a crooked nose; all of which prophecies were
speedily realized. In "The Greater Coney" (*Sixes
and Sevens*), Dennis Carnahan expatiated ironically
on the new city that had risen, Phœnix-like, out of the

ashes of the old, and the wiping-out process, which, to
his way of thinking, consisted in raising the price of
admission from ten to twenty-five cents, and having a
blonde named Maudie take tickets instead of Mickey,
the Bowery Bite.

Then the Babylonian towers and the Hindoo roof
gardens blazing with lights, the camels moving with
undulating walk, and the tawdry gondolas of artificial
Venetian streets. These were what Maisie knew,
Maisie of "A Lickpenny Lover" (*The Voice of the
City*). These things her little soul of a shop girl saw
when the millionaire painter-traveler, Irving Carter,
whose heart she had so strangely won, proposed to her
and drew his eloquent picture of a honeymoon in lands
beyond the seas. These and no more. The next day
her chum in the store asked about her "swell friend."
"Him?" says Maisie in high contempt. "Oh, he's a
cheap skate. He ain't in it no more. What do you
suppose that guy wanted me to do? He wanted me
to marry him and go to Coney Island for a wedding
trip."

But back to Bagdad. It is not likely that the Fourth
Avenue of to-day would appeal to O. Henry's imagination. But as it was twenty-odd years ago it was one of
his favorite thoroughfares. It called to romance and
reached its apotheosis in "A Bird of Bagdad." There
O. Henry pictured it as a street that the city seemed to
have forgotten in its growth, a street, born and bred in
the Bowery, staggered northward full of good resolu-
tions. At Fourteenth Street "it struts for a brief moment proudly in the glare of the museums and cheap
theatres. It may yet become a fit mate for its high-

born sister boulevard to the west, or its roaring, poly-
glot, broad-waisted cousin to the east." Then it passed
Union Square and came to the silent and terrible
mountains, buildings square as forts, high as the clouds,
shutting out the sky, where thousands of slaves bent
over desks all day. Next it glided into a medieval
solitude. On each side the shops devoted to antiques.
"Men in rusting armor stand in the windows and men-
ace the hurrying cars with raised, rusty iron bumpers,
hauberks, and helms, blunderbuses, Cromwellian breast-
plates, matchlocks, creeses, and the swords and daggers
of an army of dead and gone gallants gleam dully in
the ghostly light."

This medieval solitude foreboded an early demise.
What street could live enclosed by these mortuary
relics and trod by these spectral citizens? "Not Fourth
Avenue," answers O. Henry. "Not after the tinsel but
enlivening glory of the Little Rialto—not after the
echoing drum beats of Union Square. There need be
no tears, ladies and gentlemen. 'Tis but the suicide of
a street. With a shriek and a crash Fourth Avenue
dives headlong into the tunnel at Thirty-fourth Street
and is never seen again."

Then the squares of Bagdad. Occasionally Washington Square, or Sheridan Park, or Tompkins Square
play a part in an O. Henry story. It was in Tompkins Square that Lou and Nancy met at the end of
"The Trimmed Lamp." But outstanding are Madison
Square, Union Square, and Gramercy Park. What
background is more natural than the benches of the
former two for the human derelicts of the tales? He
shows you the Bed Liners stamping their frozen feet,

THE CAPITOL OF BAGDAD

Showing Madison Square where the Caliph found romance on park benches, mingling with the lame, the halt and the blind

and the preacher standing on a pine box exhorting his transient and shifting audience. In this Bed Line were Walter Smuythe and the discharged coachman, Thomas McQuade, the night that the red motor car, humming up Fifth Avenue, lost its extra tire as related in "The Fifth Wheel" (*Strictly Business*).

It was on a bench in the square that, as told in "The Discounters of Money" (*Roads of Destiny*), the millionaire Pilkins found the penniless young eloping couple, Marcus Clayton of Roanoke County, Virginia, and Eva Bedford of Bedford County, of the same State. It was perhaps on the same bench that Soapy of "The Cop and the Anthem" (*The Four Million*), sat meditating just what infraction of the law would insure his deportation to the hospitable purlieus of Blackwell's Island which was his Palm Beach and Riviera for the winter months. It was nearby, at least, that Prince Michael, of the Electorate of Valle Luna, known otherwise as Dopey Mike, looked up at the clock in the Metropolitan Tower and gave sage advice and consolation to the young man who was waiting to learn his fate as related in "The Caliph, Cupid, and the Clock." In "While the Auto Waits" (*The Voice of the City*), it was near the corner of Twenty-sixth Street and Fifth Avenue that the car with the white body and red running gear was parked while its owner, Parkenstacker, listened to the strange story of the girl in gray.

It was across Union Square that Hastings Beauchamp Moreley sauntered with a pitying look at the hundreds who lolled upon the park benches in "The Assessor of Success" (*The Trimmed Lamp*). It was on a Union Square bench that Murray and the dismissed police captain Marony of "According to their Lights" (*The Trimmed Lamp*), sat side by side one evening trying to think of schemes to repair their fallen fortunes. Of all the benches of Union Square there was just one which belonged to Stuffy Pete of "Two Thanksgiving Day Gentlemen" (*The Trimmed Lamp*), for the story tells that when Stuffy went to the Square to await the coming of the tall, thin old gentleman dressed in black and wearing the old-fashioned kind of glasses that won't stay on the nose— the old gentleman who had been Stuffy's host every Thanksgiving Day for nine years—he "took his seat on the third bench to the right as you enter Union Square from the east, at the walk opposite the fountain."

With Gramercy Park, O. Henry took the reader to the other extreme of society. All about that private square with its locked gates were the severe mansions of his aristocrats. There dwelt Alicia Van Der Pool before she married Robert Walmsley in "The Defeat of the City" (*The Voice of the City*). A house facing the west side of the park was the abode of the Van de Ruyslings, the illustrious family that had dwelt there for many years. To establish forever their social prominence O. Henry imparted the portentous information that the Van der Ruyslings had "received the first key ever made to Gramercy Park." In "The Marry Month of May" (*Whirligigs*), we learned that near the Park, old Mr. Coulson had a house, the gout, half a million dollars, a daughter, and a housekeeper.

XX

MORE THAT BOB DAVIS RECALLS

"I know," said Jeff Peters. "I've read in history and mythology about Joan of Arc and Mme. Yale and Mrs. Caudle and Eve and other noted females of the past. . . . About the only job left that a woman can beat a man in is female impersonator in vaudeville."
The Hand That Riles the World

BEING much concerned about the Caliph's ideas with reference to the female in both fact and fiction I roused him by means of a direct query.

"Tell me Bill," said I, "what you know about the emotional aspects arising from entangling alliances with the ladies."

"For your guidance, I presume," replied the Caliph, lifting his eyebrows and disclosing the eyes of a romanticist. "A simple question designed to draw forth from a mere student such trivial testimony as would make conversation. Do I interpret you correctly?"

"Quite so," I replied. "No man is expected to incriminate himself, but it seems to me that in a professional sense you should turn your thoughts to a subject about which the whole world is concerned. A writing man must be in constant grapple with the life from which, perforce, he plucks his characters."

"Why limit the discussion to mere authors, Major? What's the matter with letting a plumber or a book-keeper drift away from the cares that infest the day and put his mind on the grand passion."

The Caliph pulled at his cigar and shot a shaft of

smoke into space. Dreamily he closed his eyes and
went into reflection. Aware that he was philosophizing
and on the brink of revelation, I offered no interruption.

"Now if I were called upon," he continued, re-
awakening, "to establish a code of courtship for mankind—and could get a ratification from the women folk
—I would state plainly, via the preamble, that in all
matters of the heart the word o-w-n-e-r-s-h-i-p be ex-
punged. Friends of mine, who have forced confidence
upon me, are a unit in the conclusion that romance is
a form of proprietorship, that is to say a gent supposedly living a free and unencumbered existence casts
a languishing eye upon a fair woman, lets a few kind
words slip into his conversation, allows her hand to re-
pose in his for a split second and then finds himself on
a par with the leading character in *Uncle Tom's
Cabin.*" The Caliph slowly closed one eye and went
back to his cigar.

One word escaped my lips: "Slavery."

"In chains," resumed the thinker. "Manacled,
clanking in a lock step with his fate. Thus Old Uncle
Tom comes to, with the discovery that his Simon Legree
is a perfect lady who owns him body and soul. Do I
make myself clear, Mr. Man?"

"Bill, isn't that rather abrupt?" I asked. "Is bond-
age inevitable in all heart throbbing?"

"Yes! My plan would serve to abolish the institution of complete possession. The ritual would make
plain that slavery could play no part in the love affairs
of the human race. Guaranteed emancipation would
be the key note of the code."

"How would you bring about such a millennium?"

"By international agreement," answered the Caliph, emitting a cloud of smoke that for a moment concealed him.

"At The Hague?"

"Oh, nothing like that," he replied emerging from the vapor, in the manner of a genie, "but by tacit understanding among the disciples; by a clear presentation of the principles that would insure human happiness; I might say human liberty. Major, you don't seem to grasp the fundamentals of my doctrine."

"I'll admit that the abolition of the word proprietorship will be a flying start, but where does the experimentalist bring up? I wish for to know what is in yore mind, pardner."

It was not unusual for us to fall into the lingo of the West, thus reducing speech to the range limits.

"Well, hombre," he began, twirling an imaginary mustache, "for a starter, take for instance the case of a gal gettin' mashed on a good-lookin' sport, who ain't got nothin' to speak of 'cept a new bandanna handkerchief and a pup seal mustache. 'Get up behind, girl, on the bronco,' says he, 'and ride with me through yon valley,' all of which she does. And next week the sport rides on to the next valley while the frail walks back home. All wrong! I say all wrong, because bein' as how she ain't accustomed to men who act that-a-way. But like all females she figures that he is her'n and like as not will return some summer day; which he won't. The bird is unaware of the principle of ownership and forgets the terms. No matter how you look at this affair one of 'em does a heap of suffering. Remember that."

"Bill," said I, "you are dealing out old cards. That there is an ancient tale."

The Caliph tapped me on the knee and blew some smoke in my eye. "Just a minute, Mr. Man," said he, "I'm dealing a trilogy to you. The second case is the affair of *The Scarlet Letter,* which you probably read at a time in your life when such books were hidden from the inspection of the very young. Same here. But I was old enough to feel sorry for Old Doc Dimmesdale and Miss Hester. So far as I could make out, and time has not changed my viewpoint, both of these people, if left to their own devices, would have recovered from that shock and saved a whole lot of scandal in the parish. But it wasn't considered good form to let philanderers filter through their own conscience and become purified from within. Penance was publicity with the good church folk and hypocrisy was the eleventh commandment. And then again the doctrine of ownership rose up on its hind legs and demanded to know who was whose. The minister and Hester thought they belonged to each other and were prepared to pay the price for going into market without sufficient margin to carry them through a panic. With the parishioners howling around the pit, that wouldn't do at all. There must be a public record of the transaction. So Hester broke, Dimmesdale fell below par, and the crash followed with all its deplorable consequences. We have never ceased to talk about it. That is another illustration of the terrors of ownership. Why should a caress carry with it the assurance of vassalage?" he continued, warming

up to his subject. " 'I love you!' To which the
fellow-imbecile replies in a ringing voice, 'You are
mine!' And then the deluge."

Again the Caliph closed his eyes and passed into a
deep reverie. Following a respectful silence I asked
him to enunciate the third proposition of his trilogy.
My feeling was that he was getting in deeper and
deeper, rushing to the lip of a Niagara that would dash
him on the rocks.

"We now come to the autonomous ideals of the new
code," said he, picking up the thread of his discourse,
"the magnificent immunity that would reshape the
destinies of the tenderly disposed. I am convinced that
the new features of my code of courtship should be
taught like manners and made a tenet of good breed-
ing, so that one rushing into the realm of emotional
rhapsody would have in advance a proper appreciation
for its refined limits. Let it be understood that two
souls with but a single thought should regard the cul-
mination of that illusion as both the beginning and the
end of the heart's desire, rather than to classify it as
the inauguration of a permanent alliance with all its
attendant and unhappy obligations. Would it not be
a complete solution to look upon realization as a triumph so beautiful that it could not in this life recur,
instead of announcing that under new management the
business would now begin to boom? We eat, we live,
we laugh, we love ourselves to death. We come to the
table when the bell rings, laugh when another jackass
brays, love when lips are pouted against our own and
soft hands are extended. Whosoever declines any of
the proffered things is catalogued as sick, stupid or

cold. The prerogative of self-determination, or even temporary retirement for the solace of silence is denied us. Ownership obtrudes at the most inopportune times; and lacking resistance or better still, freedom, we come when called, and if we do not come we are dragged from our sanctuary and reminded that the law of possession is stronger than the mood of retirement. Of all the whip hands, the dimpled one wields the heaviest cat-of-nine-tails and the back that receives the scars is owned by the wielder of the knout. My code will recognize the right of the individual to regard great ecstasy as something that is offered by the gods and not as a tidal wave hurled upon him with the violence of a Johnstown flood, from which he cannot escape until he arrives at the morgue. Even then some well-intentioned but misdirected zealot will establish ownership of the body. But there will be no call for me to readjust the liberty of individuals. They will go on forever selling themselves for value received and the worst offenders will be those who have hearts. 'I Am the Captain of My Soul,' by Henley is a great poem, but nobody believes it. Ambrose Bierce sized it when he drafted that masterful toast: 'To woman. O that we could fall into her arms instead of her hands.'

"So you can see, Colonel, what I don't know about females in both fact and fiction," said the Caliph flipping the ashes from his robe and rising from his cushion. "So far as I am concerned everything suits me as is. But if I were called upon to serve the oppressed and bring order out of chaos—well, that's a different proposition. Rouse me in half an hour, Watson."

With that the disciple of the Caliphian Code for Courtship slipped into the ecstasy of a brief nap.

Among the writer folk, more particularly the fictionists, there has always been no end of amazement at the number of titles listed to the credit of O. Henry's pen. Less productive authors marveled at his fertility. Not a few made an exploration through his collected works in a conscientious effort to account for the secret of his fecundity. Time without end, I have heard otherwise sane writers make the claim that the Caliph had mastered a trick. The same thing was said of Lindbergh by aviators; of Bobby Jones, by golfers; of Tilden, by tennis players; of Caruso, by cabaret singers; and of the mad Poe, by idiots.

It was not my privilege to know all the processes of the Henryesque mind, nor have I strength to lift the veil behind which the delicate machinery of his horsepower was concealed. I can say, however, that he was the only noiseless operator with whom I ever came in contact. If there was grinding in his gears, not the faintest echo ever reached the outer world. Once an idea became fixed in his mind, the act of converting it into copy was a simple and progressive performance, free of commotion. When the moment arrived for him to begin production he shed his coat and vest, sharpened a few lead pencils, and without fuss or delay proceeded to create on sheets of letter size manila paper that which was clamoring to be born. His penmanship, round, flowing and legible, resembled the chirography of a telegraph operator. Each period was made in the form of a tiny x enclosed in a circle.

The punctuation was most exact and served to convey every shade of meaning that the writer intended. He made but few revisions in his manuscripts. The first draft usually satisfied him.

The title of the story in hand, and the initial letter of the first word often stirred a decorative impulse in the author. Frequently he shaded the capitals and often gave way to a playful flourish on the terminals. Some of his manuscripts bore marginal sketches, not however of the sort calculated to inflame an art collector. Nonetheless, if those whimsical creations could have survived the composing room or been saved from the furnace into which most old manuscripts conclude as ashes, they would to-day be worth more than was paid for them as originals. Intermittently he turned from the pencil to the typewriter, returning invariably to the noiseless longhand. When he was in the act of composition quiet was requisite. Only those who had the private signal could cross his threshold to the inner shrine. When interrupted he would turn his unfinished manuscript face down, receive the privileged invader most graciously, and pretend to be idle.

One morning I dropped into his apartment to secure a story three days overdue. He made a profuse apology, regretting that he had not found time to complete it.

"Only eighteen pages done. Give me until day after to-morrow," he pleaded, "and I will come across with the finished tale. How about we-all taking a little walk among the poor and winding up at some chuck-wagon for lunch?"

Familiar with his procrastinations, and observing a

wad of paper face down on the deal table that served as a desk, I urged him to stick to his job until the last page was finished.

"Colonel, it is too hot to work. What I need is air," he replied.

"You are looking," I answered, "at the one man who can supply it," and at once shot the window open. Into the room romped a gust that sent the manuscript, not less than thirty pages, flurrying to the floor. Some of it went under the sofa. The Caliph assumed the air of a guilty man, hiding his confusion while in the act of gathering, with my assistance, the loose sheets.

"Eighteen pages," I exclaimed. "Only eighteen pages. You're the bunk, Bill. What's the title of this story?"

"General, I can't say. Look under the lounge. If we can only find the first page, that may give us a hint. Mebby the title has gone out of the window. . . . This yarn is in a hell of a mess. . . . I don't imagine we ever shall know the title or what it is all about."

Page 1 was peeping from under the table. "Here it is," I announced, recovering the truant sheet.

"What is the title?" asked the fresh-air applicant, still feigning astonishment.

" 'Hostages to Momus.' "

"Who's it by?"

"O. Henry"— I counted the pages while he looked on in silence—"and there are *thirty*-odd sheets. Complete in all particulars. These go with me. You can turn out another by day after to-morrow. What was the idea about 'only *eighteen* pages?' "

"W-e-e—l," drawled the perspiring genius, his face

lighting, "I had an idea that this story, which according to the evidence appears to have been written by me, could be touched up here and there and perhaps improved. But if you're satisfied—" He paused and reached for his shaving mug. "It's an ill wind that blows nobody good. Take the damned thing."

While he was preparing for that excursion in search of a chuck-wagon I read the manuscript. One of O. Henry's best; pregnant with drama, human interest, amazing dialogue and infectious laughter. Nothing he would have done could improve it. "Where did you get the idea for this story?" I asked.

"Do you really want to know? If so, I don't mind pointing out to you the source. I found it in a book first published in 1872; a book read by most Americans —and a lot of foreigners for that matter—but apparently overlooked as the basis for an up-to-date short story."

"You didn't swipe this plot, Bill?"

"No, sir, not a syllable or a sentence," he replied with a touch of pride. "My story begins where the other fellow left off. If you have any doubts about the originality of my tale you may inspect the documents and decide accordingly."

With the shaving soap still clinging to his rubicund jowl the Caliph walked over to a book shelf and took down a volume of *The Adventures of Huckleberry Finn*, by Mark Twain. Slowly he began to turn the pages. "Do you remember the scene—here it is— where Tom Sawyer, Ben Rogers, Joe Harper and Huck Finn are in convention discussing the formation of what was to be known as 'Tom Sawyer's Gang,' when they planned to become murderers, robbers and pirates with kidnapping as a side line?"

"Perfectly. I seriously considered taking up those professions myself. Tom Sawyer's Gang was a great inspiration to me, Bill, and I am delighted to hear that you also were in sympathy with those boys. Anything that you have done to keep them before the public meets with my full approval."

"Very well, Major," replied the author of "Hostages to Momus," "here we are, chapter two. Ben is addressing his remarks to Tom. I'll read three paragraphs:

"Oh that's all very fine to say, Tom Sawyer, but how in the nation are these fellows going to be ransomed, if we don't know how to do it to them?—That's the thing I want to get at. Now what do you reckon it is?"

"Well, I don't know. But per'aps if we keep them until they are ransomed, it means that we keep them until they are dead."

"Now that's something like. That'll answer. Why couldn't you have said that before? We'll keep them till they're ransomed to death; and a bothersome lot they'll be, too—eating up everything, and always trying to get loose."

Truly, as O. Henry said, his story began where Mark Twain's left off. In "Hostages to Momus" the kidnaped bankers not only disdained any attempt to gain liberty, but turned their prison into a week-end festival which put the ransom-hunters in the pauper class.

"You will observe," said the Caliph, spraying a jet of bay rum over his countenance, "that there is a story in what a man *won't* do just as there is in what he *will* do. Every phase of human emotion is a basis for a piece of fiction. Striving for a superlative situation is all rot. The *genus homo* in his normal manifestations is quite sufficient for an author's needs. A plot without logical characters fails in advance. And characters without plots represent a school of literature with which I have no familiarity. Now, how about setting forth on the trail of that chuck-wagon. Even an author must occasionally have a date with something more substantial than the stuff of which dramas are made."

I cite "Hostages to Momus," not as an indication of O. Henry's habit, but as an illustration to show how his alert intelligence seized upon a shadow and gave it substance, mingled with delineation, and sparkling with incomparable humor. He had a feeling for life and the art necessary to record it.

From the grist mills of half-baked memories much chaff has been set afloat during the years that have accumulated since the Caliph stepped out of Bagdad into the silence. None has suffered more from the whispering chorus than he. On occasions I have heard from total strangers more amazing details concerning his life and habits than I had been permitted to know from himself. In previous chapters I have dealt fully and conscientiously with those personal matters that in the course of our acquaintance it was my privilege to observe, taking every precaution to quote him accurately and to preserve the argot of his utterances. He possessed to a marked degree the gift of lucidity. His conversation was never involved. Even in his whim-

sical flights he measured his sentences with due regard
to clarity. If an auditor failed to get the drift of his
speech O. Henry the humorist would sidetrack Sydney
Porter the philosopher, and drop to the level of the
listener. Or, not infrequently, cease talking.

He could be silent for an indefinite period, and if
need be carry on a conversation in monosyllables.
Strangers usually got on his nerves although on such
occasions there was no indication from him that he was
listening to their babble for the last time. He had a
Chesterfieldian way of saying farewell. Windbags left
at the post never had the slightest intimation that the
victim had escaped forevermore.

Sensitive to a degree, and swayed always by his own
convictions Porter established many queer friendships.
Most of these people were in complete ignorance as to
his occupation or the breadth of his fame. They knew
him only as a soft-spoken southern gentleman who was
ever in good humor. A waiter in a Third Avenue
chop house confided to me that he "figured the polite
guy to be in the cotton business." And I doubt if he
ever knew the truth, or that he was embalmed in one or
more of the Caliph's short stories. Strangers never
spotted him for a man of letters. He had none of the
manners of a Grub Street disciple. I have seen him
stroll into a Bowery bar room, place his foot on the
brass rail and milk a bartender of his Burke's peerage
without arousing the slightest suspicion in the breast
of the mixologist.

I venture to say that twenty-five years ago in New
York City there were a hundred wasters with whom

Sydney Porter had more conversation than he did with any of his intimates. Few of these men knew the identity of the blue-eyed magician who loosened their tongues.

How many cops with whom he stopped and chinned in the flicker of the old gas lamps knew that the well-dressed stranger wearing a derby hat and a four-in-hand necktie, decorated with a stick pin, was a better shot with a six-shooter than any man in Mulberry Street Police Headquarters? Not one. Nevertheless the fact remains that Bill Porter could cut all the diamonds out of big casino at thirty paces and not miss a jewel. He could have stepped into any of the shooting galleries which at that time infested Chatham Square and with either hand blow all the plaster of Paris birds into the back alley. He could handle a gun almost as dexterously as Wild Bill Hickock. The West and Central America did that for him, but his pistol plays ceased with expert marksmanship. At heart he was a man of peace, and the thought of getting a drop on his fellow-man would have sent him to the hospital with nausea.

He knew the ways of evil men and had a wide familiarity with all the arts of the grafters. He could sit at table with the powers that prey and address them in the lingo of the day. Plenty of the gentry who leaned with the Caliph on the damp mahogany referred to the incident in after years as "a jag with O. Henry." These rumors accumulating with needless rapidity brought about the widespread impression that he and the bottle were inseparable companions. There is ample evidence that toward the later years of his life the Caliph drank more than was good for him, but I have yet to meet any man who ever saw him intoxicated to the point of mental or physical incapacity. Two years before his death, in reply to a query from an Asheville, North Carolina, resident, as to how he went about the task of writing a short story, the Caliph replied:

The first step is to get a kitchen table, a wooden chair, a wad of yellow fool's cap writing paper, one lead pencil and a drinking glass. They are the props. Then you secure a flask of Scotch whiskey and a few oranges, which I will describe as the sustenance. We now come to the plot, frequently styled the inspiration. Combining a little orange juice with a little Scotch, the author drinks the health of all magazine editors, sharpens his pencil and begins to write. When the oranges are empty and the flask is dry, a saleable piece of fiction is ready for mailing.

There is something ironic about this recipe for creative literature, although great numbers of the grand army of hacks who from time immemorial practiced it, had failed to produce very much that was saleable. The Caliph refrained from stating whether the flask held a quart or a pint. In the absence of a specific quantity, and in view of the fact that during his writing career, or eleven years, he turned out more than six hundred pieces of original fiction, it is reasonable to assume that his mentality was not to any great extent impaired by the use of alcohol. He lived in a generation when hard liquor, properly distilled, was in general use and free from synthetic ingredients. Other more or less distinguished contemporary authors drank more whisky and produced less that was fit to read than the Caliph of Bagdad.

That the recollection of the dark hours in his earlier life took toll of his resistance there is no doubt in my mind. The memory of his flight to Central America, the return to his own country, there to pay the penalty, the haunting associations that grew out of that tragic chapter, left its scars upon his sensitive soul. One less delicately organized would have thrown off the fears that beset him. He lived in an agony of fear of revelation, depressed to the point of illness. Despite this ever-present dread, his sublime imagination frequently soared above the tragedy of his youth and set him free. It is in these flights that one sees his true spirit untrammeled by the past.

There has long been an impression among certain of his intimates that he had confided in me the story of his life behind the gray walls of the Columbus retreat, and that for good and sufficient reasons I had refrained from contributing to the details given circulation after his death. Such was not the case. The first and only intimation I ever received from him that there was a rift in his life came in the form of an unfinished sentence. We were discussing the trivialities that turn men from one occupation to another; accidents which influence destinies. . . .

"Some day," said Porter, "I'll tell you how I fell heir to enough spare time to take up fiction seriously. Perhaps it would be better to tell you now, so that . . ."

He stopped, bit his lip and looked out of the window.

"Go to it," I urged, anxious for the particulars bearing upon the growth of his greatness.

"No," he replied softly. "Let me write it to you. The story can be told in four lines. At least they will give you the idea."

With that cryptic remark he fell into silence, from which I found it difficult to extricate him. Familiar with his moods, I made some casual reference to nothing in particular and left him with his reflections, unaware of what he had been about to impart. Looking back upon that unfinished conversation, and recalling the abruptness of my departure, I have no regret that the whole story was not then revealed to me, as the telling of it would have caused the Caliph considerable embarrassment. Better that it should die abornin'.

Evidently he had no intention of breaking his promise to "write it" as I received from him a week later a letter in which he varied from his usual comic signature. I realized when I saw it that this was his story, the story of his whole life; the shortest short story ever written. Here it is in full:

Note the smooth, flourishing "Sydney Porter" and contrast it with the crabbed unhappy scrawl below. The first is the man he showed to the world, the successful short-story writer of 55 Irving Place; but who is this underneath—the cramped hand of the alias, the man of the shadowed years, the Columbus convict?

Aware that he had conveyed all he wished me to know, and having no desire to intrude beyond this simple intimation, I refrained from ever making the slightest reference to the subject. Nor did he again reopen it. The letter, filed away among other precious historical documents that have to do with the writer folk whose trails have crossed mine during the last thirty years, was resurrected after the Caliph's death, framed with his picture and now hangs upon my wall.

And this is the only information I ever received from the Caliph of Bagdad concerning his forced restraint from a life of freedom. Now all the world knows, and all the world forgives.

One afternoon when the atmosphere of my office was being revitalized by a visit from the Caliph, Elliot Balestier, an ambitious young author, was announced. Conscious of the beneficial effects that a glimpse of the master would have upon any student of plot and style, I invited him in.

It was a memorable meeting, for me, at least. The *entente* was complete after a few sentences and the conversation turned to the fiction market with particular emphasis upon the importance of plot and suspense, at that period the Gold Dust Twins in popular literature.

"I have a story that I call 'Chivalry,'" said the beginner, casting anxious eyes in the direction of the Caliph, "but for some reason or other it seems to lack the right kind of a finish. Do you mind—?"

"Let's have it," said the listener.

The amateur aviator spun his propeller, rose into the air and began to hum:

"Kind of a romance, located in the South; where you came from. Old Virginian, saturated with chivalry, lives alone in the country with but few neighbors. Near his estate is a deserted house that has been rented by a quiet couple; from the North. They are not the least bit hospitable and wholly disregard the social call paid upon them by the Old Virginian. Frequently he passes their home on horseback, but is never invited in. Naturally he resents this and finally comes to the conclusion that the newcomers are utterly lacking in good manners. One day while riding past their gate he discerns a white handkerchief fluttering from an upper window. This he regards as a signal of distress, which it proves to be. He rides in with all the courage of a Don Quixote and offers his services. The woman, apparently alone, hurriedly explains that she is a prisoner and begs him to rescue her from her harsh jailer who has barred the way to liberty. Fine for the Old Virginian, who pants for adventure. The next night, while the brutal jailer is visiting a near-by town, the Old Virginian, mounted on Andrew Jackson, his favorite horse, and leading a gentle mare, comes to the house, rescues the fair lady, gallops away with her to the railroad eight miles distant, flags the train and with a knight errant's farewell and a tender paternal embrace bids her Godspeed. Great! He has rescued a lady and probably encompassed the downfall of the scoundrel. The train pulls out with the rescued lady on board waving her kerchief in farewell.

"Filled with satisfaction the Old Virginian rides leisurely home, beds down his horses, and repairs to the old drawing-room, there to sit in meditation and review the night's work. While in this contemplative mood it dawns, first upon his eyes and then his intelligence, that something has gone wrong. For one thing various objects of art left to his forbears by Lafayette, Washington, Patrick Henry, and others have disappeared from the center table. Certain priceless paintings have been cut from their frames. A vandal hand has been laid on his numerous possessions. He reaches for his twenty-four carat jeweled Swiss watch, which came down from his great-grandfather and bore a photographic miniature of his wife, who had died in her girlhood. That, too, had vanished from his sagging vest pocket, filched by the shapely fingers of the charmer as she bade him farewell at the train. Treachery! The pair of Northern confidence operators had stripped him of his Lares and Penates. He invokes the curse of darkness upon all peoples residing north of Mason and Dixon's line. Morning finds him prostrated and ill in a voluminous armchair by an open window. His exhaustion is complete and his pride wounded beyond words. Chivalry be damned. . . .

"That's as far as I've got," said the narrator reflectively. "Seems to be hanging in the air. I don't know what to do with the old boy. If I leave him there he'll starve to death. Suggest something."

The Caliph, apparently in deep reflection, gazed out into the open, across his own Bagdad. After a spell of silence that seemed interminable he spoke.

"May I—?"

"I shall be grateful if you will," answered the beginner.

The author of that other "Unfinished Story" which is to-day incorporated in every living tongue and known throughout the world, summoned the Genie of his Genius.

"Let him mourn for a day or two," said he. "Southerners have a way of recovering from what seems at the time to be a death blow. You can then conclude the story about as follows."

The Caliph spoke slowly for a few moments, defined clearly his idea for a finish and departed.

The young author returned the next day with the addition which is here reprinted verbatim from the finished story:

Three days later Colonel Pembroke Pendleton sat silent and apathetic in his despoiled library and looked up gloomily at his Negro servant who had just entered the room.

"Mars Pem," said the old man softly, "dis hyer letter jes' come for you. Dere's a package down to de 'spress office, too."

The Colonel eagerly tore open the envelope. A sudden glow of happiness lighted his face. He read:

DEAR SIR:
I am returning your watch by express. After seeing the beautiful miniature within I had not the heart to keep it. Over the antiques that were taken, I have no control. If all men were like you—there would be no bad women.

There was no signature; none was necessary.

"By gad, suh," cried the Colonel, starting up with a radiant face. "Ah deserve to be thrashed, suh, for doubting a lady. Ah should have known she was actin' under duress. The loss of my silver plate and my precious trinkets is a triflin' matter. Southern chivalry is vindicated, by gad, suh!"

Judge Thomas A. Jones, Sr., enjoys the distinction of having had for a client America's most celebrated short story writer. His retaining fee—the only one the Judge would accept—was paid in friendship. A pair of gold cuff buttons, worn in life by the author and bestowed by his widow upon the counselor, are all of intrinsic value that ever passed between them. However, there were other and stronger links that bound these two men together. They hold still in the flesh and the spirit.

After meeting the Judge I can readily understand why a story-teller could cotton to him. He knows a joke when he hears one!

After Porter married Sara Coleman, an Asheville girl, and took up his residence here I saw him continuously. We had nearby offices in the Legal Building and became pretty well accustomed to one another. There wasn't a day passed but that he came into my quarters and talked about what was in his mind. He never seemed to understand his popularity. Just couldn't account for it and looked upon literature as a meal ticket. When he was ill at the Hotel Clarendon in New York, where I called upon him ten days prior to his death, he admitted to me that he was in need of funds.

"Recently the doctors have been fixing me out with a number of complications that cost money. There doesn't seem to be in the pathological record a single within-the-reach-of-all disorder that fits my case," said he. "I made application for a cheap symptom, but the medical sharks cannot supply any in the present market. On that table by the window you will find the first pages of a story entitled 'An Experiment in Neurasthenia.' As my legal adviser you are entitled to know that the stuff is biographical. With the returns from that story I propose to pay my doctor bills."

For the short story entitled "A Retrieved Reformation," from which Paul Armstrong made the dramatization "Alias Jimmy Valentine," Porter received the sum of $250. I advised him not to sell the dramatic rights without a percentage of the royalties. He said the yarn was not worth a nickel more than $250 and that he was satisfied. When the play was produced and became a great success I went to a performance with the author of the original story. He applauded every act and complimented Armstrong on the dramatization. I learned that the royalties totaled $800 a week, none of which went to Porter. "Aren't you sorry," I asked, "that you didn't keep a string on some of that easy money?" "Not at all, Judge," he replied. "When a truly great dramatist puts a kick into one of my short stories and gets his money back I'm tickled along my entire vertebræ. The stuff I sold him is nothing in comparison with what he gave the public. Glad it's a hit."

One week-end he visited a friend who had a manor house up in the hills back of New England. The room in which he slept was unduly spacious and contained at one end a large fireplace. At breakfast the host asked his distinguished guest how he liked the sleeping accommodations. "Extremely," answered Porter. "The open fire was so damned hot that I was blistered and the bed was so far north that my breath formed icicles. A man occupying a revolving chair in the middle of the room could be fairly comfortable. Never before have I met a barbecue and a blizzard under the same roof." There was nothing harsh about his humor. I never heard him utter a joke that would wound. Nor have I ever read a line from his pen that left an unpleasant taste.

Judge Jones handed down a book from the top of his desk and opened it. "Read the inscription in this volume. I received it in 1909 after he and I attended a performance of 'The Four Million'."

The lines are quoted in full, spelling and all:

"To Marsa Tommy Jones in commmmmemmoration of our evening on seeeeeing The Four Million—for he's a joooly good felllow. O. Henry."

The book was a first edition, published in 1906, worth to the Judge with the signature the full amount mentioned in the title. The lines were written all askew as though Mr. Porter were lit for fair. The Judge has other books from O. Henry but that copy is the prize of his collection. He alone knows how often the pages have been thumbed.

"Madison Cawein, the Southern poet," continued his Honor, "told me that Kipling said to him in Montreal, on the occasion of Kipling's last visit to America, that the United States was threatened with 'mobocracy,' and that O. Henry was the one living man who could leaven with his pen the class and the mass. Well, he has done that, and his soul goes marching on."

"Why," I asked, "was he buried here in Asheville?"

"Probably because this was his last residence and the home of his wife. But, if you ask me, I think his remains should lie at the corner of Forty-second and Broadway."

In 1915, I attended at the old Delmonico restaurant on Fifth Avenue, an informal dinner given to Colonel

William Taylor, at that time editor of a popular weekly periodical to which O. Henry occasionally contributed during his lifetime.

The guests, representative men and women writers, numbering about one hundred, had been friends and intimates of O. Henry in the days gone by.

As toastmaster of this particular dinner I assumed certain prerogatives, one of which was to place upon my left an empty chair; a chair before which there was a place card; a chair that was reserved for the visiting wraiths, if you will.

"Just whom do you expect?" asked Taylor after I explained what was intended. "Be careful that these phantoms don't take the dinner away from you."

"It is my hope that they will," I replied. "If the speakers become infected with the illusion that the old masters are present this dinner will be the hit of the year. One addressing a jury of immortals has got to be good."

After the coffee, I announced that Edgar Allan Poe, Henry Harland, Marion Crawford, H. C. Bunner, Frank R. Stockton, Bill Nye, Artemus Ward, Frank Norris, Richard Hovey and others might drop in and occupy the seat on my left, and urged the speakers to address themselves to the delegates from Olympus, and not to me.

Taylor was right: The ghosts took the dinner away from me—as I had hoped they would—the speakers acquitting themselves brilliantly. Wit, wisdom and philosophy ran riot. When the mirth was at its summit I asked for silence in order that I might present O.

Henry—"who has just arrived." I offered him the empty chair and a cup of black coffee.

Before the phrase "needs no introduction here," had died on my lips the widow of the author of "The Four Million" and others, entered the banquet hall on the arm of a gentleman with whom "Will," the name by which Mrs. Porter always addressed her husband in life, had long been associated. Instantly, the guests arose, joined in acclamation and in concert urged the new arrival toward the speakers' table.

Colonel Taylor, alive to the importance of the moment, produced an extra chair and placed it beside the one occupied by the shade. Upon taking her seat Mrs. Porter asked me who was to sit between us. "The Caliph of Bagdad," I whispered across the chasm.

For a moment, which seemed to be an age, she fell into silence, and then in the most matter of fact tone replied, "I might have known Will would be here to-night."

No finer demonstration of understanding could have been made. All in the room seemed to feel with Sara Porter that she had come into The Presence. Here was an overtone of harmony between the spiritual and the intellectual. Those who spoke addressed the Caliph as though he were there in the flesh. We all talked of the lean days when Bill Porter first appeared on the Island of Manhattan, of the bay window at 55 Irving Place, where he sat behind the drawn curtains, unknown, unsung, and wrote tales that were destined to bring him fame; of the subway, Madison Square, the Bowery, the East River and that mythical world which he peopled with the creatures of his imagination.

And his widow, proud of the homage bestowed, heard all, understood all, shared all until the farewell toast was offered and the party broke up.

We got away from Delmonico's about twelve. The night was cold and clear, with bright stars gleaming overhead; the traffic falling into diminuendo. Ambitious taxi-cab drivers hailed belated fares and honked away. A few remaining diners, bidding Mrs. Porter good-night, were grouped at the corner of Forty-fourth and Fifth. Down the Avenue came rolling an old-time hansom cab, echo of the past, the Jehu cracking his whip from the high box.

The Caliph's widow lifted her hand. The ancient vehicle came in to the curb. "Yes, Lady," said the cabman blowing on his fingers.

"Would you—," said Mrs. Porter, with a furtive smile meant for her escort, "as it isn't far to the hotel, would you mind—if I drive home with Will?"

"I quite understand," said he, bowing her into the hansom.

Automatically, the glass doors folded, the cabby cracked his whip and Sara Porter, bolt upright, rode away in the company of her immortal.

XXI

THE WIDE APPEAL OF O. HENRY

I walked the streets of the City of Insolence, thirsting for the sight of a stranger face.　　　　　*A Ruler of Men*

HUNDREDS of thousands if not millions of his countrymen and countrywomen have read and found delight in O. Henry's stories. Scores of imitative authors have strained after the magic twist of his method. The best of them have failed to reach it. Much has been written about him. Yet, paradoxical as it may seem, he has only partially received his meed of serious critical appreciation, and very little of that has come from home. In that there is a subtle tribute.

Americans have so taken it for granted that every one knows O. Henry and his stories that in writing about him they have confined themselves to some single side or aspect of his work, to his association with this city or that city, his interpretation of the activities of the engaging confidence man, or his championship of the little shop-girl. Nicholas Vachel Lindsay, for example, saw him as the "little shop girl's knight" who "always worked a triple-hinged surprise to end the scene and make one rub his eyes."

> And be it said, amid his pranks so odd
> With something nigh to chivalry he trod—
> And oft the drear and driven would defend—
> The little shop girl's knight, unto the end.

374

Only the critics of other lands have approached him to sum him up sweepingly. The voice of Canada was heard when the genial Stephen Leacock wrote of "The Amazing Genius of O. Henry." Arthur St. John Adcock has told of England's sentimental and practical reception of O. Henry. Mr. I. F. Marcosson has elsewhere told that Sir James Barrie has found so much entertainment in O. Henry's stories that one of his pet diversions is retelling them in Scotch, which, by the way, must be an extraordinary and appalling performance when one thinks of Jeff Peters expounding his philosophy of life in the dialect of Thrums. There is considerable of a French audience for O. Henry. The French novelist, Maurice De Kobra, has translated many of the O. Henry stories, and in introducing them has written of O. Henry as he is seen from the Gallic angle.

It is significant that Leacock, Adcock, and De Kobra have all singled out one story to be placed above all the rest. That is not "A Municipal Report" or "An Unfinished Story," which most Americans are likely to mention first, but "The Furnished Room." Of that tale Stephen Leacock said: "It shows O. Henry at his best as a master of that supreme pathos that springs, with but little adventitious aid of time or circumstance, from the fundamental things of life itself. In the sheer art of narration there is nothing done by Maupassant that surpasses 'The Furnished Room.' " St. John Adcock singled out the story to echo Professor Leacock's appreciation. In Paris one day some winters ago M. De Kobra and Arthur Maurice indulged in an O. Henry "fanning bee." "Which one do you like best?" was asked. "The Furnished Room," was the Frenchman's instant reply. "And after that?" "The Gift of the Magi."

Which one do you like best? The question suggests one very extraordinary aspect of the O. Henry appeal. That so many persons differ as to their favorites among his tales is the finest possible tribute to the edifice that he built in the span of his brief working life. To illustrate the point in the simple and most direct way, suppose symposiums, or plebiscites, or what you will, were held to find out which were the most popular stories of Maupassant, Stevenson, Poe, Kipling, and Bret Harte. It would be fairly easy to guess at the general result.

For example, selections from Edgar Allan Poe according to a dozen different tastes would all include "The Purloined Letter" and "The Fall of the House of Usher," and "The Cask of Amontillado." All the lists devoted to Maupassant would find "La Parure" ("The Necklace") very near the top. Picking ten tales from Stevenson, nearly all readers would begin with "The Pavillion on the Links," or "Sire de Maletroit's Door." A Bret Harte list without "The Luck of Roaring Camp" is inconceivable. A dozen lists setting down the favorites among Kipling's short stories might run to some fifteen different titles, but all of them would certainly contain "The Man Who Would Be King," "The Drums of the Fore and Aft," "The Finest Story in the World," "Without Benefit of Clergy," and "The Brushwood Boy." With O. Henry the case is very different. Such is the variety of his appeal that there is no handful of his tales that stand out as meaning all things to all men. Actually it is almost impossible to find two readers who are even in remote agreement as to what his best stories are.

That variety of appeal is best illustrated by the story of an experiment of seventeen years ago. *The Bookman*, then edited by Arthur B. Maurice, in its issue for June, 1914, printed ten lists of ten stories apiece, representing the individual preferences of O. Henry readers. Those asked to contribute to the symposium were for the most part either themselves writers of fiction, or for some reason or other were in a position to judge relatively of the quality of the various tales. In addition to the lists elicited there were accompanying letters that contributed bits of O. Henryana.

For example, Booth Tarkington, sending in his ten favorites, added the comment: "The ten are not his best stories. I don't know what his 'best' are, of course. These ten are what you asked for—the ten I have enjoyed most. There is one I wanted to include. The boy who went to war after the girl flouted him and came back to the town here and said to her (she was married then) 'Oh, I don't know—maybe I could if I tried'; but I couldn't remember the title and couldn't find it."

Of course, the story for which Mr. Tarkington was mentally groping was "The Moment of Victory."

One letter in particular calls for full quotation. It was the letter that accompanied the list of the favorites of O. Henry's widow, Mrs. William Sidney Porter. To her the stories *were* Porter:

After all [she wrote], I am not sure that it is the story—good as it is—for O. Henry's own face lifts from a Nashville "roast" that was given the story and I hear his puzzled: "Why did it offend?" "Do you see anything in it that should offend?" "The Fifth Wheel"—and we stand together in Madison Square in the deep snow, looking at the line waiting for beds. When we turn away ten men have found shelter. The recording angel must have seen us there some of the snowy nights of 1908. He must have known that when we turned homeward there were times when O. Henry had not a dollar fifty left in his pockets.

One story in Mrs. Porter's list likely to surprise many readers is "Madame Bo-Peep of the Ranches." There is a reason for its inclusion. That story figured largely in Mrs. Porter's own life. In the spring of 1905 her mother returned to Asheville after a visit to Greensboro and said to her: "Your old friend Will Porter is a writer. He lives in New York and writes under the name of O. Henry."

O. Henry. In my desk lay "Madame Bo-Peep" and I loved her. I wrote O. Henry a note. "If you are not Will Porter don't bother to answer," I said. He bothered to answer. The letter came as fast as Uncle Sam could bring it. "Some day when you are not real busy," he wrote, "won't you sit down at your desk where you keep those antiquated stories and write to me? It'd be so pleasant to hear something about what the years have done for you, and what you think about when the tree frogs begin to holler in the evenings." Thus after many years a boy and girl friendship was renewed. Last in my list, but first in my heart, is "Adventures in Neurasthenia"; the new title, "Let Me Feel Your Pulse," the publishers gave. It

SARA LINDSAY COLEMAN PORTER

*O. Henry's second wife, to whom he was married in Asheville,
North Carolina, in 1907*

brings back the little office in Asheville, the pad, empty except for the title and words: "So I went to a doctor." So often at the last the pad was empty. The sharp pencil points in their waiting seemed to me to mock the empty pad, the weary brain. The picture is too vivid.

It was the story that was told by the various lists that was remarkable. No one list bore the slightest resemblance to any other list. Only two stories, "A Municipal Report" and "An Unfinished Story," were duplicated as a first choice. Booth Tarkington, for example, began his list with "The Ransom of Red Chief," the reasonable preference of the creator of Hedrick Madison and Penrod Schofield for a delightfully diabolical boy. George Barr McCutcheon selected "The Tale of a Tainted Tenner"; other leaders were "A Tempered Wind," "The Rose of Dixie," "A Harlem Tragedy," and "The Defeat of the City."

Sixty-two different titles out of a possible one hundred represented the various preferences; most of them appearing in but one list. Of course there were a few general favorites. "An Unfinished Story" led, with seven mentions, followed by "A Municipal Report" with six mentions. Then came "A Lickpenny Lover," "The Gift of the Magi," and "The Furnished Room" with four mentions apiece; and "Mammon and the Archer" and "Let Me Feel Your Pulse" with three mentions apiece. The tales dealing with Little Old Bagdad on the Subway seemed to have the widest appeal. Sixty-five of the one hundred stories contained in the ten lists were tales of New York.

XXII

O. HENRY AND THE STAGE

F. P. ADAMS AND ALEXANDER WOOLLCOTT REMEMBER

I'm really afraid that all the stage is a world, anyhow, and all the players men and women. "The thing's the play" is the way I quote Mr. Shakespeare.
The Thing's the Play

O. HENRY wrote his stories with his own necessities, the demands of the editor, and the entertainment of the reader in mind; never with the thought of their ultimate possibilities for the stage or the screen. The latter institution in his day had emerged from its flicker and custard pie infancy. Thoughts of the stage, and above all of the fabulous profits to be derived from a success, were constantly with him in the last year or two of his life. Reverting to his Aladdin days, he dreamed of the theater as another Wonderful Lamp which had only to be rubbed to evoke the Jinn bearing chests of gold.

Occasionally the dream was in a measure realized. When Channing Pollock's "Roads of Destiny" was presented on the stage the program carried a line of credit to O. Henry and O. Henry's estate had a share in the profits. Yet Mr. Pollock has told that the origin of the play had really nothing to do with the O. Henry tale. His story is that in the spring of 1915 he ran into Charles Klein, who was to have sailed some days before on the steamship *Philadelphia*. Klein explained the delay. He had been worried thinking how easily

380

the German underseas boats might "get" a vessel as
slow as the *Philadelphia;* so he changed his plans and
sailed on the *Lusitania.*

When the *Lusitania* had gone down, and Klein with
her, Pollock was haunted by the conversation of the
previous week. Was it Fate? Had Charles Klein been
destined to die that way? What would have happened
had he sailed on the *Philadelphia?* It occurred to
Pollock to write a play, showing a man doing four different things, and coming to the same end through all
of them. He wrote it, and called it "The Moving
Finger," with apologies to Omar Khayyam, and sold
it to a producer. Then he recounted the plot to a
friend, who asked pointedly: "Have you ever read O.
Henry's 'Roads of Destiny'?"

"I had," says Channing Pollock, "and I read it
again, and wondered whether I was an unconscious
plagiarist. What should I do; what *could* a reputable
author do under the circumstances? I solved the problem by a sort of post-facto purchase of the dramatic
rights of the earlier story, and, having arranged to
give up a share of my royalties, decided that I might
as well have the value of a familiar title, and called my
opus 'Roads of Destiny.' Under that name it was
produced. Soon afterwards I discovered what O.
Henry probably discovered soon after his tale was
printed—that, in all literature, no plot is more common. It occurs seven times in the *Arabian Nights.*"

But the epitome of O. Henry's association with the
stage and stage people is the story of the play that was
made, based upon his "A Retrieved Reformation."

As "Alias Jimmy Valentine," it was the metropolitan
hit of a year, and in the United States road companies
kept it alive for many years thereafter. In England
it scored a success as "Jimmy Sampson." A French
stage version was made by Mr. Maurice Tourneur, and
a Spanish translation of the English version was acted
in Madrid. Yet practically the only reward that Porter derived from it was the sum of five hundred dollars, paid in advance, whereas the profits of Paul
Armstrong, who made the adaptation, exceeded one
hundred thousand dollars.

Fully one hundred of the O. Henry tales should be
preserved through the medium of the screen, with its
modern technique and resources. These stories are
admirably fitted to that form of presentation, in the
hands of an intelligent director, calling for little altera-
tion. Early in the year 1925 the Fox Film Corpora-
tion bought certain rights to the O. Henry stories with
the idea of giving them adequate pictorial interpretation. But with the enthusiasm and lack of judgment
often characteristic of the industry those in immediate
control of the enterprise refused to heed or even to
listen to professional advice.

They thought merely in numbers. They knew that
there were approximately two hundred and fifty O.
Henry stories. Years before some one hundred and
twenty of these had been filmed in an amateur way,
and were therefore unavailable. Those in control
thought only of the one hundred and thirty remaining
titles, not realizing that the earlier sifting had thoroughly exhausted all the tales with screen possibilities.

The result was that for the new screen presentations bearing the O. Henry name entirely new stories had to be written, most of them having not the slightest relation to the original text.

The intimate stories of O. Henry's relations with the theater have been told by Franklin P. Adams and Alexander Woollcott. Various theatrical managers had a part in them, conspicuously Mr. George Tyler. Early in 1909 a Chicago manager wrote to Mr. Adams saying that he had a star and wanted a play for him. The manager had seen a story by O. Henry in Collier's, "To Him Who Waits," that was just the thing on which to base the proposed play, and suggested that Messrs. Adams and Porter collaborate on the dramatization. The idea appealed to Mr. Adams. He recalls:

I called on O. Henry and we discussed it at length. His other pseudonym was Barkis. We agreed to collaborate, both of us to work on the dialogue and both on the lyrics. And as it happened it was almost a complete collaboration. Hardly an independent line was written.

We were interested in the piece and anxious to please the manager, who had gone out of his way to get us . . . O. Henry and I would convene nearly every afternoon and talk the thing over, outlining scenes, making notes of lines of dialogue, tentative ideas for lyrics, etc. . . . We enjoyed working at this time. It was fun blocking out the plans and O. Henry was simply shedding whimsical ideas for lines and situations.

To the reader acquainted with the plot of "To Him Who Waits" it will be apparent that the industrious

dramatists strayed rather far from the story that had
first caught the manager's eye. Probably they dismissed it entirely from their plans. The work became
a kind of comic opera, built about an anthropological
expedition to Yucatan to delve into the theory that
the American Indian was descended from the ancient
Aztecs. O. Henry called this *aztechnology*, and "The
Enthusiastics" was at first suggested for the title, a
suggestion which did not please the manager, who said
that it sounded like the title of an amateur performance
given by the Lincoln Memorial High School. The
eventual title, which Mr. Adams credits to O. Henry,
was "Lo," taken from the line of Pope. "Lo" appealed
to the manager who said that it would be easy to ad-
vertise and would look well in type.

But the troubles of the authors were only beginning.
They had supposed that in the construction of a
musical comedy the librettist first wrote some verses
and the composer then evolved a melody to fit them.
"But," says Mr. Adams, "most of our songs were constructed to fit tunes the composer had already written." Then came disagreements with the manager,
who engaged another man to rewrite the book. After
that the original collaborators had to rewrite the dialogue all over again. "O. Henry never worked harder
or more conscientiously on anything in his life," says
Mr. Adams. "He lost weight. He worried." Day
and night they worked on the comedy. Again they
sent on the completed script, this being the third or
fourth rewrite. As they mailed it O. Henry recited
in a singular minor key:

> Dramatization is vexation;
> Revision is as bad;
> This comedy perplexes me
> And managers drive me mad.

Finally "Lo" was produced, the first performance being given in Aurora, Illinois, August 25, 1909. Late that night there was a doctoring up of the second act. "Lo" played for single nights in Waukegan, Illinois, and Janesville, Wisconsin; and then opened a week's engagement in Milwaukee. For fourteen weeks it lasted and then breathed its last in St. Joseph, Missouri. Some of the lyrics of "Lo" have survived. For example, there was one, "It's the Little Things That Count," which might fit into a musical comedy of any time. It ran:

GIRL— Little drops of water, little grains of sand,
Make the mighty ocean and the pleasant land.
BOY— Little drops of seltzer, little drops of rye,
Make the pleasant highball, when a man is dry.
BOTH—It's the little things that count, ev'rywhere you
go;
Trifles make a large amount. Don't you find
it so?
GIRL— Little deeds of kindness, little words of love,
Make our life an Eden, like the heaven above.
BOY— Little drops of promise, made to little wives,
Make us little fibbers all our little lives.
BOTH—It's the little things that count, ev'rywhere you
go;
Trifles make a large amount. Don't you find
it so?

That song was collaboration, and presumably rather more Adams than Porter. But entirely O. Henry's

was "Snap Shots," with its suggestion of James Whit-
comb Riley and Poe, and which began:

Watch out, lovers, when you promenade;
When you kiss and coo, in the deep moon shade.
When you're close together in the grape-vine swing,
When you are a-courting or philandering.
Mabel, Maud and Ann, Nellie, May and Fan,
Keep your eyes open for the Snap Shot Man!

> Snap! Shots! Hear the shutter close!
> What a world of roguishness the little snapper
>   shows!
> Click! Click! Caught you unaware—
> Snap Shot Man'll get you if you don't take care!

Incidentally the work of collaboration was done
partly at Franklin P. Adams's home at 16 Manhattan
Avenue when Porter could be induced to journey that
far from his accustomed haunts, and partly in Porter's rooms in the Caledonia. Porter's preference for
his own quarters was natural enough. There it was
always possible to break the monotony of forced crea-
tion by occasional visits to a convenient sideboard in
quest of the stimulation that he found a spur to creative work.

The failure of "Lo" was discouraging, but Porter
for the rest of his life continued to dream of dramatic
success and above all of the material rewards that it
brought. A master workman in his own field, he was
still an amateur in the business of play construction,
and at that later period of his career lacked the energy
and application necessary to learn the game from the
beginning. The O. Henry of 1904 might have done

it: not the O. Henry of 1909. The years of hard work and harder living had somewhat softened him. "As a playwright," says Alexander Woollcott in *Shouts and Murmurs*, "O. Henry was a little brother to that forlorn fellow who figures in Augustus Thomas's reminiscences and whose successive lodgings in New York were always traceable by stray bits of mss. which never progressed beyond the brave beginning: 'Act I. Scene I. A Ruined Garden.' To that family of dramatists O. Henry belonged. It was a large family. It still is." Yet there were many managers ready to encourage him, believing that there was a mine in his talent if wisely directed. George C. Tyler was conspicuously the manager who hoped to make O. Henry a playwright, again and again writing him urging him to try. First he tried to make O. Henry prepare a dramatic version of the story "A Retrieved Reformation." After many delays and broken promises he lost patience and wired an offer of five hundred dollars for the stage rights. The offer was accepted by wire and then by the following letter:

Asheville, North Carolina.
October 27, 1909.

My Dear Mr. Tyler:

I hereby transfer to you the entire dramatic rights etc. of the story you write me about—the title is "A Retrieved Reformation." I am glad to be able to hand you over anything you might be able to use.

But I want you to let the $500 that I owe you still remain owing, for I'm going to write that play yet and soon.

I've been in bad shape for a long time both as to

writing and refunding. I'm wrestling with a bad case of neurasthenia (so the doctor says) but I'm getting back into shape again. I am living about six miles out of Asheville and spend most of the time climbing hills and living out of doors. I have knocked off twenty pounds weight. I eat like a drayman and don't know what booze tastes like. In fact I'll be better than ever in a week or two. I got out the scenario of "The World and the Door" some days ago and began to plan out the acts and scenes. I'll surprise you with it as soon as I get down to hard work.

I deeply appreciate your leniency and kindness and intend to "come up to scratch" yet with the goods.

So the dramatic rights of the "Retrieved Reformation" are yours and if you strike another story you like take it too.

In the meantime I owe you $500 and am going to pay it and remain

Sincerely ever,
SYDNEY PORTER

P. S. If you want a more formal assignment to the rights of the story, send on the papers and I will sign 'em.

The dramatization of "A Retrieved Reformation" was turned over to Paul Armstrong on a royalty basis. George Tyler mailed to Porter every week a duplicate copy of the box office statements. At first the situation appealed to Porter's sense of humor, and he never seems to have felt the slightest resentment at the disparity between Armstrong's reward and his own. But in time the constant reminders began to grate a little. Again from Asheville he wrote:

MY DEAR MR. TYLER:

I had expected to be in New York before this but I am not. I have been putting in all my time getting in good shape for future campaigns, and doing practically no work at all. Have entirely recovered my health and feel fine and fit. I have barely done enough writing to keep the possum from the door since I've been down here, but I think I have gained greatly thereby.

Got a little proposition to make to you.

If you'll advance me $500, I'll come to New York, establish myself in some quiet rural spot of the metropolis known only to yourself and your emissaries and go to work and finish a play. I will not let my whereabouts or even the fact that I am in the city be known to any one but you; and I will give all my time and energy to the play.

As collateral, I can only make over to you the dramatic rights of all my stories until the work is done. The new play, "Alias Jimmy Valentine" inspired me to believe I can do something for both of us.

If you will do this let me know immediately and I will come.

Of course, if you don't care to do it, it won't affect our future relations. But I want to get into the game, and I'll stick to you exclusively till we try it out.

Yours as ever,
S.P.

In January, 1910, he was again writing:

MY DEAR MR. TYLER:

I will be brief. Why I want the money in a lump sum is to make a quick getaway. Your proposition is better than mine, but it lacks the hastiness and expedition necessary to a big theatrical success. As I told you I have been busy down here for about four months getting rid of cirrhosis of the liver, fatty degeneration of the heart, and neurasthenia—none of which troubles I have ever had. But I am about as nervous and reflexactionary as the hind leg of a frog as shown in the magazine section of any Sunday newspaper. The country and the mountains have been worth more to me than money—I am almost as strong and tough as a suffragette.

But I have (by order of the old Doctor) avoided work gladly and cheerfully. Consequently I have about as much money lying on hand as was left lying around the box-office at the last performance of "Lo."

Now suppose we have a few moments' conversation as heart-to-heart as an editorial on chicken salad in the Ladies' Home Journal by Edward Everett Hale.

I owe something in the neighborhood of $500 down here that should and shall be paid before the obsequious porter of the So. Ry. Co. can have the opportunity of brushing the soot off the window-sill of Mr. Pullman's car onto the left knee of my new trousers. I'm not after money now—it's transportation, and a chance that I want. I can't work the proposition out in the short story line; but it's slow, Colonel, slow. I want to get into the real game, and I'll stake my reputation as the best story writer within a radius of Asheville that we can pull it off.

Here's what I need in order to start things going.

I've got to pay up everything here and leave a small bunch of collateral with my long suffering family to enable them to purchase the usual cuisine of persimmons and rabbits for a while.

I will do this.

If you will send me the necessary sinews, I will start for New York on Wednesday or Thursday of next week. I will, on arrival, secure a room with privileges of bath three flights above, and phone you the next morning. Thenceforth I am yours and Mr. Ford's until results have been accomplished. I will place all my time at your disposal until the play is finished. My proposition is not unselfish—I expect to make it profitable to myself as well as to you.

Proviso—

Don't give it away to any magazine, or anybody else, that I am there. I will be in retirement and working for you as long as may be necessary. My mail will be sent here as it has been, and forwarded there. My family will remain here during the summer. . . . They seem to like the idea of my returning to New York, although I have been reasonably kind to them.

Now listen.

You know how much "front" counts. I'm not afraid of New York police and editors; but if I arrive there in a linen suit, with helmet and tennis shoes, what would Big Bill Edwards do but to shovel me into a cart and dump me into the East River?

So get busy with your telegraph blanks. Send me $750 *by wire* when you get this and I'll strike New York Thursday at the latest. I've got to have some margin, and you'll get my exclusive services thereby. Take another chance. You can't lose.

I am enclosing you as rather poor collateral the rights to my stories.

I hate to make any new dickers with the magazine people and that's why I put the matter so strenuously to you. I know now how much better (financially) the stage business is; thanks to you.

Tell Oom Paul Armstrong that I hope he'll crack the safe for all it's worth in "Alias Jimmy Valentine." I got the press notices that you sent me.

I'm awfully sorry to have to come back to work and write a better play than Mr. Armstrong has—but I need the money—he won't mind.

With best regards,
S.P.

P.S. To summarize—$750 by wire—not by A.D.T. —satisfaction guaranteed—or money refunded.

This letter was followed by a telegram:

Like to have funds. Do wire to-day. Will positively
be there on time. Have cut out spending and Chianti.

Then a second telegram:

Will arrive at noon Monday if four hundred wired
to-day. Exclusive work guaranteed until satisfactory.

And a third telegram:

Wire balance. Am waiting at the depot.

In all something like $1,200 was advanced. The last
request was met on account of the play to be written
from the story "The World and the Door." Then,
according to Mr. Tyler through Mr. Woollcott:

So I wired the balance, but the telephones from the
modest and secluded lodgings never came. The first
tidings came from a hospital, to which O. Henry had
been taken with pneumonia. He had received the
money, retained the margin, and started North. But
once he found himself at the gates of Bagdad he had
stood wide-eyed for a moment and then drifted happily off to the bazaars, stumbled on some old cronies,
and given himself over to celebrating his return from
exile. I never saw him again, and the great American
play, "The World and the Door"—was never written.

XXIII

THE LAST O. HENRY STORY

SUPPOSE there had never been any Old Man of the Sea, or suppose that he had been shaken off and defied in the early New York days. What might O. Henry have achieved had he lived to man's allotted span of three score and ten? Were he alive to-day he would be in his sixty-ninth year. It was approximately at that age that George Du Maurier, finding a new profession, was setting the world on fire with "Trilby" and then going on to write "The Martian"; it was approximately at that age that William De Morgan was beginning a fruitful literary career.

Other conspicuous short-story tellers, Poe, Stevenson, and De Maupassant, died young. But Poe, dying at forty, was mentally burned out; Maupassant dying at forty-three, was worse than burned out; it was necessity and a stern courage that moved Stevenson, who died at forty-four, to toil at Vailima with a tired and flagging brain. But there is always the feeling that the work of these men had been done; just as there is the feeling that Thackeray had done his work at fifty-two and Balzac at fifty-one.

With O. Henry the case was different. Excesses and perhaps his physical heritage had taken their toll from his body. But there was no evidence of any exhaustion of the mind. His life as a story-teller had

393

been brief. He was almost forty when he began seriously to pour out in fiction his treasures of invention
and observation. Until very near the end, when ill
health interrupted his work, there was never any per-
ceptible slackening of the pace. Among his last stories
were many of his best. The O. Henry of 1908 and
1909, producing such tales as "The Enchanted Profile," "The Moment of Victory," "The Rose of Dixie,"
"Thimble, Thimble," "The Third Ingredient," "Best-
Seller," "A Municipal Report," and "Let Me Feel
Your Pulse" or "Adventures in Neurasthenia," which
was not published until after his death, was a far finer
workman than the author of "Georgia's Ruling" or
"Whistling Dick's Christmas Stocking."

Most important of all, he still believed in himself,
saw visions of a riper achievement in the future. "I
want to get at something bigger. What I have done
is child's play to what I can do, to what I know is in
me to do." He was planning to write his first long
novel, and had finished eight pages of it in manuscript.
An unfinished letter, published in the issue of the
Bookman for the month following his death illustrates
his purpose, his mood, and his vigor.

My idea is to write the story of a man—an individual,
not a type—but a man who, at the same time, I want
to represent a "human nature type," if such a person
could exist. The story will teach no lesson, inculcate no
moral, advance no theory.

I want it to be something that won't or can't be—
but as near as I can make it—the TRUE record of a
man's thoughts, his description of his mischances and
adventures, his TRUE opinions of life as he has seen it

and his absolutely *honest deductions*, comments and views upon the different phases of life that he passes through.

I do not remember ever having read an autobiography or a piece of fiction that told the TRUTH. Of course, I have read stuff such as Rousseau and Zola and George Moore and various memoirs that were supposed to be window-panes in their respective breasts; but, mostly, all of them were either liars, actors, or posers. (Of course I'm not trying to belittle the greatness of their literary expression.)

All of us have to be prevaricators, hypocrites and liars every day of our lives; otherwise the social structure would fall into pieces the first day. We must act in one another's presence just as we must wear clothes.

The trouble about writing the truth has been that the writers have kept in their minds one or another or all of three thoughts that made a handicap—they were trying either to do a piece of immortal literature, or to shock the public or to please editors. Some of them succeeded in all three, but they did not write the truth. Most autobiographies are insincere from beginning to end, and about the only chance for the truth to be told is in fiction.

It is well understood that "all the truth" cannot be told in print—but how about "nothing but the truth?" That's what I want to do.

I want the man who is telling the story to tell it—not as he would to a reading public or to a confessor—but something in this way. Suppose he were marooned on an island in mid-ocean with no hope of ever being rescued; and, in order to pass away some of the time he should tell a story to *himself*, embodying his adventures and experiences and opinions. Having a certain respect for himself (let us hope) he would leave out the "realism" that he would have no chance of selling in the market; he would omit the lies and self-conscious poses, and would turn out to his one auditor something real and true.

So, as truth is not to be found in history, autobiography, press reports (nor at the bottom of an H. G. Wells), let us hope that fiction may be the means of brining out a few grains of it.

The "hero" of the story will be a man born and "raised" in a somnolent little Southern town. His education is about a common school one, but he learns afterward from reading and life. I'm going to try to give him a "style" in narrative and speech—the best I've got in the shop. I'm going to take him through all the main phases of life—wild adventure, city, society, something of the "underworld" and among many characteristic planes of the phases. I want him to acquire all the sophistication that experience can give him, and always preserve his individual honest *human* view and have him tell the *truth* about everything.

It is time to say now, that by the "truth" I don't mean the objectionable stuff that so often masquerades under the name. I mean true opinions, a true estimate of all things as they seem to the "hero." If you find a word or a suggestive line or sentence in any of my copy, you cut it out and deduct it from the royalties.

I want this man to be a man of natural intelligence, of individual character, absolutely open and broadminded; and show him how the Creator of the earth has got him in a rat-trap—put him there "willy-nilly" (you know the Omar verse) ; and then I want to show what he does about it. There is always the eternal question from the Primal Source—"What are you going to do about it?"

Please don't think for half of a moment that the story is to be anything of an autobiography. I have a distinct character in my mind for the part, and he does not at all—

Thus the letter ends, leaving the inference that the incompleted line should have gone on to say that the "hero" of the projected story was in no sense to be confused with William Sidney Porter.

The last years will be glossed over briefly. They were spent in Asheville, North Carolina, with occasional returns to the Bagdad that had come to mean so much to him. There was a spirit of homesickness for the "big city" in his letters written from the South. He complained of too much scenery and fresh air, and said that what he needed was a "steam-heated flat with no ventilation or exercise." He had his wish. It was in New York, in the Caledonia, that the fatal stroke came, on June 3, 1910. He was hurried to a hospital on West Thirty-fourth Street. There, retaining consciousness to the end, he died two days later, with his last breath asking for more light, in order that he might not "go home in the dark."

The last O. Henry story was one that he did not write or live to see, but it was one that would have appealed to his whimsical sense of the topsy-turviness of things. His funeral was held in the Protestant Episcopal Church of the Transfiguration, better known as the Little Church Round the Corner, in West Twenty-ninth Street. The story is Will Irwin's story.

Mr. Irwin had been unaware of O. Henry's death until informed by Franklin P. Adams. William Griffith and Gilman Hall made arrangements for the funeral to take place at 11 o'clock in the morning, Tuesday, June 7, and Mr. Irwin was asked to be one of the pallbearers. Somewhat ahead of time, he repaired to the church and there found Richard Harding Davis,

another of the pallbearers.   No other member of the
funeral party had appeared.

While they were waiting in the garden that sur-
rounds the church there came the sound of merry
laughing voices as three motor cars drew up to the
street curb at the garden gate.   The cars were all
filled and among the occupants Davis and Irwin recognized an acquaintance, a magazine art editor.   Singling him out they sought explanations.

The new arrivals were a wedding party for which
arrangements had been made a day or two earlier.
"At what hour?" asked Irwin.   "Eleven o'clock in the
morning," was the reply.   "But that's the exact time
set for O. Henry's funeral.   There must be some mistake."   The art editor saw the point.   "A funeral takes
precedence over a wedding.   Leave the matter to me.
But don't say a word.   I don't want these friends of
mine to be married with any superstitious feeling of
bad luck.   I'll invent some excuse for the delay."   He
gathered the gay party together, and explained that
there had been an error in the matter of setting the
time for the wedding and that they would have to come
back later.   Reëntering the cars the wedding guests
drove away.

The funeral starting somewhat late, they were back
again before it was over.   It was a glorious early summer day.   The church windows were open, and Will
Irwin's vivid memory is of the mingling sounds of the
solemn rites and the laughing voices in the garden.
Then and there the thought came to his mind: "What
an O. Henry story!"

XXIV

BOB DAVIS AT THE GRAVE OF THE CALIPH

ON an April morning in 1929, I walked into an Asheville, North Carolina, flower store to select a simple wreath, one that would not seem obtrusive beside the headstone of him who of all men was the least obtrusive.

"May I know," asked the kindly woman who waited upon me, "where this wreath is to be used?"

"In the sunlight, and under the stars," I replied. "To last as long as may be; rain or shine."

"Is the deceased a man, woman or child?"

"It is for the grave of O. Henry."

"You are a stranger here," she said softly. "And you have come . . ."

"From New York; for one purpose."

"You shall have a wreath," said she, "and with my compliments. A wreath of immortelles. My only request is that when you stand at the grave, you wear in your lapel a live carnation; his favorite flower. Could you do that for me? I am Mrs. Otto Busick." Bowing, I accepted the fragrant pink boutonnière from the same hand that twenty years before had served Will Porter.

He lies facing the northwest. In the distance shimmers the French Broad River, and beyond the blue

399

peaks. A valley in foreground, so near that one could almost step from the lip of the hill into its lush verdure, merges into a deep wild forest now touched by the warmth of spring.

An oblong granite block rests at the head of the mound. Two lines, two dates, are chiseled:

```
WILLIAM  SYDNEY  PORTER
   1862              1910
```

Neither coping nor foot-stone are there. Three mottled yellow pansies in full bloom, and a few buds occupy the green sod that shelters the Caliph of Bagdad. In close proximity are shafts and markers, tombs and marble figures adorning the graves of his neighbors. Simplest of all is his own last resting place. The great master of the moods of men, the supreme delineator of the foibles of the living, has a permanent monument in the hearts of his readers; his tower is the printed page.

A wanderer moving along the by-paths, ambles down the gentle slope. We pass the time of day . . . we talk of the pervading peace and quiet . . . his eyes fall upon the granite stone . . . he voices the inscription: "William Sydney Porter." A light breaks.— "Is this the grave of O. Henry?"

"Yes."

"Why then isn't his pen name on the headstone?"

"I understand that in life he expressed a desire to

be buried in this manner, with no reference to his *nom de plume.*"

"Did you know him?"

"Slightly. I don't believe any one enjoyed absolute intimacy with him. He was not especially communicative in conversation, although to his readers he gave himself utterly."

"What sort of a looking man was he? I've read everything he ever wrote and have seen several pictures of him, but they don't seem to do him justice. Describe him, if you will."

"Stout, heavy chested, florid in tone and slow in movement. His shoulders were wide, his carriage erect. His head was massive, the brow broad and the eyes open."

"What color?"

"Blue as the sky at times. When he laughed his whole face lit up. The voice was pitched in a low key. . . . He spoke with a pronounced southern accent, combining deliberate gestures with his speech. . . . A better listener than a talker, but a marvelous audience under all circumstances."

"Where did he learn so much of life?"

"By living it, I suppose. He had considerable of that thing called experience."

"Which accounts for his sense of humor. I've all his books and would give much to have his signature in any one of them. When I get low spirited I read O. Henry. When I find other men in the same mood I recommend O. Henry. And to-day by accident I find the grave where he has come at last to rest. I see that some one has placed a wreath against the headstone. No card . . . I wonder who?"

"Probably," I answered, "one of The Four Million."

INDEX